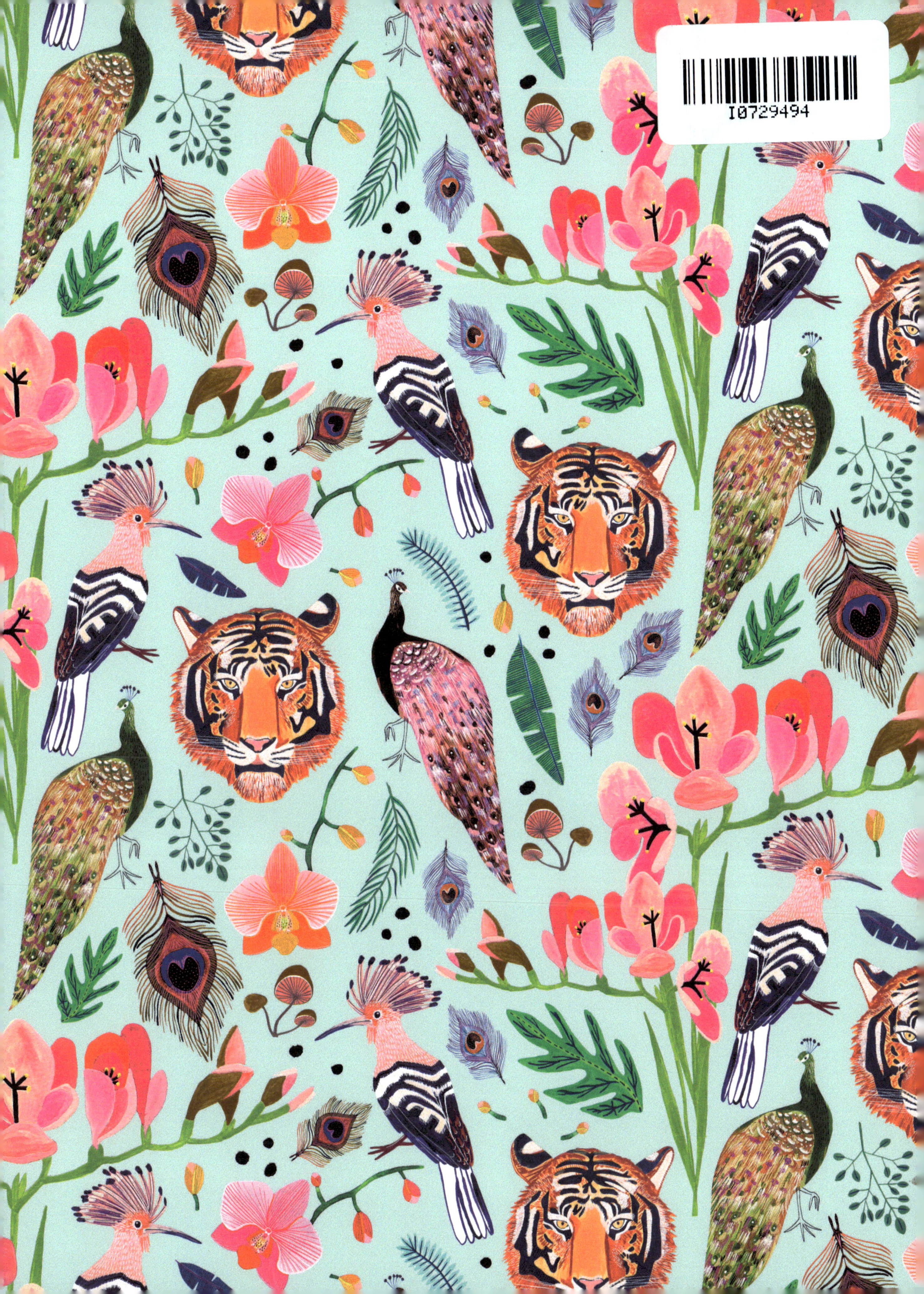
I0729494

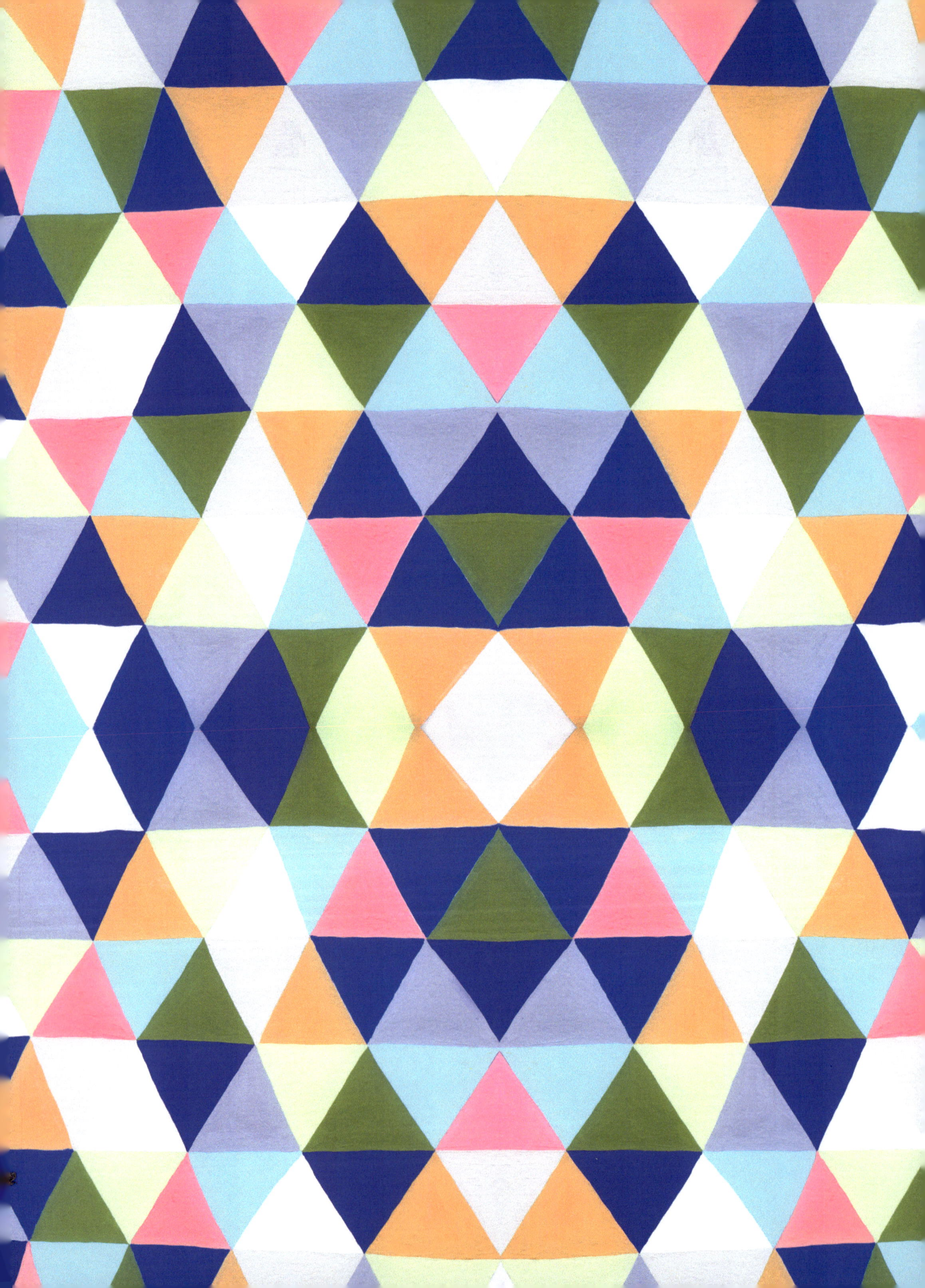

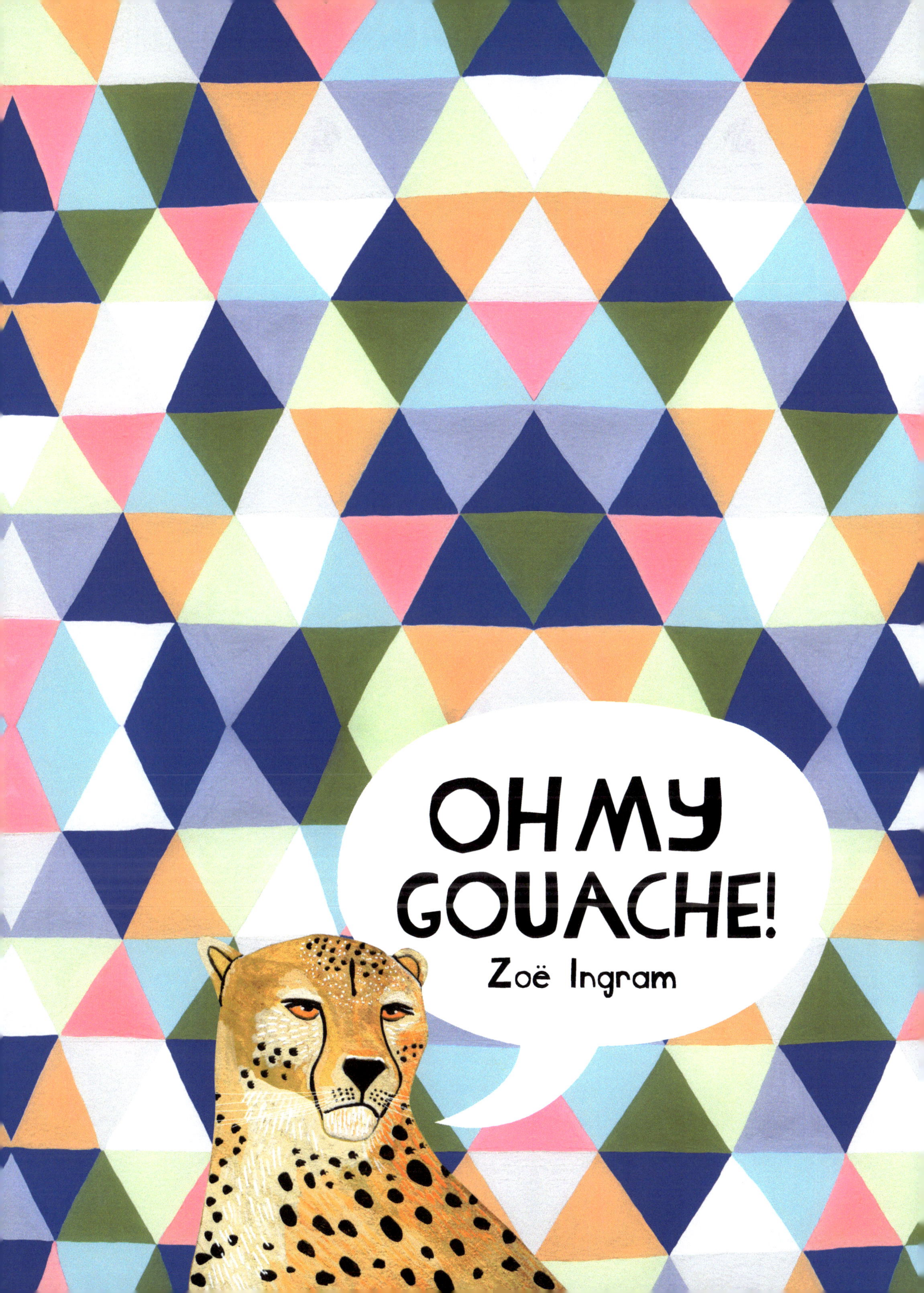

OH MY GOUACHE!
Zoë Ingram

For my two teachers and early mentors,
Jane and Mark, both of whom had such
a positive influence on me, introduced me
to gouache and taught me most of what I
know about the medium.

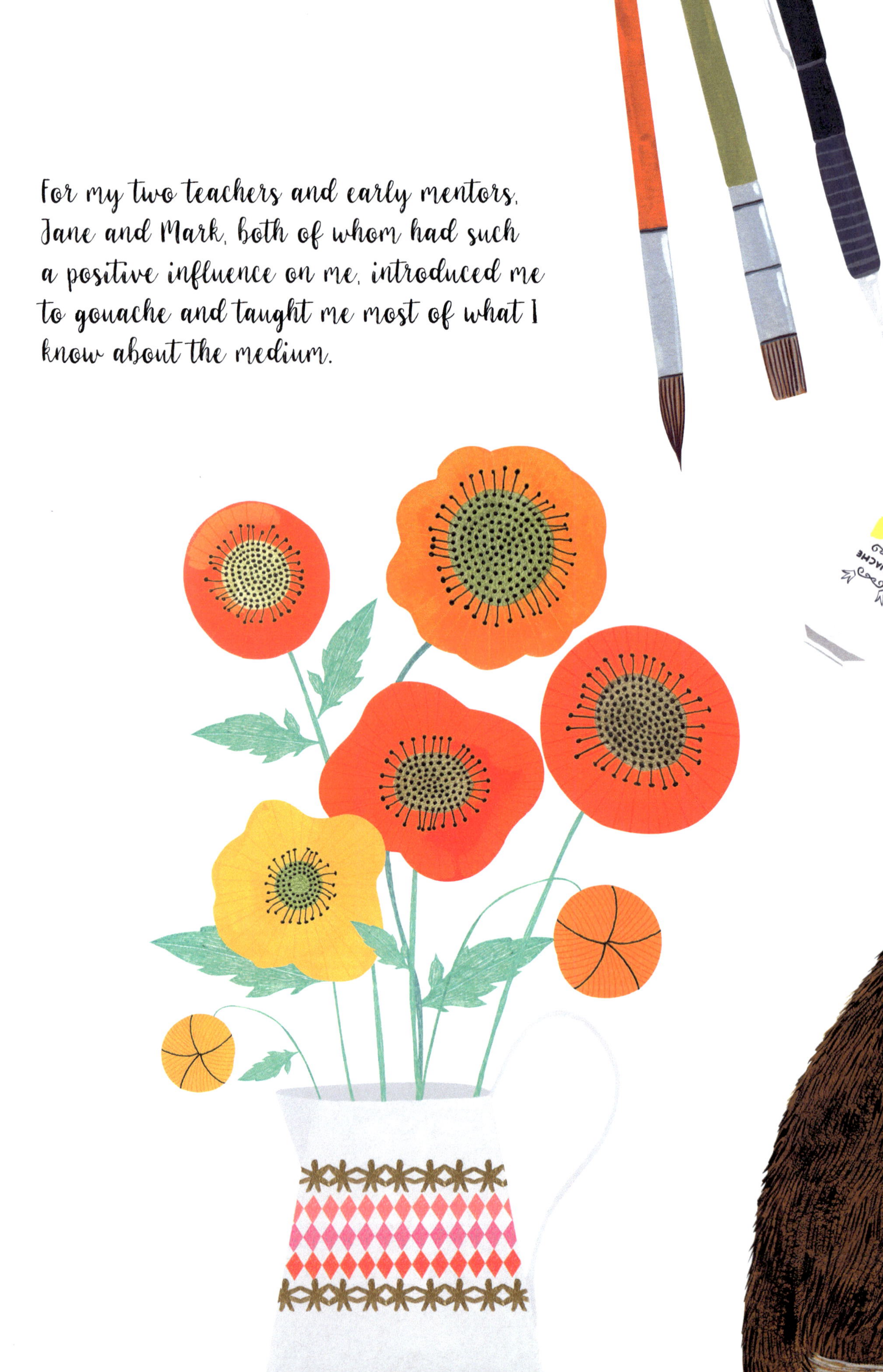

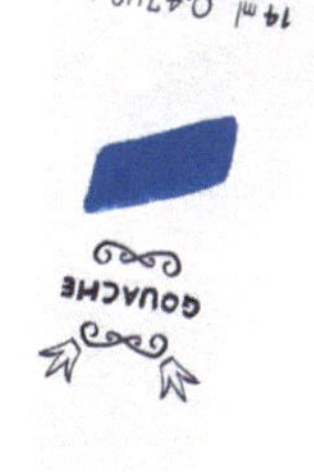
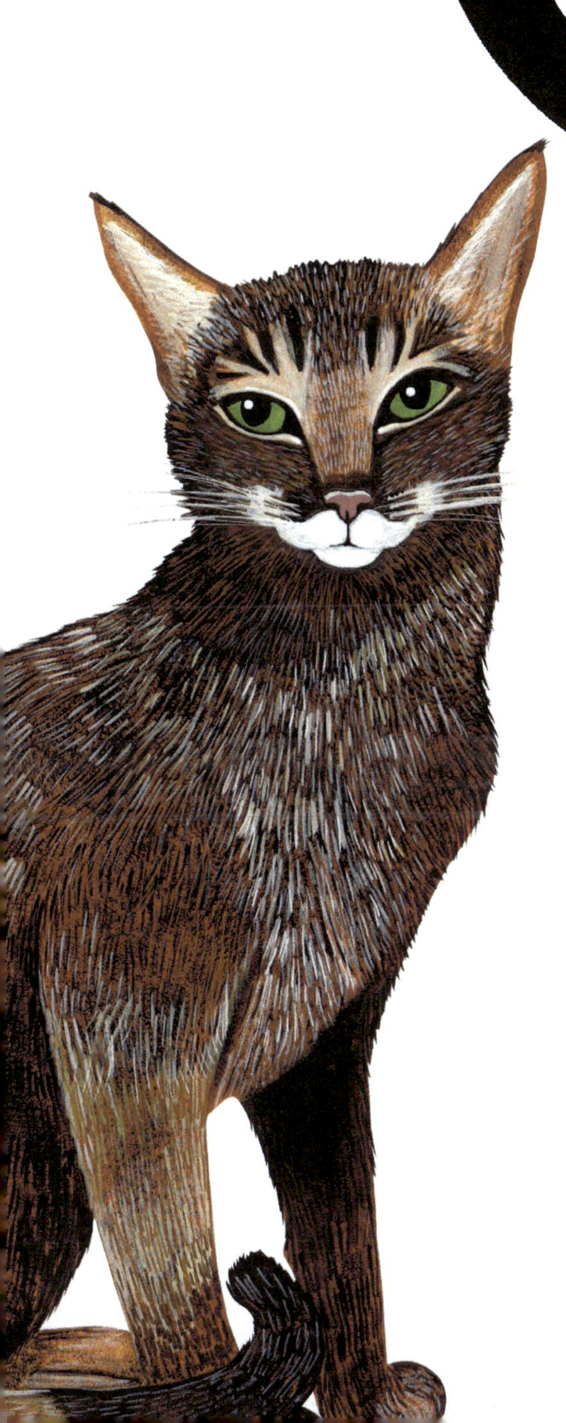

OH MY GOUACHE!

Zoë Ingram

THE BEGINNER'S GUIDE TO PAINTING WITH OPAQUE WATERCOLOUR

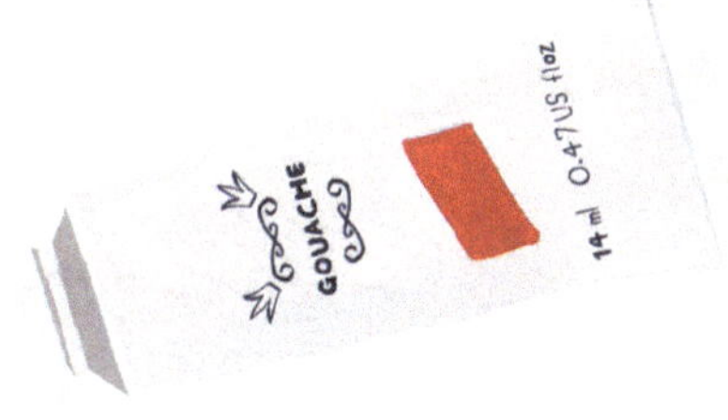

DAVID & CHARLES
—PUBLISHING—

www.davidandcharles.com

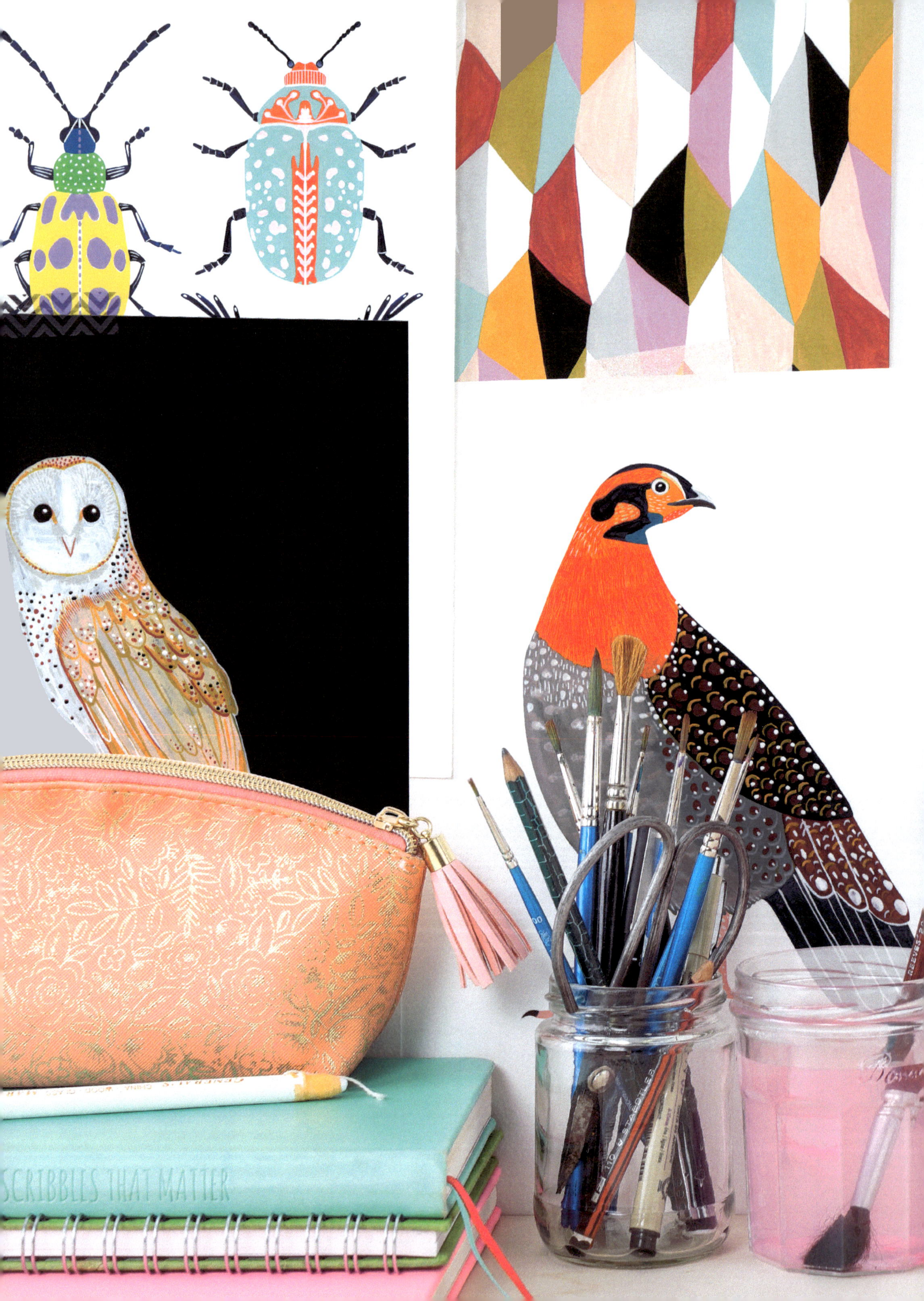
SCRIBBLES THAT MATTER

Contents

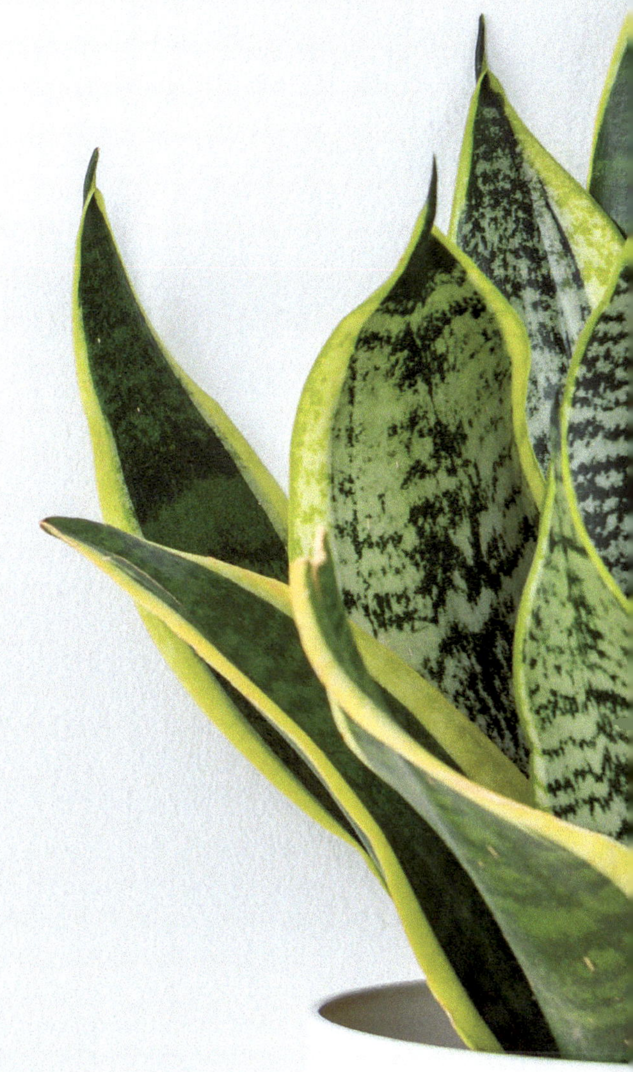

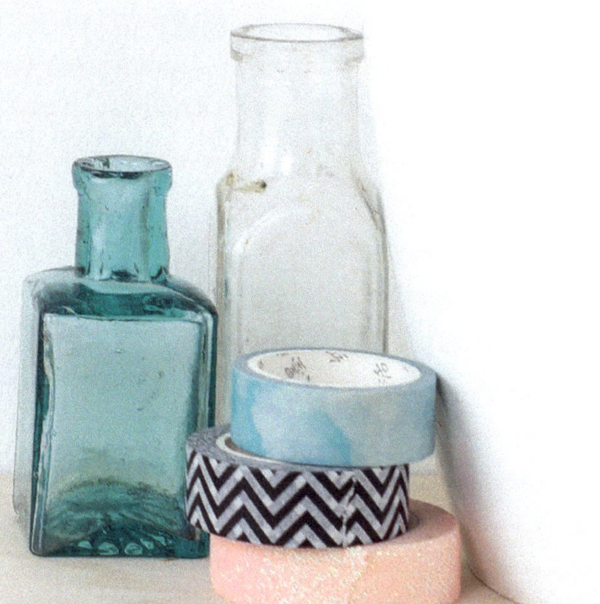

Oh my gouache!

We're going to have some fun with this wonderful medium.

First, let me introduce myself. I'm Zoë Ingram, a Scottish artist and illustrator. I've been working in the creative industries for over 20 years. My background is in printed textiles, and I later moved into the graphic design world. For the past eight years, I've been following my passion by creating artwork professionally for a wide range of clients who are publishers of books, magazines and newspapers, fabric producers, home-decor manufacturers and gift and stationery companies. I use gouache paint extensively in my everyday work, and I'm going to share with you as much as I possibly can about getting started with gouache.

I'll take you through some of the basics and explain what you'll need to get going: paint, tools and paper. I'll then go over some of the more common techniques that I use every day. Finally, there are 11 projects that you can follow along with or use as a springboard for your own ideas. Think of these projects as examples or starting points for what you might want to paint, not as a 'paint it this way' manual.

Gouache really is my first love when it comes to choosing a painting medium. It's a lot less intimidating than some other paint mediums, so I hope you're inspired to take that first step and begin creating. Finding a little time each day to paint will not only make your work better through practice, but it's also a perfect opportunity for you to do something you enjoy. At the time of writing this book, we find ourselves in the middle of a global pandemic and a worldwide climate crisis, both of which are overwhelming. Painting and art can help to express some of the emotions that you may be feeling during challenging times.

Welcome to the wonderful world of painting with gouache!

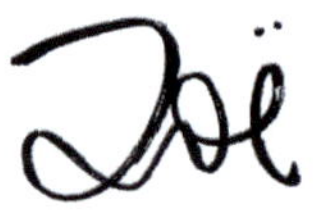

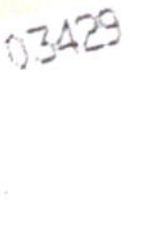

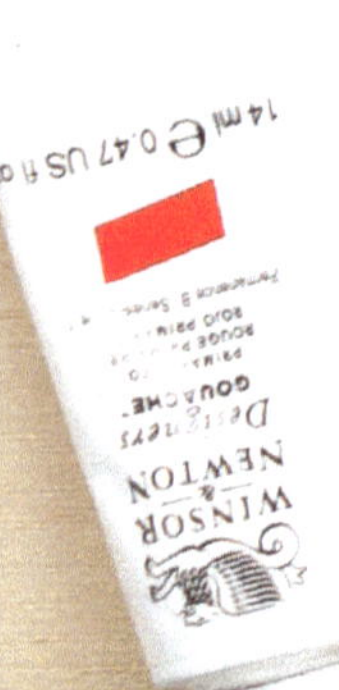

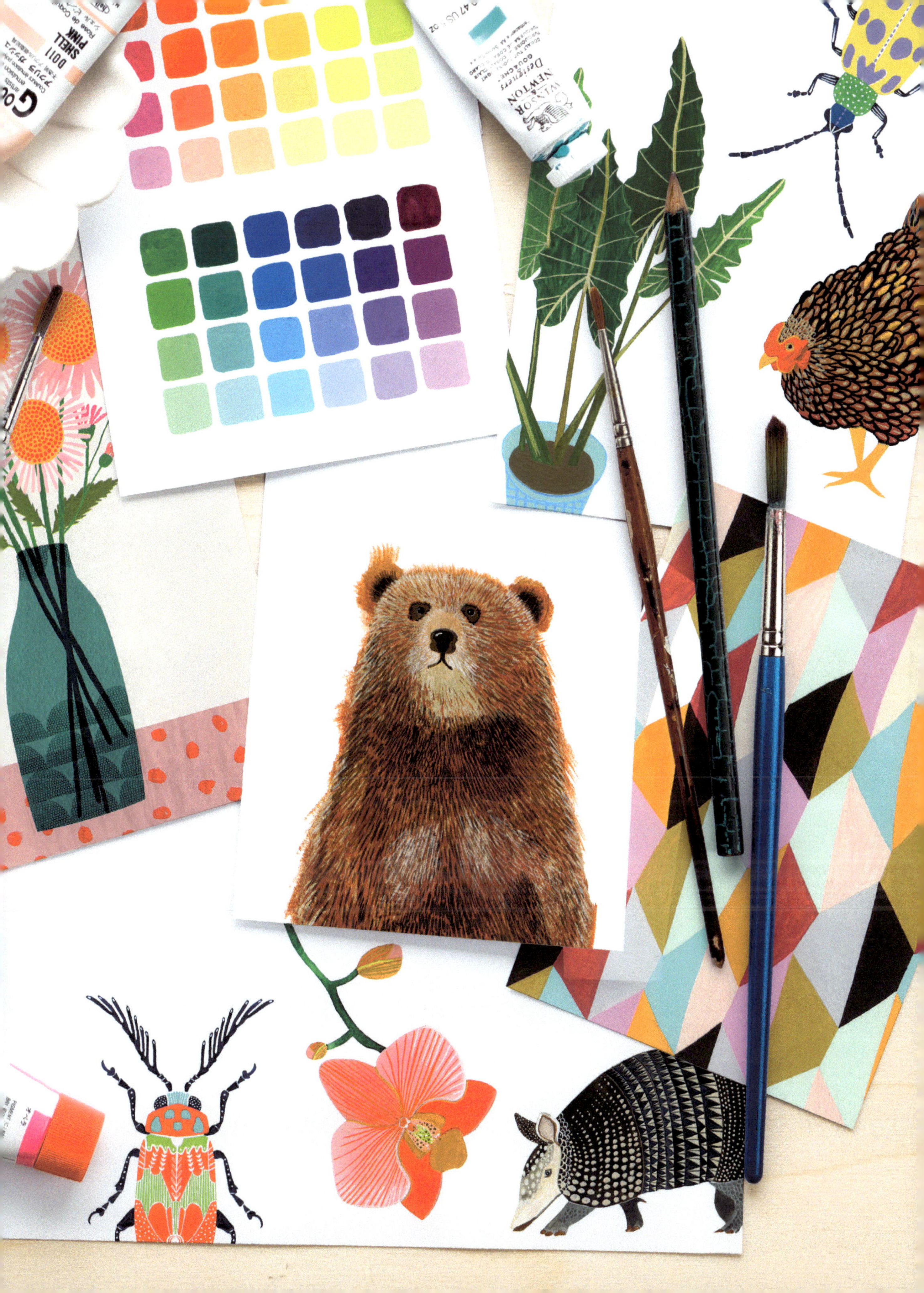

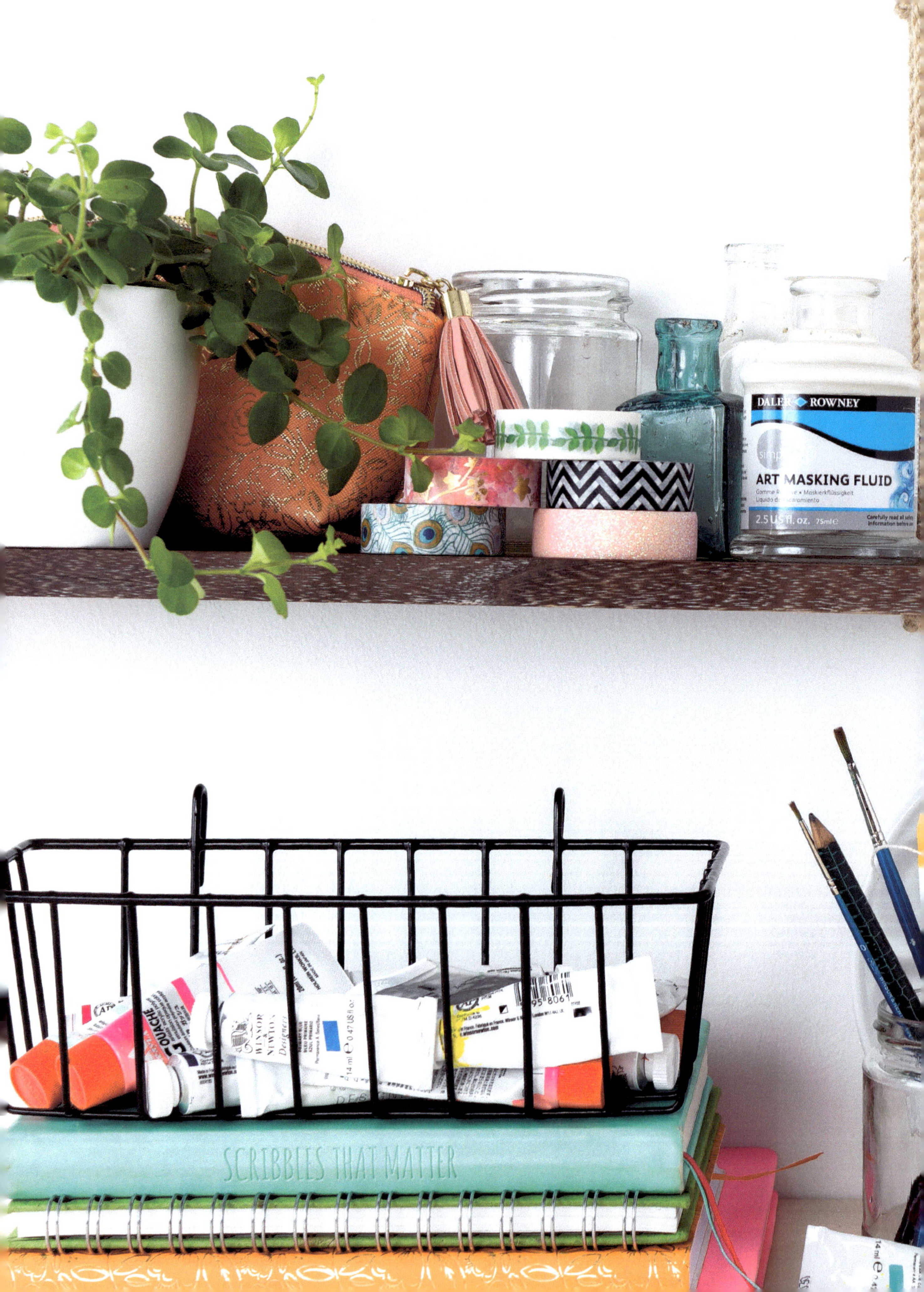

DALER · ROWNEY
simply
ART MASKING FLUID
Gomme à masquer · Maskierflüssigkeit
Líquido de enmascaramiento
2.5 US fl. oz. 75ml
SCRIBBLES THAT MATTER

MATERIALS AND TOOLS

Besides paint, you'll need a few other things to get you started with gouache. There are lots of tools and materials to choose from, and I remember literally breaking out in a cold sweat when I first walked into an art shop as a new artist. But don't worry – you don't need everything straight away, and we'll go through the basics over the following pages.

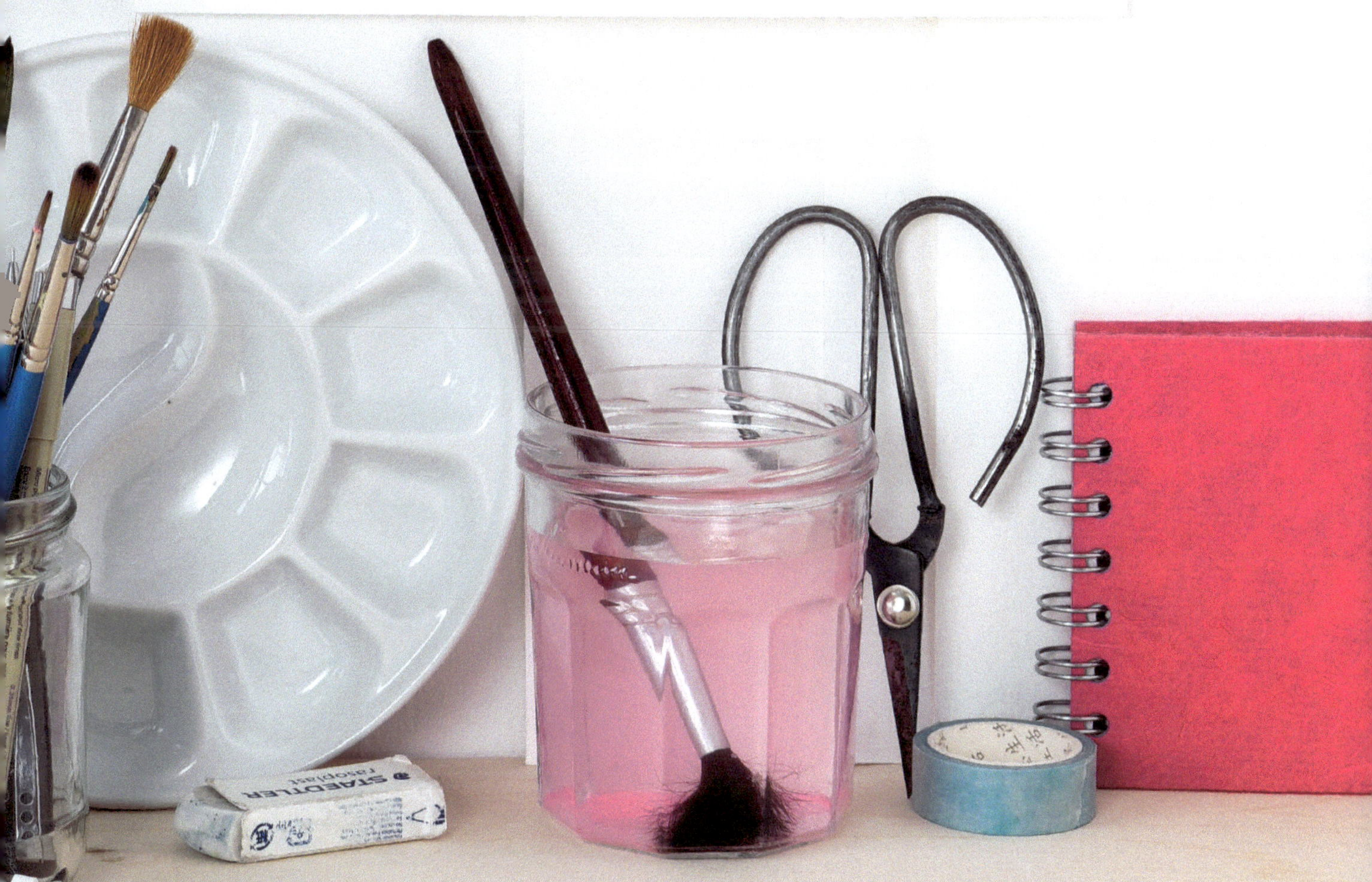

The Paint

Gouache:

[*goo-ash, gwash or goo-uhsh*] **noun**

A method of painting using opaque pigments ground in water and thickened with a glue-like substance.

Opaque watercolour of the type used in gouache painting.

A picture painted using the gouache method.

The pronunciation of gouache varies from person to person and can sound like 'gooash', 'gwash' or 'goo-uhsh'. The term originated in France in the eighteenth century, but the earliest gouache paints are known to have been made in ancient Greece and Egypt. These early gouache paints were very similar to tempera paints, which are usually semi-opaque compared to gouache as we know it now.

There are some very well-known painters who used gouache in their work, one of whom is the French artist, Henri Matisse. He used gouache to achieve the flat, bold colour he's famous for in his paper cut-outs. Another fantastic artist who historically used gouache is Paul Klee. Both of these artists are favourites of mine and I'd definitely recommend looking at their works for inspiration.

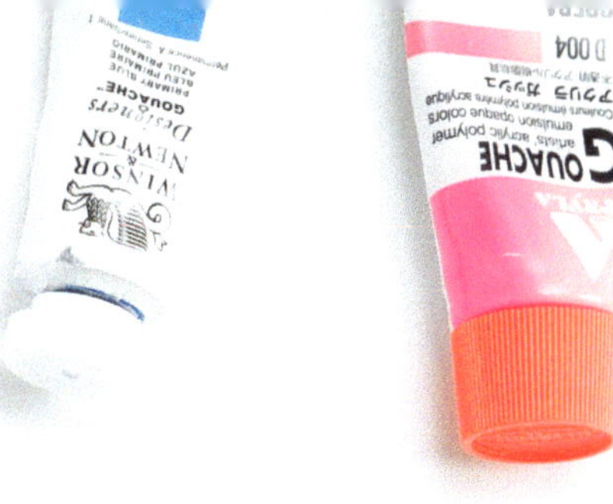

How it works

As the definition states, gouache is water-based paint that is essentially made up of pigment, binding agent and water, producing an opaque, flat, matt finish. The flat opaqueness of the paint gives a solid graphic feel and has no reflection or sheen, which makes photographing or scanning your work much easier. This also means that the paper doesn't show through, unless you dilute the paint so much that it becomes like watercolour paint. Gouache paint dries fairly quickly, too, which I find to be a big bonus. Light colours usually dry slightly darker than they look when wet, and dark colours can look slightly lighter when dry. This could be due to the opaqueness of the paint absorbing light rather than allowing light to pass through to the paper underneath as it does with watercolour paint.

Choosing your paint

Primary colours are usually the most affordable and sometimes come in beginner sets, which I'd recommend starting with as a bare minimum. Add white and you have all you really need to get going. I'll show you how to mix many colours from these four paints! You can add more non-essential colours to your toolkit as you need them. I use certain colours straight from the tube because they're so unique and hard to replicate by mixing.

In addition to traditional gouache, there is a particular kind of hybrid gouache paint that is gouache mixed with an acrylic element: acrylic gouache. I use both types of gouache in my work. Acrylic paint is polymer based, which means that when it dries, it can't be reconstituted or blended with water. I like the permanence of acrylic gouache, and I'll be using it in the elements of the projects in this book where I wanted to keep the layers distinct.

Pure gouache, however, can be reconstituted once it has dried out on the palette and, to an extent, on the paper. All you need to do is add water to the dried-up paint and – voila! – you can use it again. For this very reason, take care when using it wet on already dry paint because the layer underneath can be lifted and muddied with any new addition over the top. This doesn't apply if you're painting directly on top of acrylic gouache.

Gouache is, in my opinion, the easiest of paint mediums to use. It's very forgiving and fun to use. It's also versatile. Gouache paint can mimic watercolour or can give the opacity of oil paint if used with less water. You can use it to paint large, smooth, flat blocks of background colour and the finest lines and details.

Brushes and Palettes

Choosing brushes, paper and palettes can be a bit overwhelming and confusing as a beginner. If you're buying your essential toolkit in an art store, remember that you can ask for help if you're unsure. The staff are generally very knowledgeable and can help you to find the right tools for the job. The more you practise, the more familiar you'll become with the materials that you work with, and you'll soon have the confidence to seek out just what you need without assistance.

Here are my top tips to get you started.

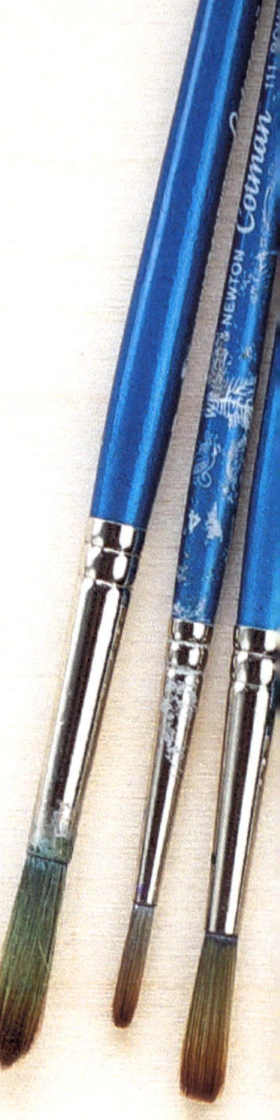

Brushes

I have a million brushes, old and new, big and small, square and round, but I tend to gravitate towards the same faithful brushes over and over. You'll find, through practice, which types and makes of brushes you prefer to work with and that suit your painting style. I like a mixture of sizes because I sometimes paint in a quick, expressive painterly fashion, yet I also paint quite tight images with a lot of detail and flat colour, so having tiny brushes is a necessity. I almost always go for synthetic brushes that are intended for watercolour use.

There are various types of brush on the market, sometimes too many to choose from: round, rigger, one stroke, angled, filbert, long handle, short handle, mops, wash brush and fan. To begin with, I recommend a set of round brushes in a variety of sizes, as these can cope with washes, solid colour, lines and detail.

BRUSHES ARE USUALLY SIZED FROM 0000 (SMALLEST) TO 24 (LARGEST). SIZES 0, 2, 4, 6, 8 ARE A GOOD STARTING POINT, AND IF YOU WANT TO ADD VERY FINE DETAILS, SOMETHING SMALLER LIKE A 00 OR EVEN 000 IS HANDY TO HAVE IN YOUR KIT.

Palettes

I've tried a lot of different palettes in the past and my favourite by far is an old white ceramic plate. The surface is smooth, which makes it easy to mix the paint, and, because it's white and doesn't discolour or stain, it's easier to see the colours that I'm mixing. You could use an old white plate that you were going to throw out, or hunt for one in a thrift shop. Disposable paper palettes are a great option for using on the go or if you really don't have the energy to clean up after a day of painting; you simply remove the top sheet and throw it away when you need a fresh palette.

Plastic palettes are an option, too, although I find that they're harder to clean and tend to stain, and I like my palette to be fresh and clean for the next load of paint. Some palettes have compartments so that your paint doesn't run into the other colours, but I prefer to have a simple flat palette. You can buy palettes that have a lid to cover and seal in unused paint, which is a great idea, but you can achieve the same result by wrapping plastic food wrap over your palette to keep your paint fresh and to stop it from drying out.

Paper

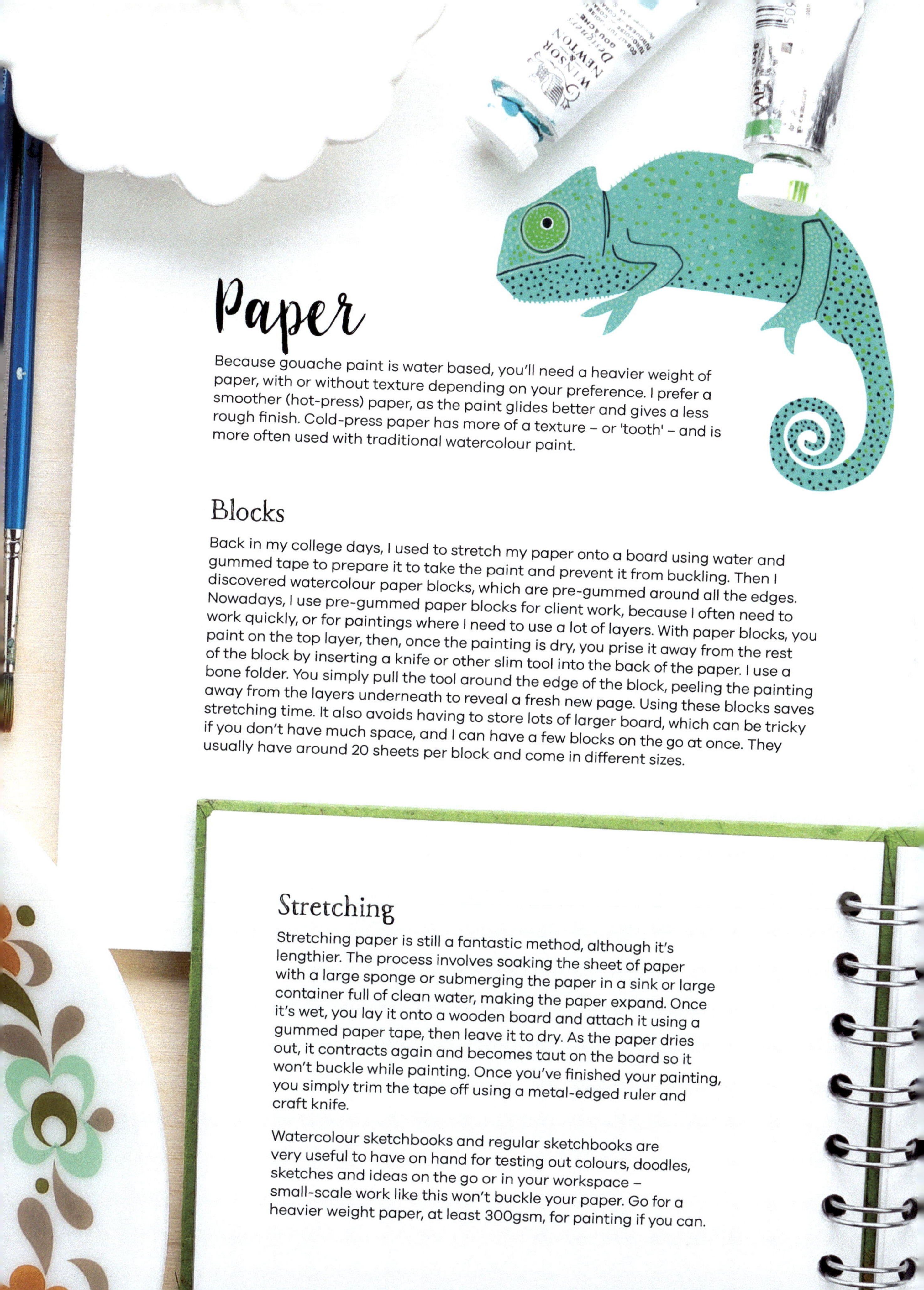

Because gouache paint is water based, you'll need a heavier weight of paper, with or without texture depending on your preference. I prefer a smoother (hot-press) paper, as the paint glides better and gives a less rough finish. Cold-press paper has more of a texture – or 'tooth' – and is more often used with traditional watercolour paint.

Blocks

Back in my college days, I used to stretch my paper onto a board using water and gummed tape to prepare it to take the paint and prevent it from buckling. Then I discovered watercolour paper blocks, which are pre-gummed around all the edges. Nowadays, I use pre-gummed paper blocks for client work, because I often need to work quickly, or for paintings where I need to use a lot of layers. With paper blocks, you paint on the top layer, then, once the painting is dry, you prise it away from the rest of the block by inserting a knife or other slim tool into the back of the paper. I use a bone folder. You simply pull the tool around the edge of the block, peeling the painting away from the layers underneath to reveal a fresh new page. Using these blocks saves stretching time. It also avoids having to store lots of larger board, which can be tricky if you don't have much space, and I can have a few blocks on the go at once. They usually have around 20 sheets per block and come in different sizes.

Stretching

Stretching paper is still a fantastic method, although it's lengthier. The process involves soaking the sheet of paper with a large sponge or submerging the paper in a sink or large container full of clean water, making the paper expand. Once it's wet, you lay it onto a wooden board and attach it using a gummed paper tape, then leave it to dry. As the paper dries out, it contracts again and becomes taut on the board so it won't buckle while painting. Once you've finished your painting, you simply trim the tape off using a metal-edged ruler and craft knife.

Watercolour sketchbooks and regular sketchbooks are very useful to have on hand for testing out colours, doodles, sketches and ideas on the go or in your workspace – small-scale work like this won't buckle your paper. Go for a heavier weight paper, at least 300gsm, for painting if you can.

Texture-Making Tools

Making textures is such a fun and lively way to incorporate depth and interest into your work, and the good news is that you can use practically anything. Of course, brushes are an excellent place to start. Try using old, splayed bristle brushes and scrub the paint around to see what happens.

Experiment with different tools to get different effects. The end of a cotton bud makes a great 'dot' mark-making tool, for example. An old rag, cotton-wool balls, a brayer (a roller with a handle used in printmaking), a toothbrush or an eraser are also exciting to try out and use.

The main thing is to have fun and build a collection of textures that you can use in your work, either as a library of techniques or as painted papers for collage. You could even scan the textures and digitize them to add texture to your work in Photoshop (see Techniques: Digitizing).

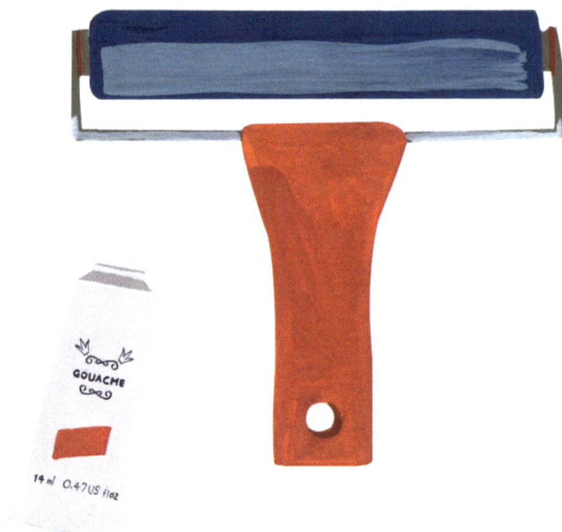

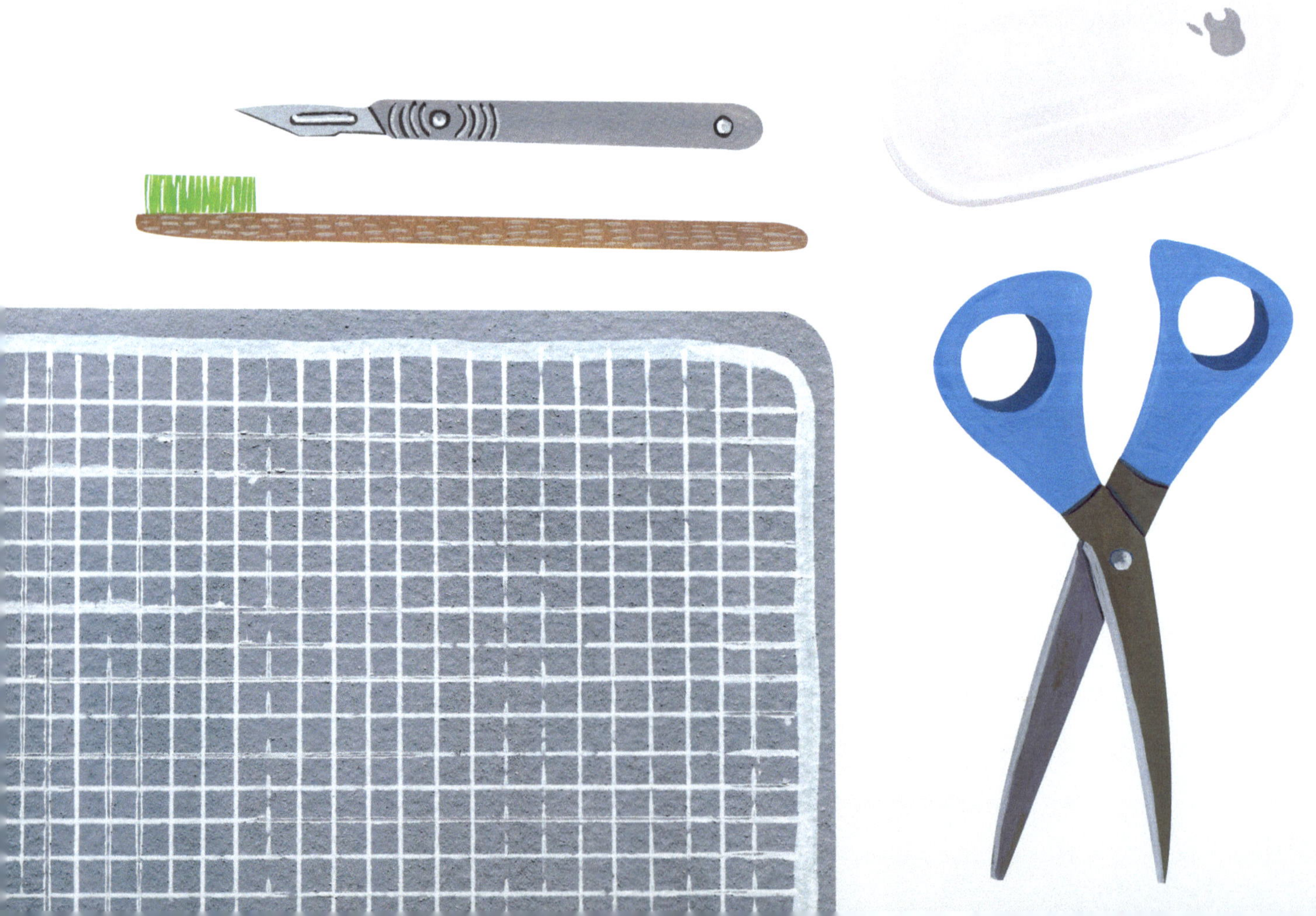

Other Tips and Tools

Here's a handy list of some other things you might find helpful to have in your work area. Some, like old jam jars, you're likely to find around your home. Others you may like to buy especially.

- Sketchbook – for trying out colour combinations, mark making and sketching ideas.

- Masking fluid – to mask off areas that you want to keep unpainted.

- Artist's masking tape – as above, but can give you a lovely straight edge or create a white frame around the paper.

- Pencils – for sketching or for drawing in details to finish off your painting. You'll need some lighter colours and maybe a white china marker pencil for darker backgrounds (see Techniques: Dark Backgrounds).

- Erasers – to get rid of any stray lines once the painting is finished or for tidying up your sketches.

- Gloss – Gouache paintings can get damaged if splashed accidentally with water, so you can seal your finished painting with a gloss medium or spray fixative. I tend not to do this, as brushing a wet gloss or varnish over gouache can have the same effect as adding water, lifting the paint and possibly smudging it and ruining the painting. Also, be aware that if you add gloss, the colours may shift slightly with the extra layer.

- Scanner – If you're going to edit your paintings in any way, be it colour adjustments or removing white backgrounds, you'll need a scanner to transfer the painting to your computer.

- Hairdryer – Although gouache tends to dry very quickly, especially if you're in a warmer climate, a hair dryer can help to speed up the drying process in between layers of paint if you're in a hurry.

- Scissors/craft knife – Tools for cutting paper are handy to have if you like to use collage in your work.

- Cutting mat – Using a cutting mat makes cutting paper safer and will prevent damage to other surfaces.

- A board, gummed tape and watercolour paper – if you decide to try stretching your own paper.

- Jars – Water jars are essential. I like to use old, cleaned-out jam jars and have a big stash of them! If you know you're going to be painting a large amount of the same colour, or need to mix up a few colours in larger quantities, it's handy to have little pots with lids to keep the paint airtight. This stops it from drying out and you won't have lots of waste. I use old glass spice jars that I've cleaned out, but you could also use little plastic takeaway containers or small glass jars.

- Paper towel – I lay my brushes down flat on a paper towel after I've rinsed them to prevent the water running down into the handles, which would ruin the brushes over time. Paper towel is also good for wiping off excess paint from your brushes.

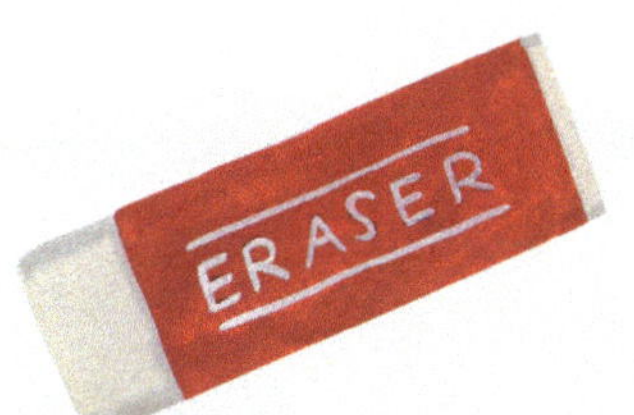

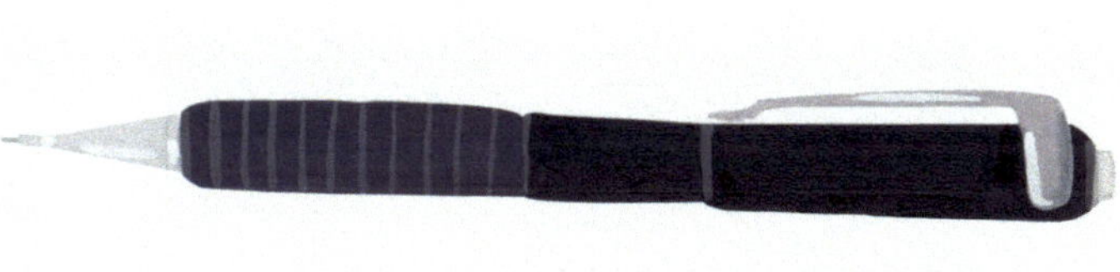

COLOUR

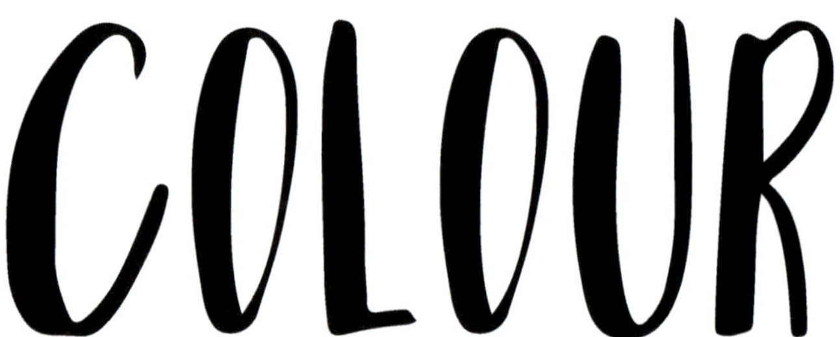

Colour is pure magic. For me, colour is one of the most crucial elements that can take a piece of artwork from good to great. It can be seen as a defining part of a style or brand, making your artwork instantly recognizable. Most importantly, the application of colour is fun!

Colour can stir up emotions, create a mood and set a tone. I liken colour in a painting to music in a movie; just as music can enhance the feeling the director is trying to portray, colour can do the same thing for your painting. It reinforces a message and conveys impact, and the interaction between two or three colours placed next to each other can create a visually exciting piece. Be bold and courageous with your colour.

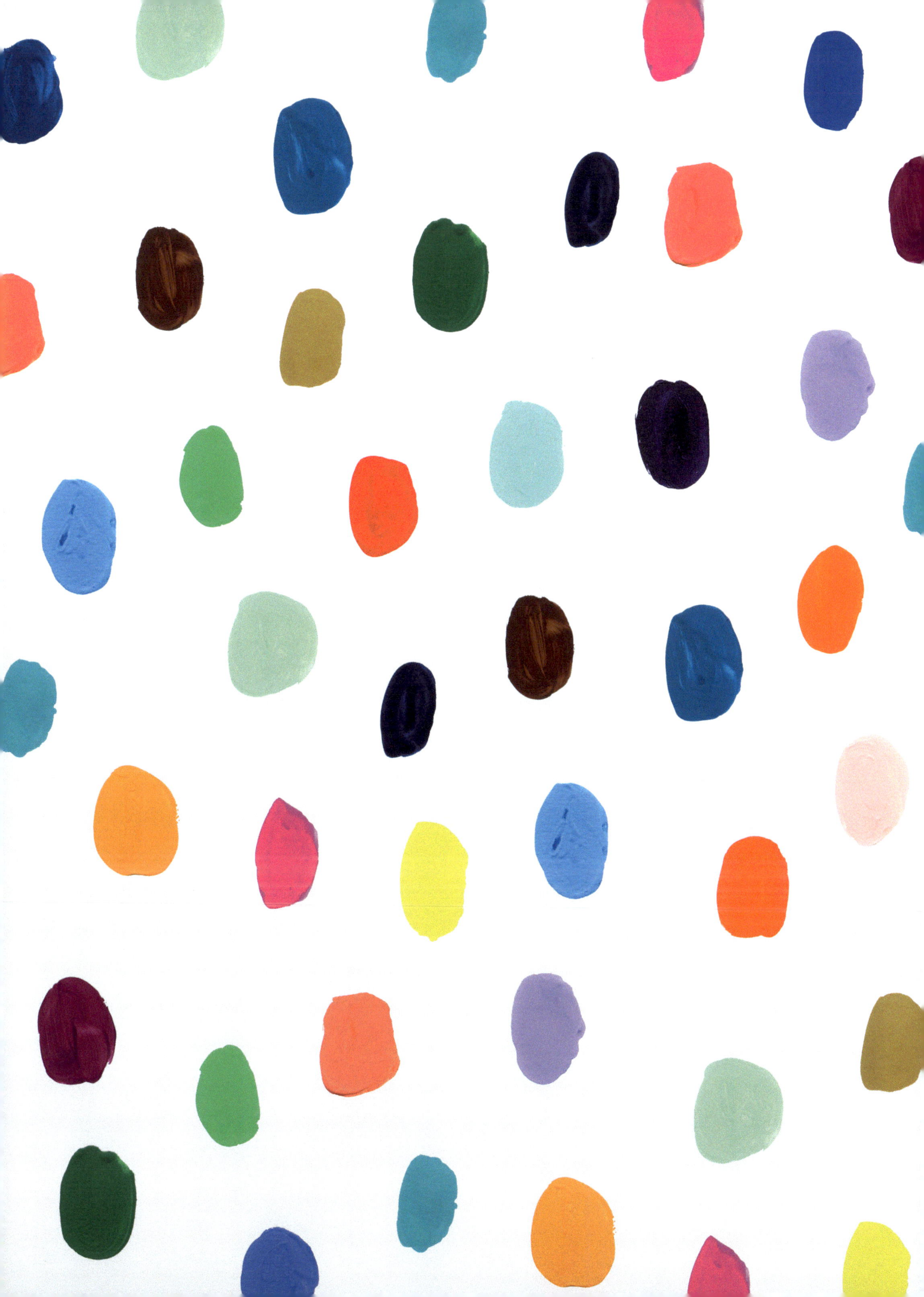

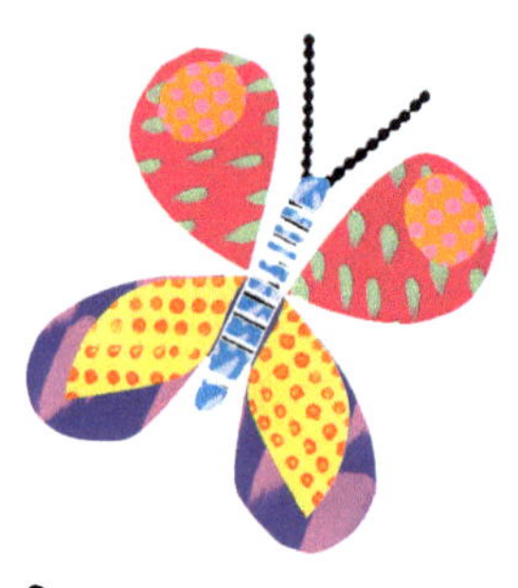

Inspiration

Colour inspiration is everywhere. For me, one of the most obvious places to start is nature. Flowers, foliage, animals and birds are a constant source of inspiration, and mother nature certainly knows how to put on a spectacular colour show.

Other inspiration for me can be in the form of food, vintage textiles and wallpapers, retro signage and packaging, street signs, clothes, architecture, interiors, sunsets, movies, travel and other cultures and a million other things. I'm always taking photos with my phone of things that catch my eye.

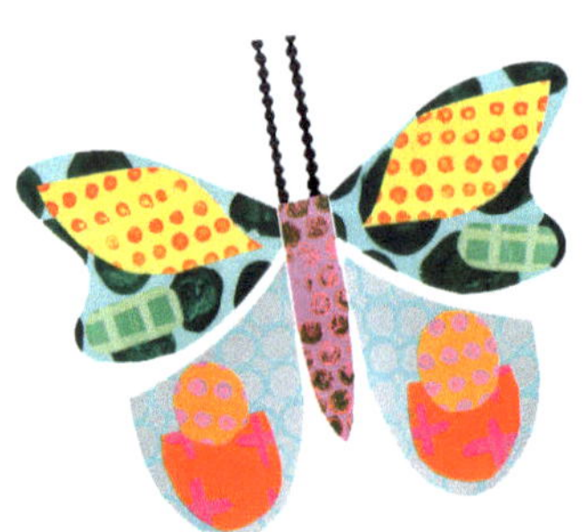

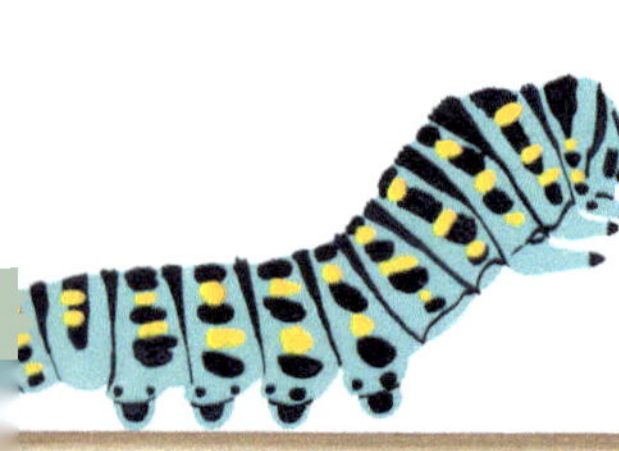

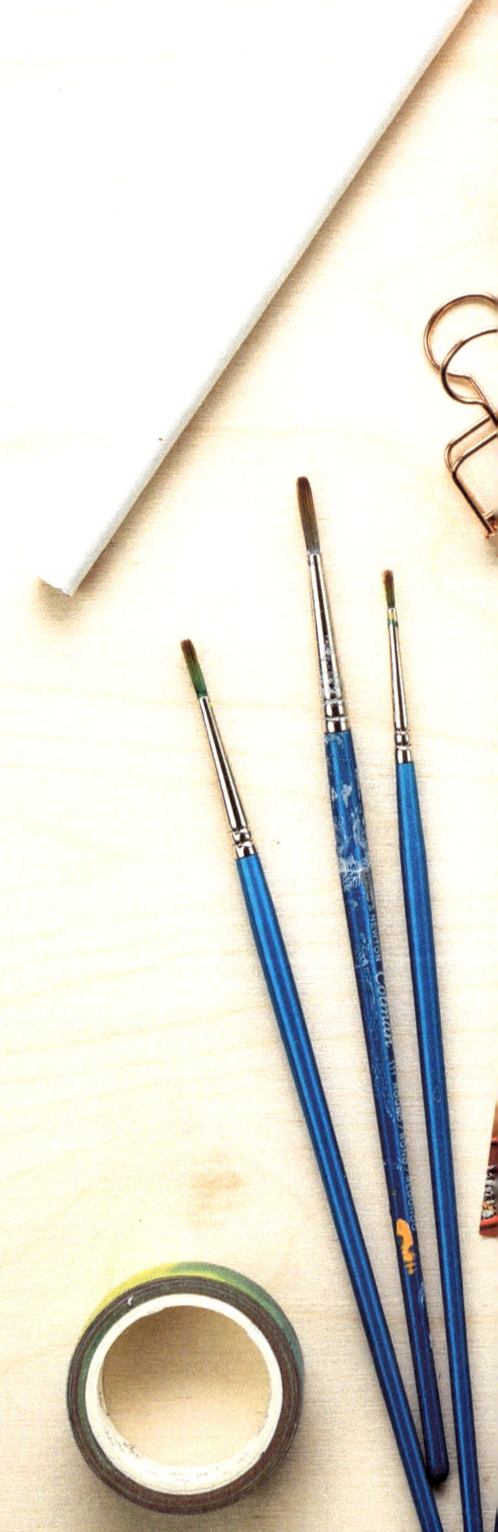

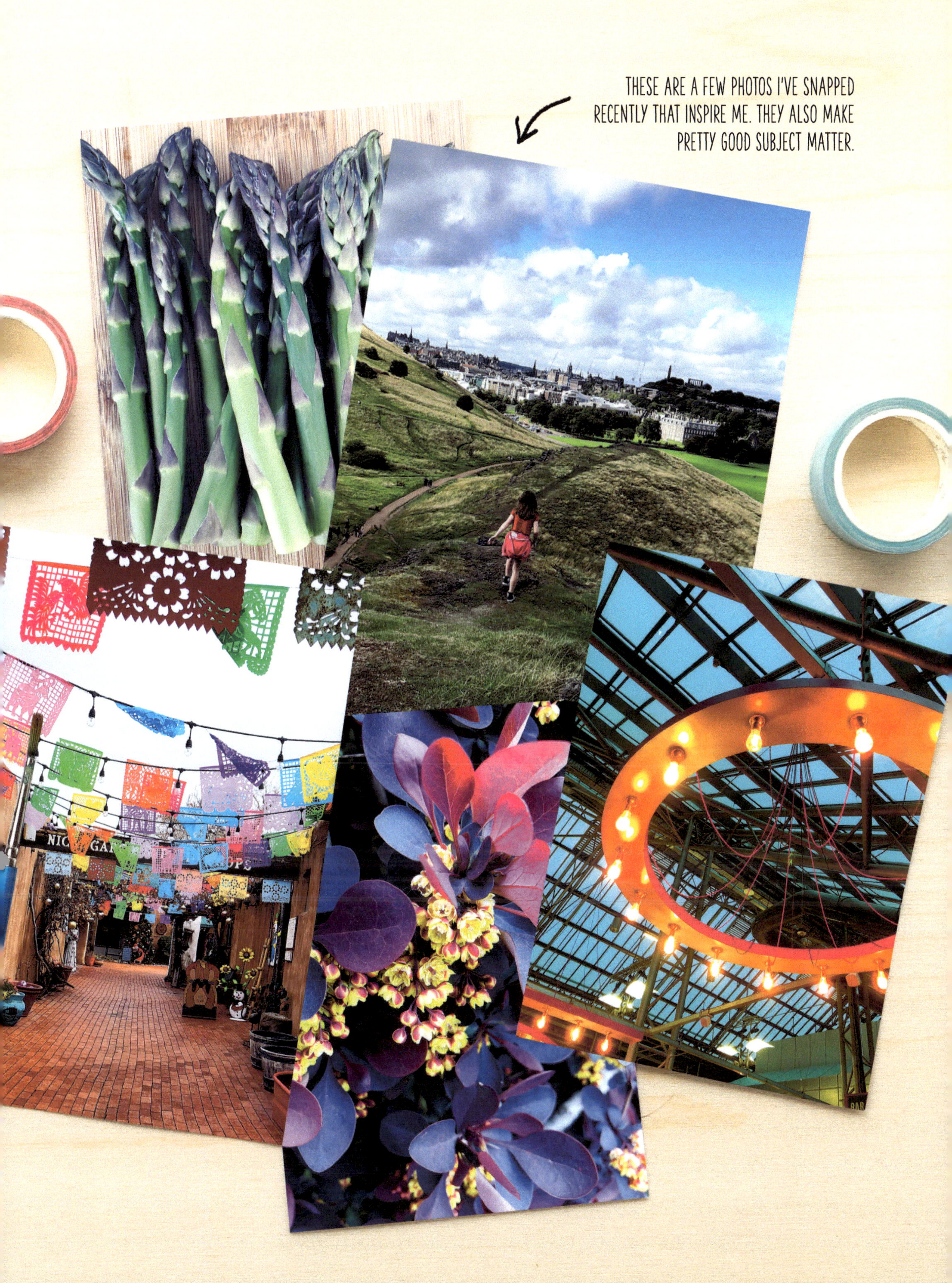
THESE ARE A FEW PHOTOS I'VE SNAPPED
RECENTLY THAT INSPIRE ME. THEY ALSO MAKE
PRETTY GOOD SUBJECT MATTER.

Colour Theory

To figure colour out in painting, we need to strip it back to the basics. Knowing how we can use colour in our art involves a little science, but don't be scared off by that – it's very straightforward when we break it down. Having a general understanding of colour will ultimately make your experience with gouache painting more enjoyable.

First, I want to show you how easy it is to make a myriad of other colours from just three basic primary colours. Here's what you need to know before we do that.

In colour theory, colours are organized on a colour wheel, grouped into three categories: primary, secondary and tertiary colours. Think of it like this:

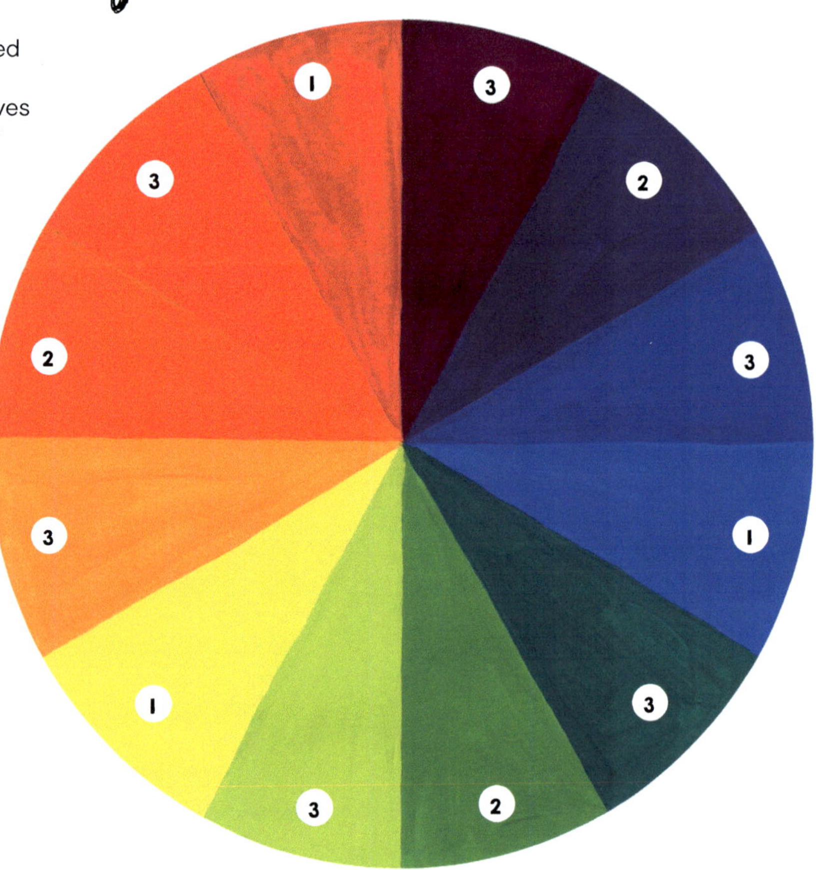

THE COLOUR WHEEL IS A USEFUL TOOL IN COLOUR THEORY. IT'S A SIMPLE VISUAL REFERENCE FOR ANALOGOUS, COMPLEMENTARY AND DISCORDANT COLOURS (SEE OPPOSITE).

1. Primary Colours – The Parents

In art, the three primary colours are considered to be red, blue and yellow. On the colour wheel, they're placed at equidistant points. The number of colours that you can create from these three basic colours is almost limitless.

2. Secondary Colours – The Children

When the primaries are mixed together, they make children – three new colours are created. Green is created by combining blue and yellow primaries, orange comes from combining yellow and red, and purple is made with red and blue.

3. Tertiary Colours – The Grandchildren

The remaining six colours on the wheel can be created by mixing combinations of primary and secondary colours.

How colours interact

Analogous Colours

Colours that are close to each other on the colour wheel are considered to have a harmonious relationship and are known as 'analogous colours'. When used together, they create a harmonious, soothing effect.

Complementary Colours

Colours that are directly opposite each other on the wheel are known as 'complementary colours' and create a lovely vibrancy when they're placed next to each other. Blue and orange, purple and yellow, and red and green are complementary colours. Mixing two complementary colours together will make brown.

Discordant Colours

Colours that are discordant are almost opposite/complementary on the wheel, but not quite. This pairing tends to be neither soothing nor vibrant, but is instead interesting and stimulating. An example of discordant colours would be orange and the green/blue between blue and green in the colour wheel. Discordant colours work well next to neutrals – colours that aren't part of the colour wheel, such as black, white, taupe or grey.

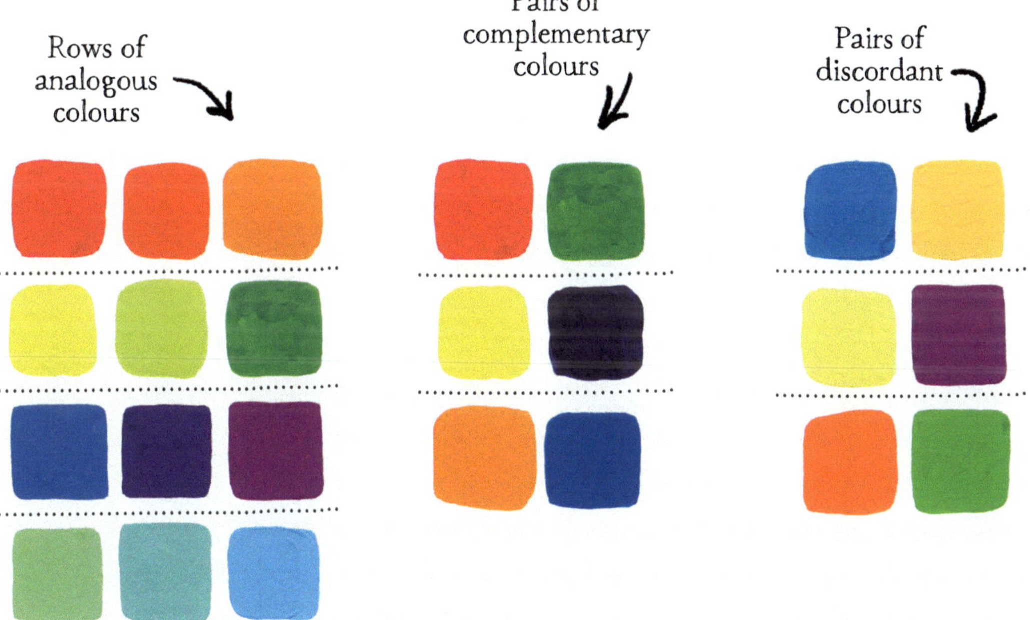

Colour Mixing

When you add black and white to the primary, secondary and tertiary colours, you can achieve almost endless tints and shades. There are a few simple guidelines when it comes to mixing with white and black.

Tints

Any colour that appears on the colour wheel is known as a 'hue'. Adding white to a hue will create a tint of that hue – a lighter, less intense version of the colour.

Shades

On the other hand, adding black to a hue will create a darker, more intense shade. Pre-mixed black absorbs a lot of light, so try to avoid using it where possible. It's better instead to create your own black by mixing all three primary colours together, creating an almost-black/grey colour (see Colour Exercise 2). In the following experiment, you can see the difference between the pre-mixed black straight from the tube (6) and the black that I mixed by combining blue, red and yellow in varying quantities (5). The pre-mixed black is a lot harsher. Ultramarine mixed with burnt umber can also produce a pretty good almost-black.

Experiments in mixing tints

For each of the following colours, I've added white gradually to show how the tints transform as the white content increases. I used a tube of permanent white in this example (see Colour mixing gouache: Recommended Colours for a Beginner Set).

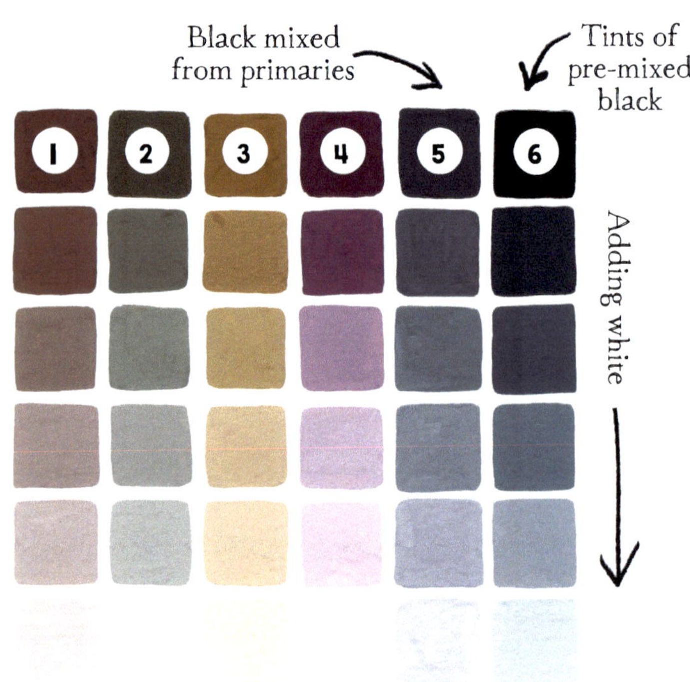

Column 1: Brown mixed from red and green.

Column 2: Olive green mixed from red and green, with the emphasis on green.

Column 3: Light brown mixed from blue and orange, leaning towards a more orange base.

Column 4: Violet and yellow with more violet.

Column 5: My mixed black created by mixing all three primaries together, gradually adding more blue, red or yellow until they cancelled each other out.

Column 6: Ivory black straight from the tube.

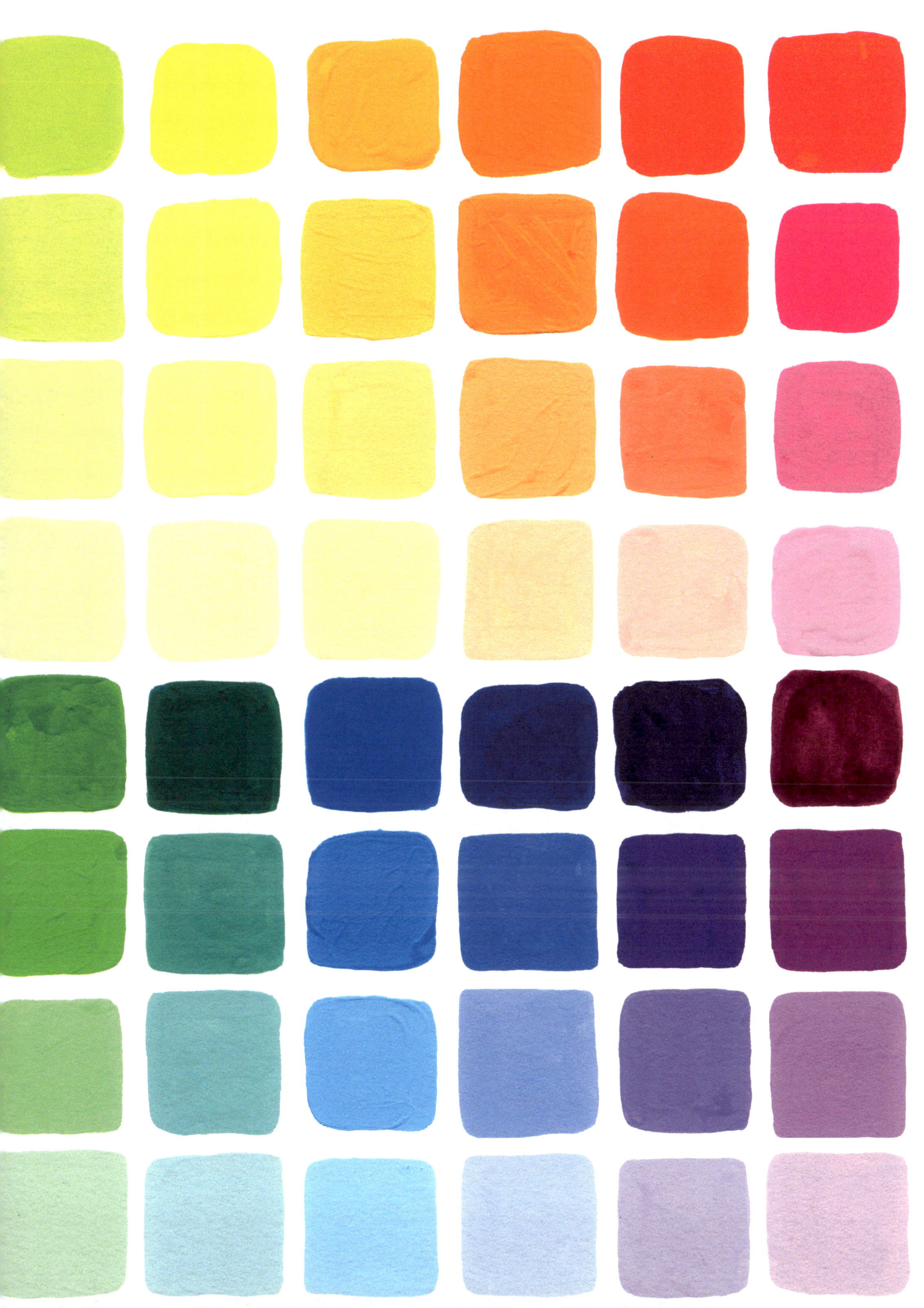

Colour mixing gouache

There are a few tips and tricks when it comes to mixing gouache paint, which I'll outline here, that will give you a great start with this medium. In the beginning, it can be tricky to get the right consistency balanced with the colour you're trying to mix, but don't feel put off. Practice makes everything better.

Consistency

Gouache paint is best used in a loose cream consistency. To achieve this, take some paint from the tube onto your mixing palette and then add clean water with your brush until the paint has the right consistency. You can also use it in a more watered-down fashion, similar to watercolour paint – just add more water. At the other end of the consistency spectrum, use little to no water for a thicker, more textured, painterly finish. Through practice, you'll eventually be able to tell by feel when you paint whether the consistency is right. It has a fairly sticky feel if it's too thick and needs more water. You ultimately want your brush to glide across the paper with ease. Keep a spare piece of paper or your sketchbook close by to test colours and consistency before applying paint to your artwork.

Water

I use two water jars while I'm painting and regularly change the water. This is important because it prevents your colours from getting 'muddy' while mixing. I use one jar for washing off the colour and the other for lifting clean water onto my palette to mix the paint.

Quantity

Sometimes it's difficult to judge how much paint you need, and this is something that you'll learn through practice, too, although I still occasionally squeeze way too much paint onto my palette. Remember, you can always add more if you need it, but it's more difficult to remove paint if there's too much. If you want to mix up larger quantities of a certain colour, it's a good idea to do that in an airtight jar or container so that you can put a lid on it and save it for later (see Materials and Tools: Other Tips and Tools). Trying to match a colour if you run out can be a real headache.

Recommended Colours for a Beginner Set

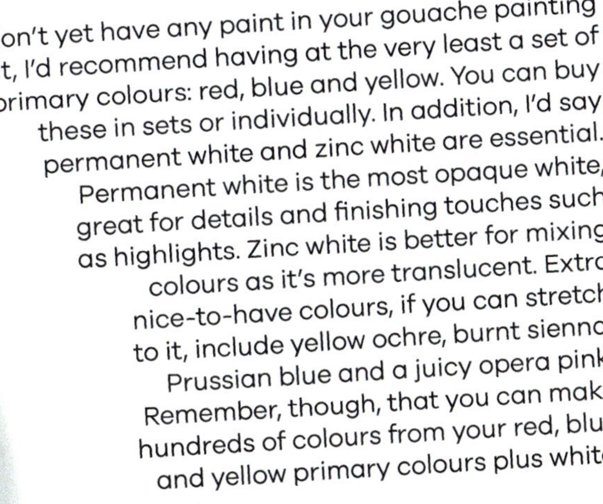

If you don't yet have any paint in your gouache painting toolkit, I'd recommend having at the very least a set of primary colours: red, blue and yellow. You can buy these in sets or individually. In addition, I'd say permanent white and zinc white are essential. Permanent white is the most opaque white, great for details and finishing touches such as highlights. Zinc white is better for mixing colours as it's more translucent. Extra nice-to-have colours, if you can stretch to it, include yellow ochre, burnt sienna, Prussian blue and a juicy opera pink. Remember, though, that you can make hundreds of colours from your red, blue and yellow primary colours plus white.

Getting To Know Colour

Colour Exercise 1:
Paint a colour wheel.

For this exercise, we're going to use basic primary colours to make secondary and tertiary colours. You'll be amazed at the magic as you mix the three parent colours.

1. First, draw a circle using a pair of compasses or draw around a small plate. Divide the circle into 12 equal wedge-shaped pieces.

2. Squeeze a little primary red paint straight from the tube onto your palette. Add some water to get the consistency right (see Colour: Colour Mixing), then paint the red into one of the triangular wedges. Leave three wedges blank and then on the fourth do the same with primary blue. Skip another three wedges, and on the fourth paint primary yellow.

3. Next, mix red and blue on your palette to make purple, then paint it into the blank in between the blue and red wedges, leaving a blank at either side. Do the same with blue and yellow to add a green wedge, then red and yellow to add orange to the wheel. Be careful to keep the colours balanced – not too red, too blue or too yellow.

4. Lastly, make the tertiary colours by mixing the secondaries (green, purple and orange) with a touch more of each primary colour, then paint into the corresponding wedges in the wheel.

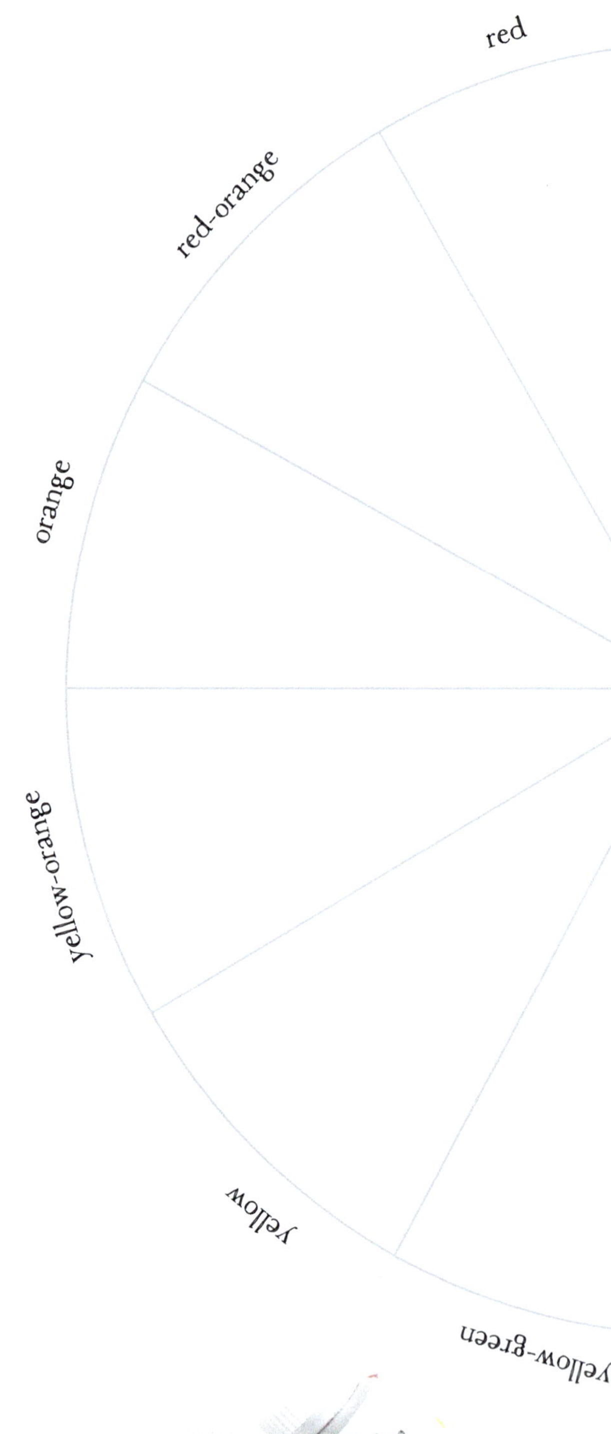

Colour Exercise 2:
Mix your own black.

Using all three primary colours, try mixing your own black. When you start this process, the mixture will probably be either very blue or too red, so just think about what you need to add to neutralize it. Does it need more yellow? If you feel like it, once you have a good black mixture, you could try adding white gradually to get an idea of how neutral your black is (see Colour: Colour Mixing).

Making black with red, yellow and blue

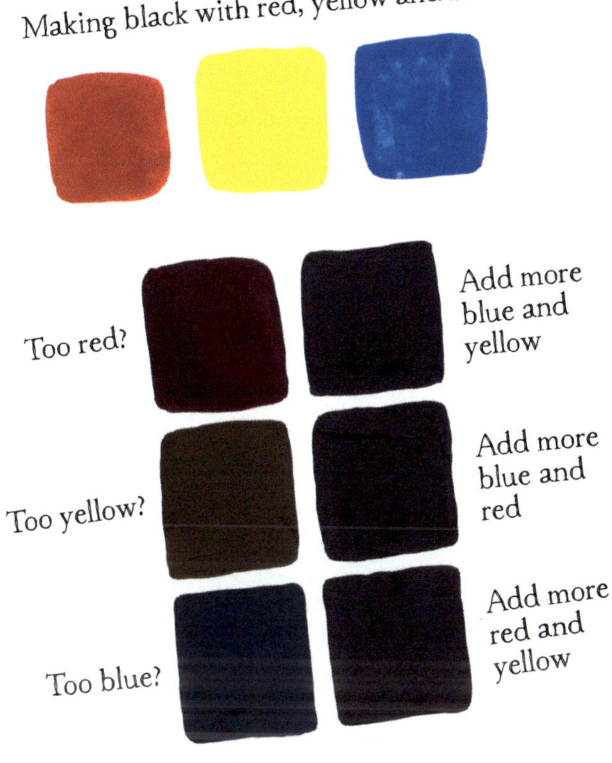

If you want to try mixing more colours before you start painting, make a grid and mix up some other hues, tints and shades like the examples shown in the Colour Mixing experiment. These experiments and exercises will help you to feel more confident when mixing colours for painting, and they're handy to keep as a reference.

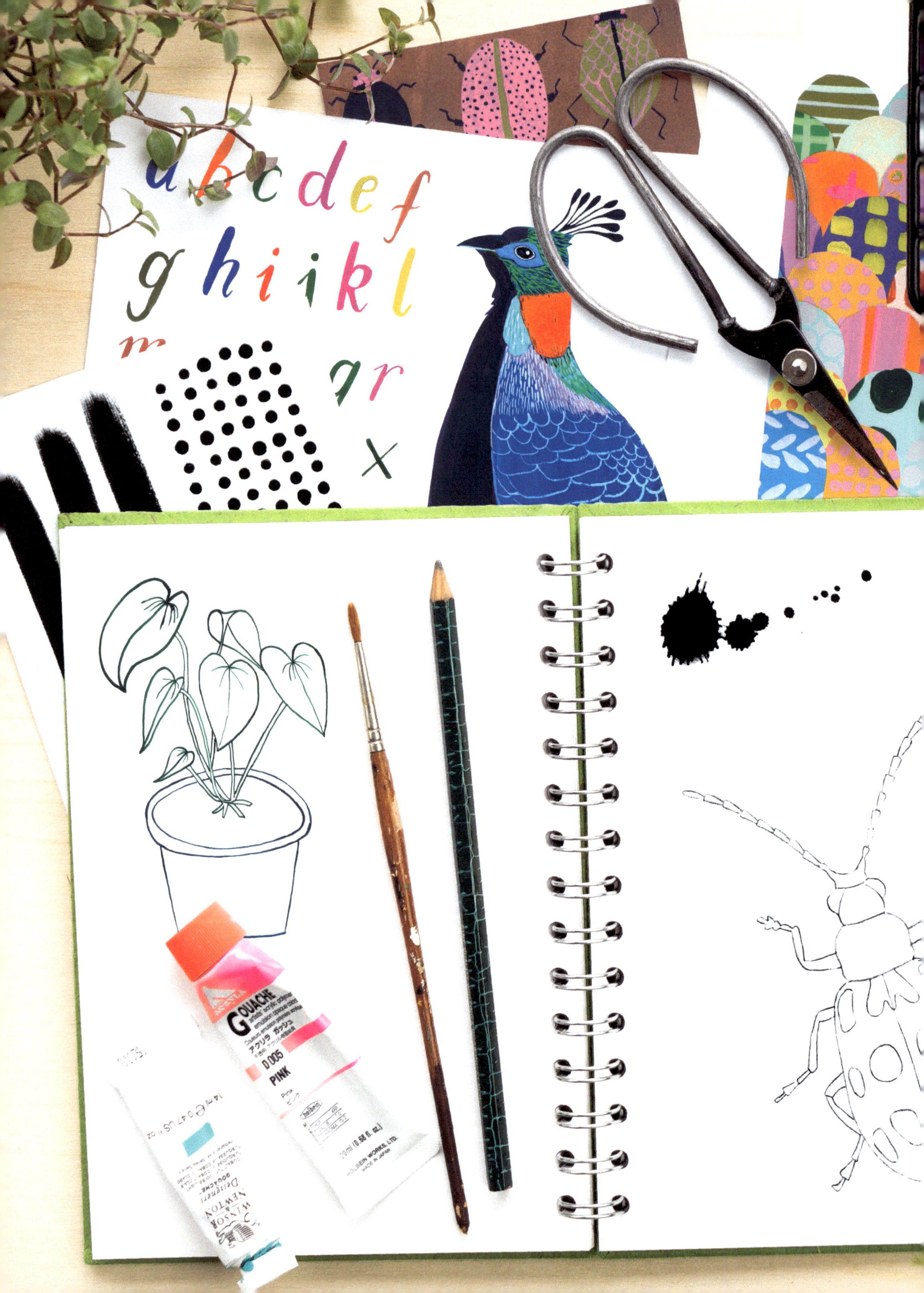

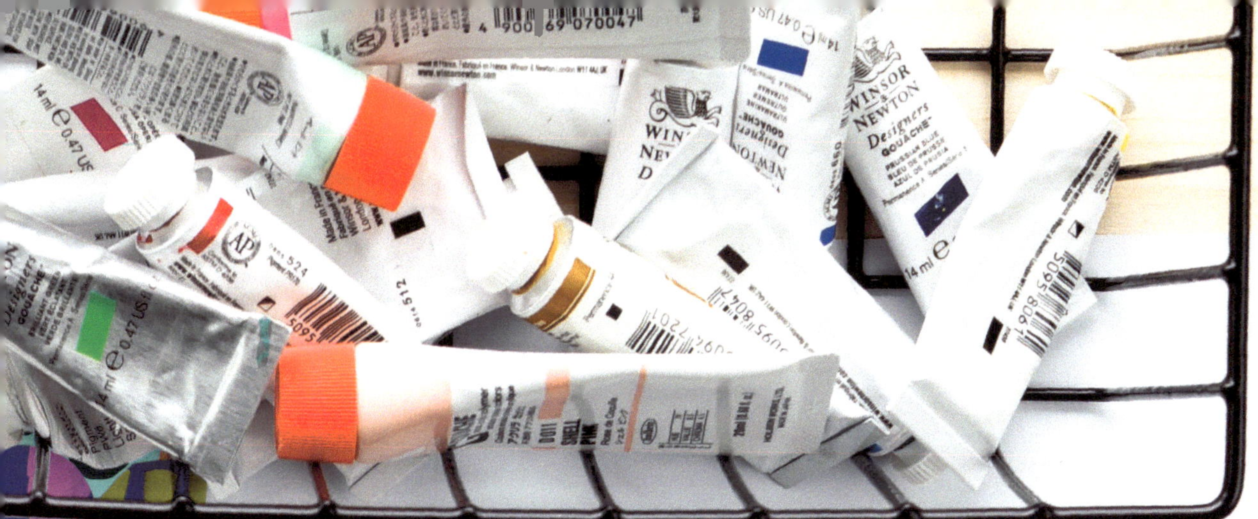

TECHNIQUES

Over the next few pages, I'm going to show you some techniques that I use in my work with gouache paint. I've also included some techniques, such as sketching and digitizing, that aren't paint, but they are a part of my process. Within each piece of work that I create, I can use multiples of these techniques.

Each technique has a little exercise at the end for you to try that will help you understand how you can use the medium.

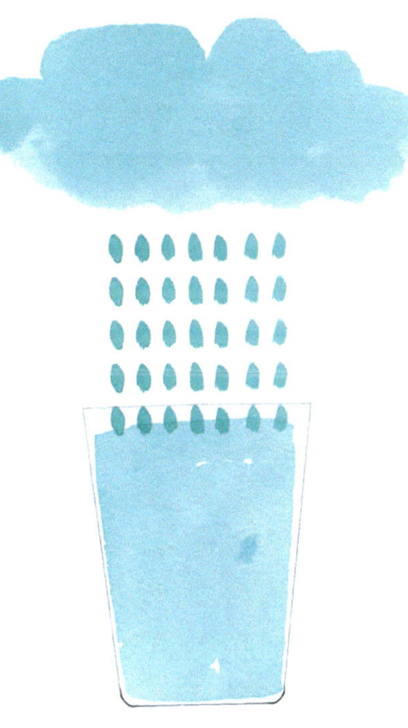

Sketching

When it comes to sketching, all you really need is some paper, a decent pencil and an eraser. I love using Pentel Twist-Erase mechanical pencils in either 0.5 or 0.7 size, as there's no need to sharpen the lead – a simple click is all that's required. They also have a handy little eraser on the end that's great for getting rid of small lines.

I tend to sketch things out before I begin to paint, as I like to get the overall shape of the item that I'm going to be painting. I don't usually include a lot of extra details in my sketches. The spontaneity comes from the paint itself, not the sketch, and, unless you have very thin watery paint, your pencil lines will disappear as soon as you begin to paint over them.

So, I like to think of my sketch as a simple guide for the overall shape rather than a detailed drawing. I generally like to use photos as reference, but I sometimes sketch from life, too.

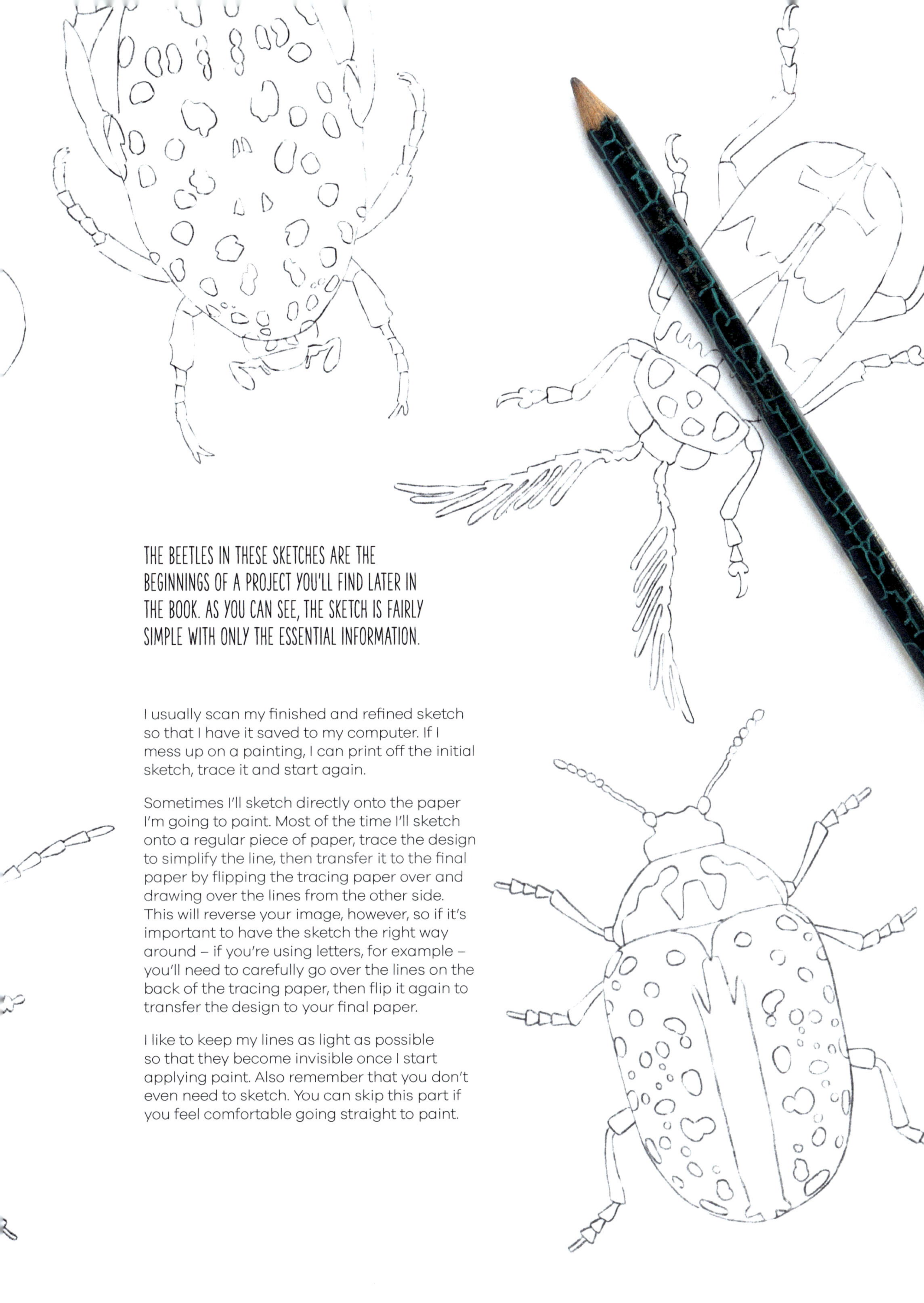

I usually scan my finished and refined sketch so that I have it saved to my computer. If I mess up on a painting, I can print off the initial sketch, trace it and start again.

Sometimes I'll sketch directly onto the paper I'm going to paint. Most of the time I'll sketch onto a regular piece of paper, trace the design to simplify the line, then transfer it to the final paper by flipping the tracing paper over and drawing over the lines from the other side. This will reverse your image, however, so if it's important to have the sketch the right way around – if you're using letters, for example – you'll need to carefully go over the lines on the back of the tracing paper, then flip it again to transfer the design to your final paper.

I like to keep my lines as light as possible so that they become invisible once I start applying paint. Also remember that you don't even need to sketch. You can skip this part if you feel comfortable going straight to paint.

Find your sketch style:

Find three or more things from your kitchen and simply sketch them using a pencil. You can use your sketchbook or some sheets of plain printer paper. It could be bottles of sauce, spice jars, mugs or cooking utensils. If objects like this aren't your thing, choose some objects that appeal to your own sensibility. Try using a continuous line for some, but also make more detailed sketches. This will help you to define your own style and enable you to naturally decide how and what to draw.

Washes

The great thing about gouache is that you can most definitely water it down to create a watercolour effect. It doesn't always have to be opaque and flat. Gouache typically has more densely packed pigment particles than watercolour. The more water you add, the more you'll spread those pigment particles out, giving that translucent watercolour look. You don't need much paint to achieve this effect.

Gouache paint is lovely when used as a wash. You can apply it to wet paper or load up a big brush to create a beautiful background. Think about where more transparency is needed in your work – for example, to depict water or liquid.

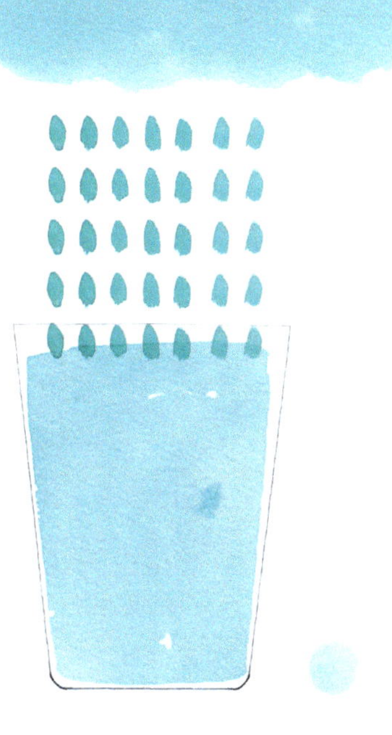

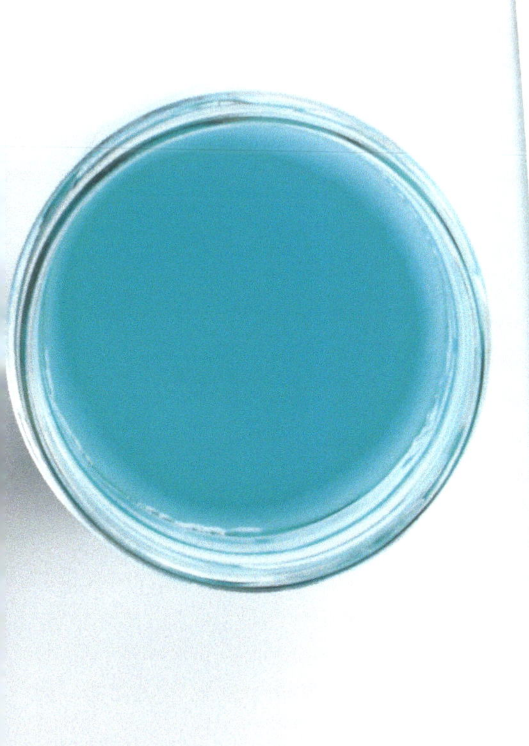

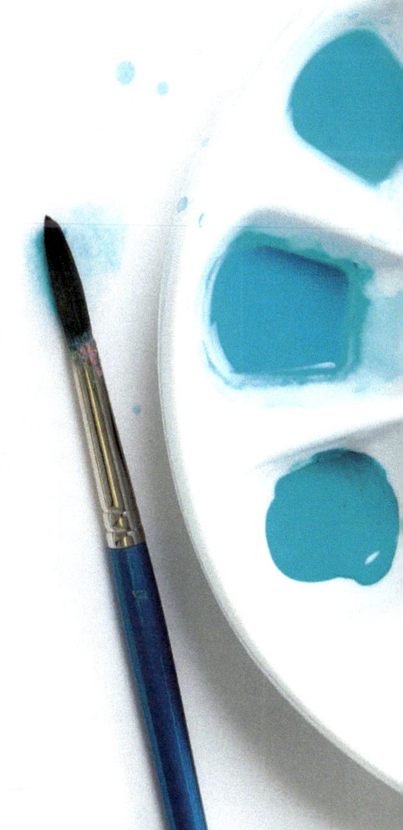

Overcome the blank page

At the start of a painting, I lay down thinner paint to map out shapes. I then build up more opaque layers once the first layer has dried. Sometimes, facing a blank white page can feel intimidating and scarily overwhelming, so laying down a wash of colour like this, either before or after sketching, can really help to kick-start the process.

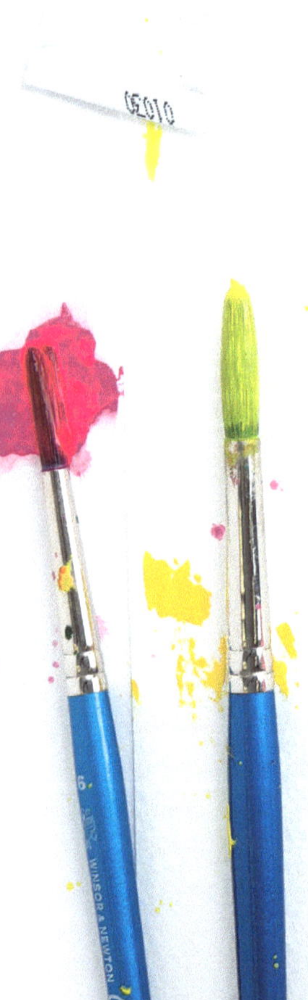

I PAINTED A LIGHT WASH TO GET ME STARTED ON THIS OWL. IT HELPS ME TO SEE AREAS MORE CLEARLY AND THEN I CAN BUILD UPON THOSE LAYERS.

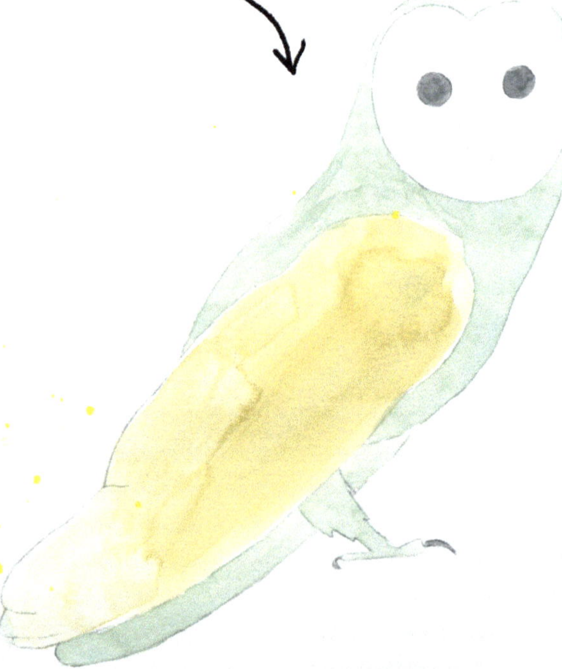

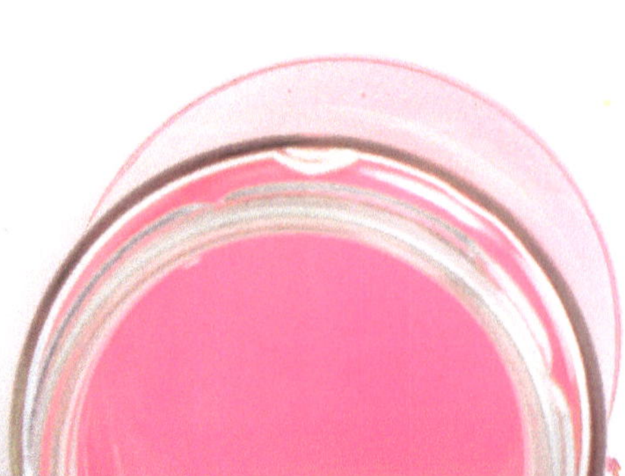

AN ABSORBING TECHNIQUE

Soak up any excess water with the corner of a tissue or a cotton bud and you'll notice how easily the colour underneath is lifted from the paper.

1. This mushroom has a wash treatment, and I added some detail over the stem with white gel pen.

2. Using a wash as a background is also a lovely technique when combined with linear drawing over the top so that the translucent background shows through. Notice how the paint has pooled in areas to create a lovely watery effect.

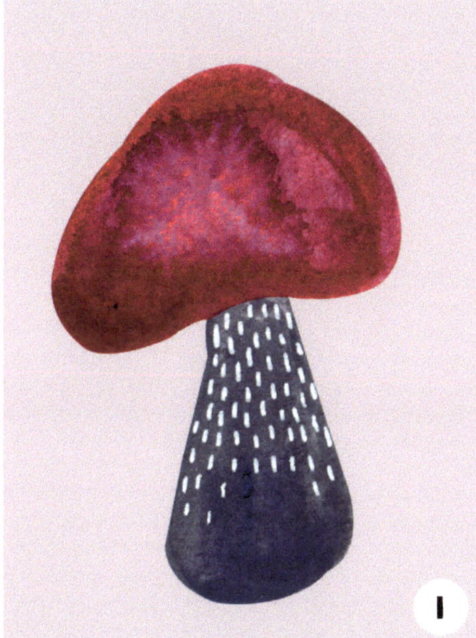

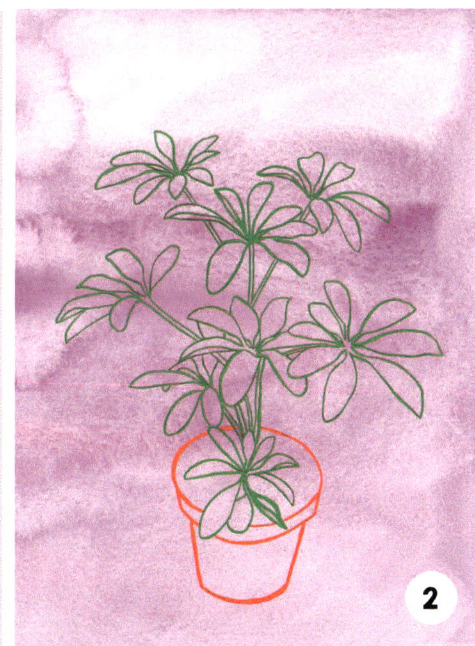

Feeling wishy-washy

Roughly draw four to six squares on a page of watercolour paper and, using a fairly large brush, fill each square with a different wash. Use different colours in each square and experiment with different amounts of water in the paint. Try blending more than one colour together on the page and, once the paint has dried, add droplets of water on one of the squares with a paint brush. You could also try painting a check or gingham with different colours to see how the colours interact when they overlap each other.

3. Two colours placed next to each other on a cold-pressed, rough textured paper.

4. A check pattern with two colours crossing and intersecting to see how the more translucent paint reacts.

5. This page was covered in a green wash and allowed to dry. Water was then dropped onto the sheet and the droplets soaked up by a cotton bud.

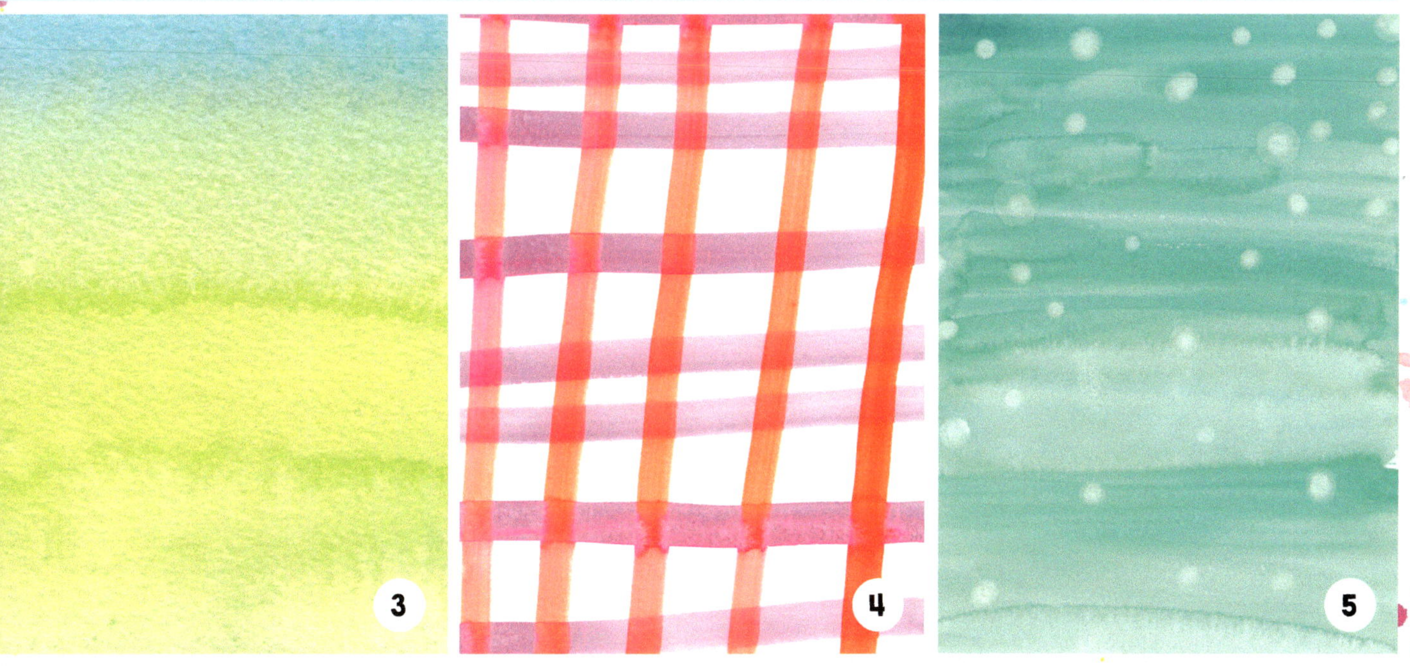

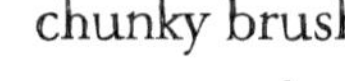

embossing tool

Mark Making

Mark making with gouache paint is a really fun way to introduce textures and depth to your painting. You can keep it simple by using various sizes and shapes of brush, but, if you're feeling adventurous, why not try using some alternative implements in a spot of experimentation?

You can use mark making in your paintings to create interest. Simple black on white works really well for mark making, especially if you later want to scan and use your textures digitally to enhance your paintings. I also absolutely love painting sheets of paper with brightly coloured marks to use in collage projects.

chunky brush

elastic band

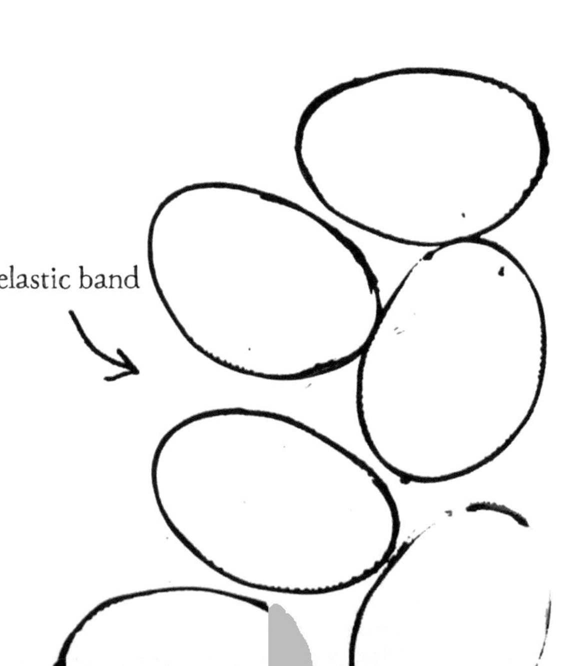

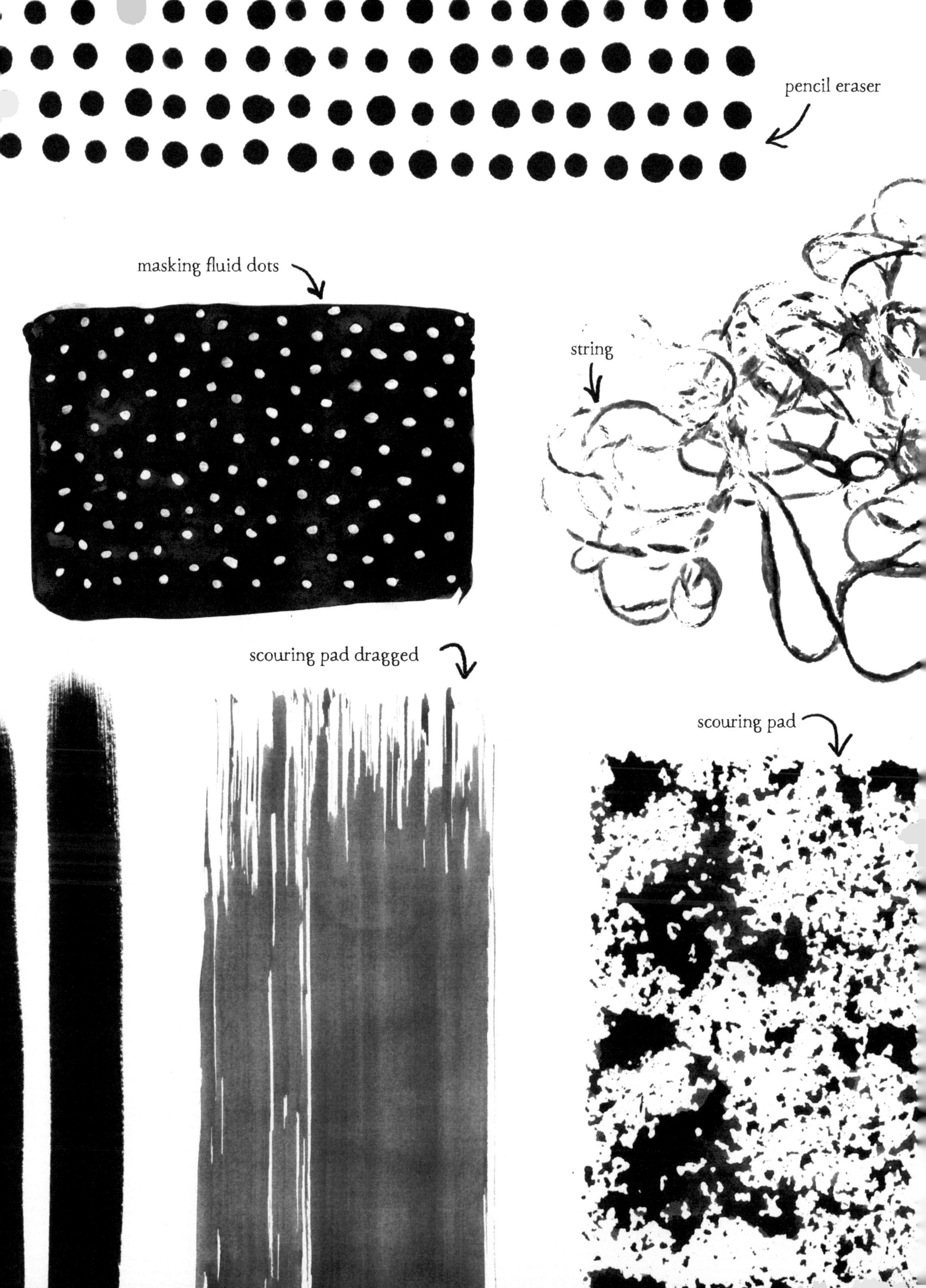
pencil eraser
masking fluid dots
string
scouring pad dragged
scouring pad

Add some colour...

For the following patterns, I used a variety of items that I had to hand around the house and used them in a technique very similar to printing. I painted the sheets of paper in solid colours and once they were dry, I chose a different colour to make my marks. Later in the book, I use some of the mark-making papers shown here to make an abstract collage (see Techniques: Collage).

As you can see from these examples, you could use a wide variety of everyday items. Get creative and see what you can come up with.

1. Aqua circles on grey

The end of a rubber bottle stopper.

2. Pink dots on orange

The end of a cotton bud dipped in paint and pressed onto the paper.

3. Aqua on pale yellow

A toothbrush flicked onto the page and then scrubbed.

4. Red on pale salmon

A very chunky brush loaded with paint and simply dabbed onto the page in a repetitive fashion.

5. Pale blue stripe on green

A small brush dragged across the page.

6. Dark green on aqua

A medium-sized brush held vertically and twisted in a circular motion.

7. Pale blue on grey

Scrunched-up paper towel dipped into paint and dabbed and scrubbed onto paper.

8. Green dots on pink

Bubble wrap painted and then pressed onto the paper.

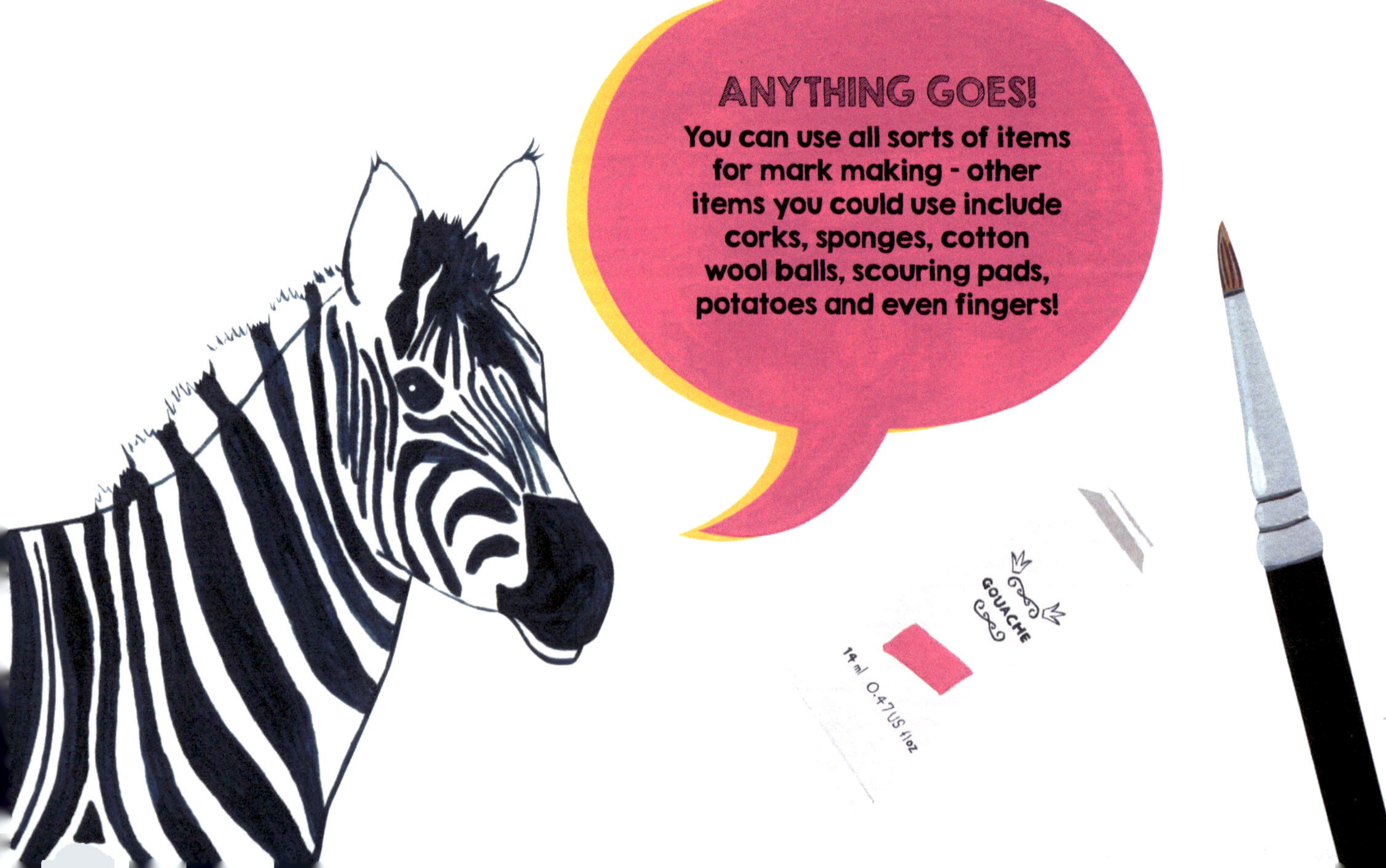

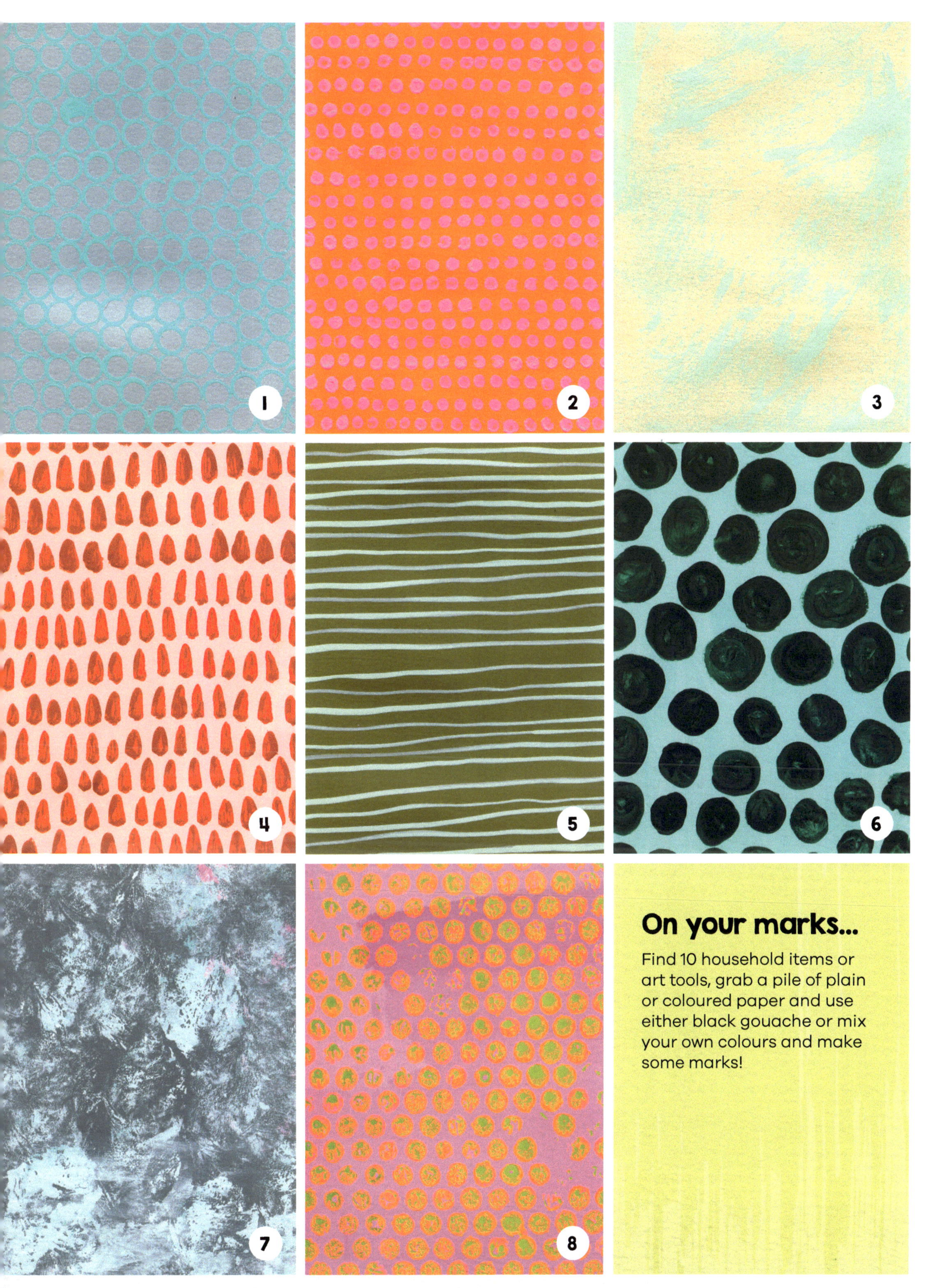
1
2
3
4
5
6
7
8
On your marks...
Find 10 household items or art tools, grab a pile of plain or coloured paper and use either black gouache or mix your own colours and make some marks!

Line Work

Drawing with my brush is one of my favourite things to do. It gives such a sense of freedom compared to working with a pen and really allows for beautiful organic lines. Wavy, dotted, dashed and solid lines make interesting features in painting – either as added details or as a simple line "drawing". You can also create straight, crisp lines using masking tape.

1. On the sloth, I used quite a long-bristled brush to achieve the long, straggly, dangling fur texture that sloths are known for. I painted the lines in a downward motion and directed them away from the sloth's head.

2. It's easy to achieve clean lines with the masking method. Here, green masking tape has been applied where I wanted to leave the paper beneath blank. Paint over the whole sheet.

3. Once the paint is dry, removing the tape reveals the sharp lines of the pattern. You could use masking fluid to achieve a similar effect.

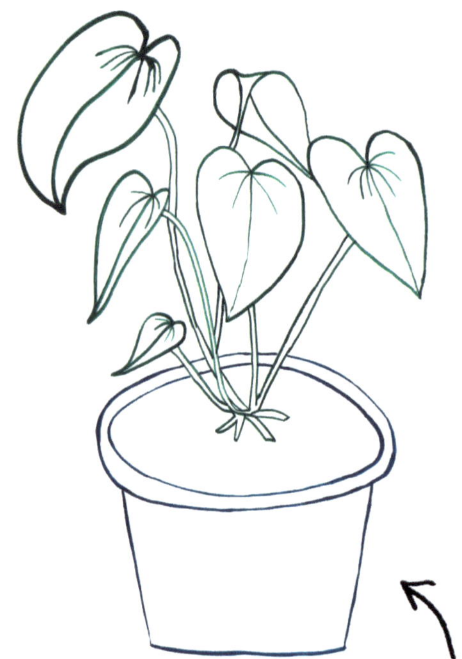

SKETCH IN PENCIL FIRST OR GO FREESTYLE, AS I HAVE WITH THIS POTTED PLANT TO GIVE NATURAL-LOOKING FORM TO THE LEAVES.

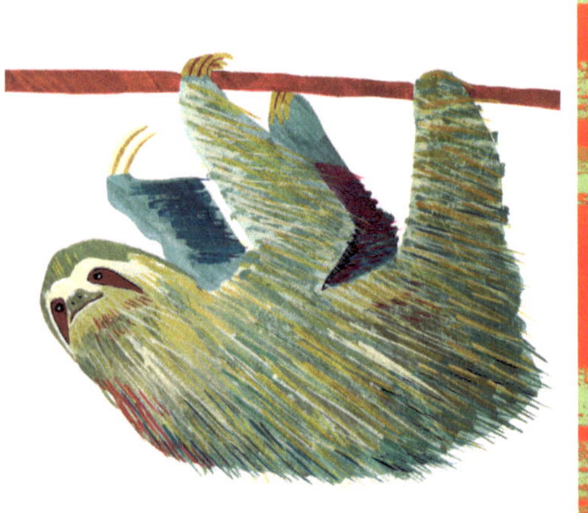

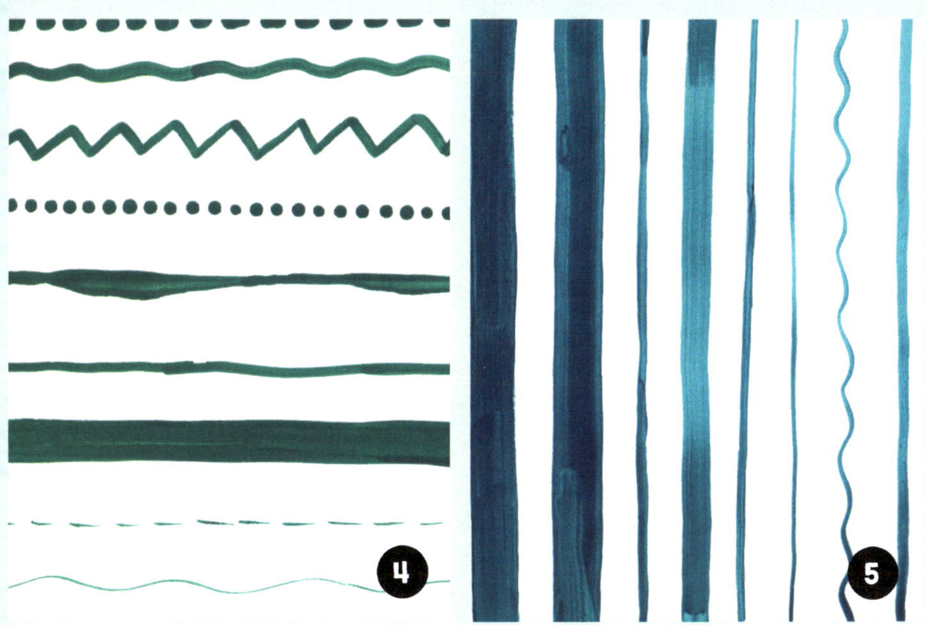

Practising your lines

See how many different types of lines you can draw with the same brush (4). Adjust the pressure and angle of the brush for different thicknesses and weights (5). Then try replicating feather, fur and petal textures similar to my examples below.

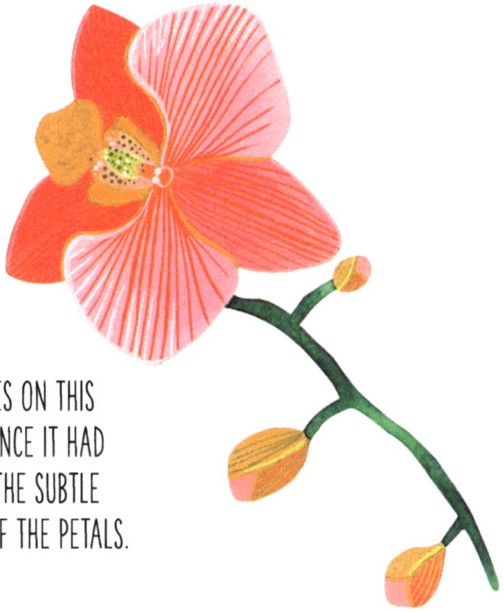

USING A VARIETY OF BRUSH SIZES HERE, I'VE CREATED LINES OF DIFFERENT THICKNESSES.

I USED TONAL LINES ON THIS PAINTED ORCHID ONCE IT HAD DRIED TO CREATE THE SUBTLE RIDGED TEXTURE OF THE PETALS.

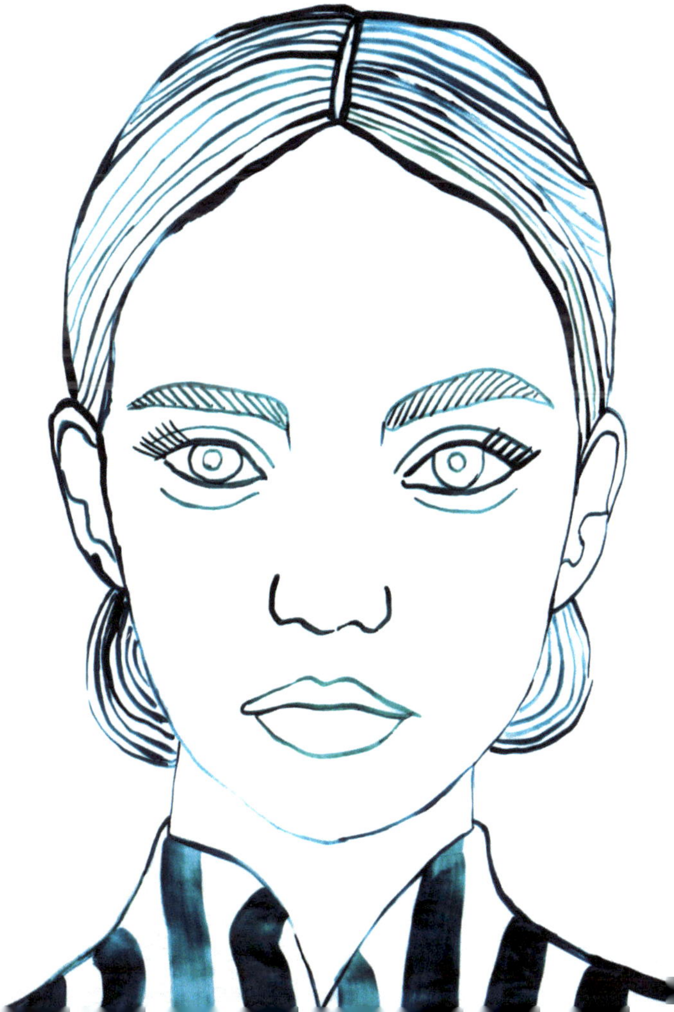

THIS FINISHED PAINTING SHOWS HOW I'VE USED LINES TO CREATE FEATHER SHAPES. I'VE USED AN ALMOST BLACK COLOUR TO RENDER THE FEATHERS IN VARYING SCALE.

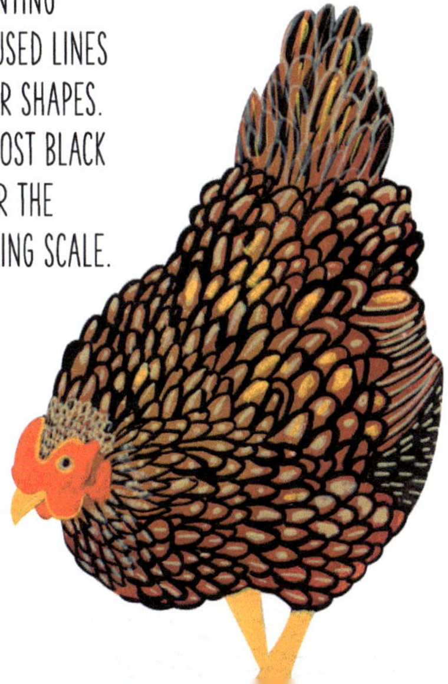

Shapes and Edges

Gouache, by its very nature, produces very crisp edges. All that's needed is a good brush and a steady hand. Easier said than done! But don't fear. To keep edges crisp for angular or geometric shapes, you can use artists' masking tape (see Techniques: Line Work). Masking fluid, which is a liquid that you can paint onto the page, blocks or masks out an area of the painting in a more organic way, producing softer shapes while maintaining the crisp edge. Once the masking fluid is dry, it rubs off easily with an eraser or a finger to reveal the shape underneath.

Edges can also be rough or blended. For example, for painting the rough edge of fur, you can use your brush with very little paint so as to give a drier consistency, then flick or scrub the brush to get the fine hair effect – as highlighted in this bear painting.

Cut and paste

If you're familiar with Photoshop, another way to sharpen and tidy up edges is to scan your painting and cut around the shape using a tool such as the pen tool, eraser, magic wand or magnetic lasso (see Techniques: Digitizing). You could also do this manually with scissors or a sharp craft knife. This allows you to be very free and non-literal in the painting – there's no need to be neat around the edges as you're going to cut out the shape.

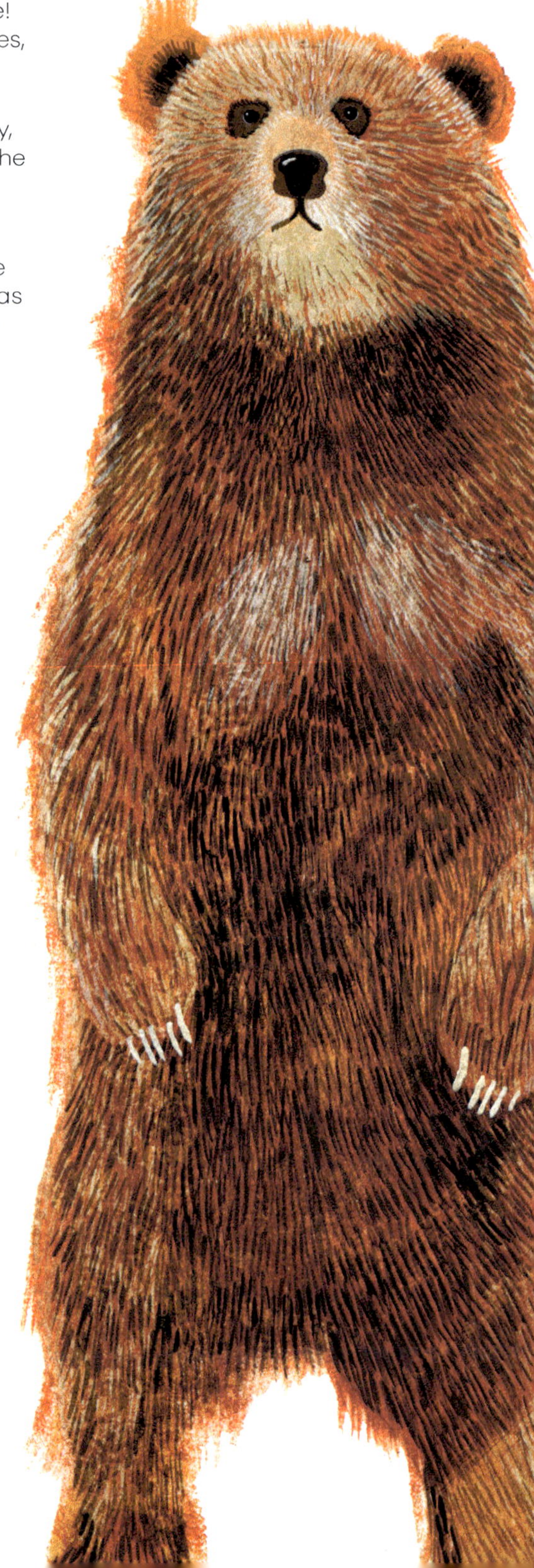

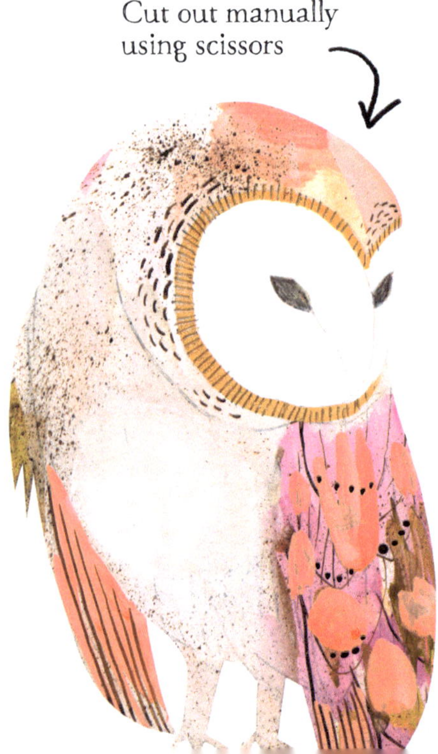

Cut out manually using scissors

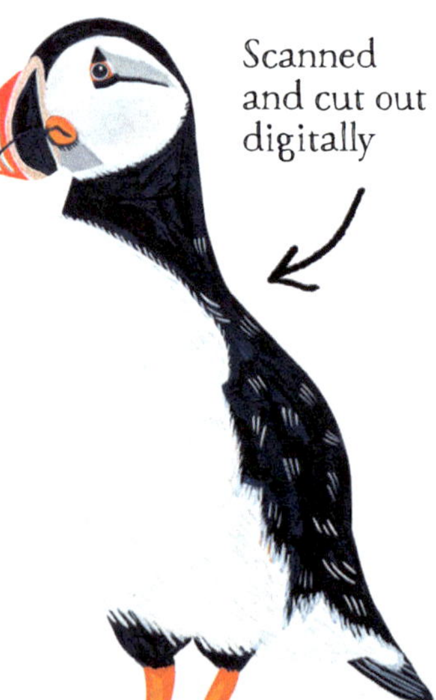

Scanned and cut out digitally

Gridlocked

Make a grid with artists' tape, placing all the horizontal strips first and all the verticals afterwards (or vice versa), so that you can remove the tape easily. Paint each square of paper exposed between the strips with a different colour (1). Once dry, peel the tape away (2). You're left with perfectly aligned painted squares (3).

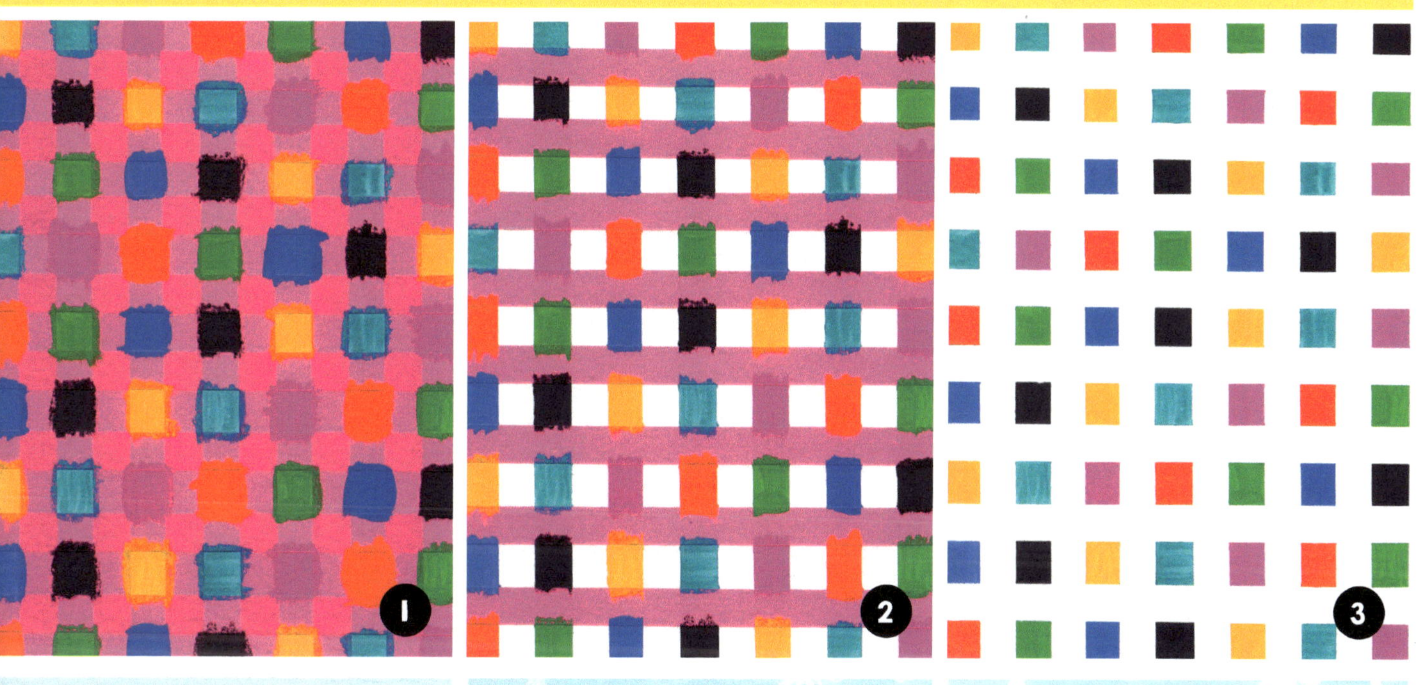

Mask off

Using masking fluid, paint some simple shapes. Once dry, paint a wash over the top (4). Leave the paint to dry, then rub away the masking fluid with an eraser to reveal the shapes underneath (5).

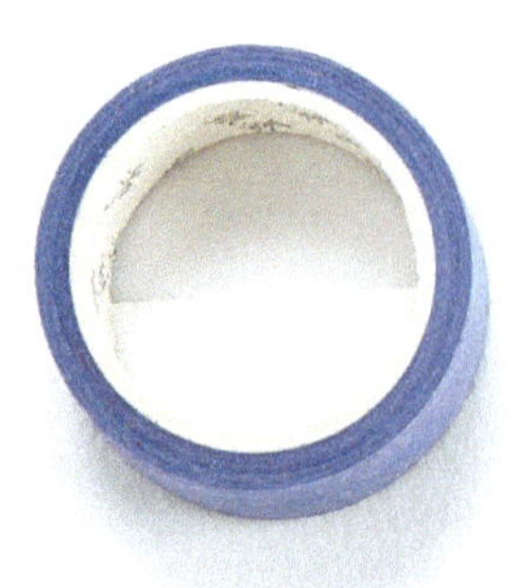

Lettering

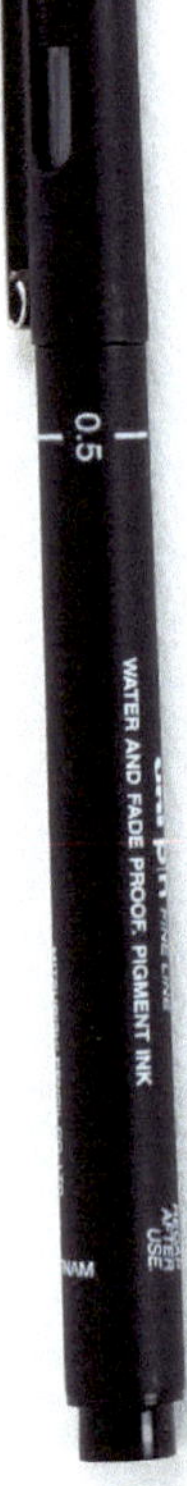

Before digital, gouache was used extensively in graphic design for posters and typography – so using gouache for lettering is perfect.

Letterforms are simply shapes, each with their own set of characteristics. This makes painting letters very enjoyable. Lettering can add another dimension to your work. Quotes are great to hand letter. The best way to start with lettering is to look at letterforms from existing typefaces. Signage on packaging and shop displays provide great inspiration, too.

With lettering, you can draw the shapes using a line or you can block in the shape with solid colour. You could use some paper that you've previously painted for collage, cutting out your own letter shapes. Add an extra decorative layer for even more interest, as I've done with the fun letter 'T' opposite, painted with a tiger pattern.

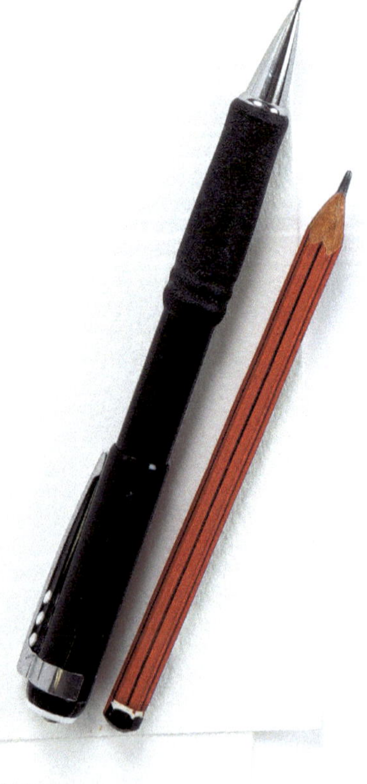

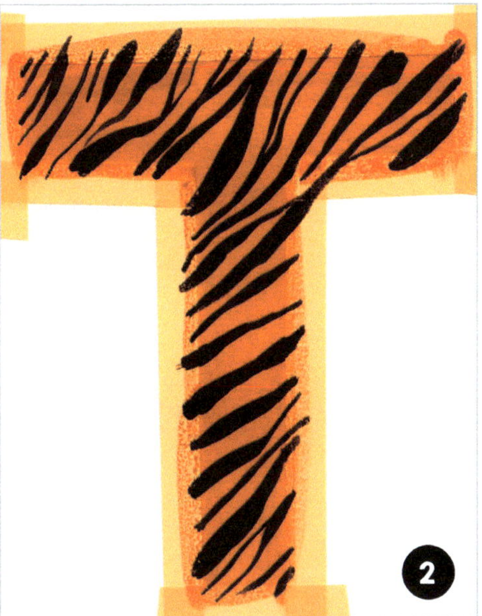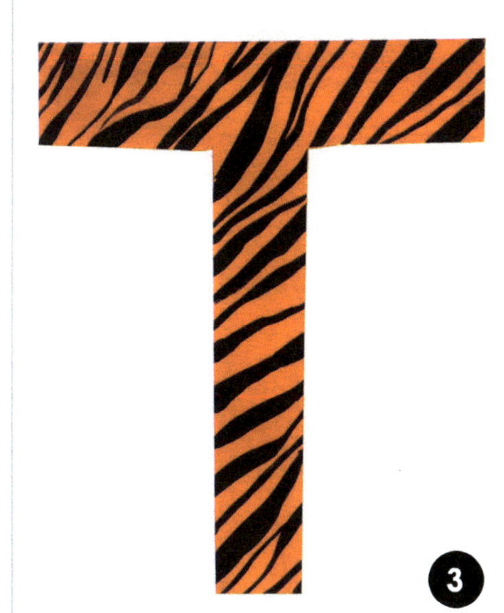

A tiger comes to 'T'

1. Mask out the letter shape using tape. Paint a solid colour within the boundaries of the tape and leave to dry.

2. Make some diagonal tiger stripes over the solid background colour, using lines in a darker colour. Leave to dry.

3. Peel off the tape once dry to reveal a lovely crisp edge.

Free and easy

Now let's try painting freehand lettering on a bright background for a bold and vibrant painting. Begin with a brightly coloured piece of card that you've bought off the shelf or painted yourself. For this example, I've used yellow card. You can draw some faint guidelines in pencil to make sure everything lines up centrally on the page, then erase them later.

4. Take a slightly darker but bright colour and freehand paint the letters OMG in a vertical format.

5. Sprinkle some stars around the letters using the same colour paint, or choose a different colour.

6. Once the paint is dry, finish off with little white highlights to decorate the letters and stars. I dipped the tip of a round eraser dipped in paint, then pressed it onto the page.

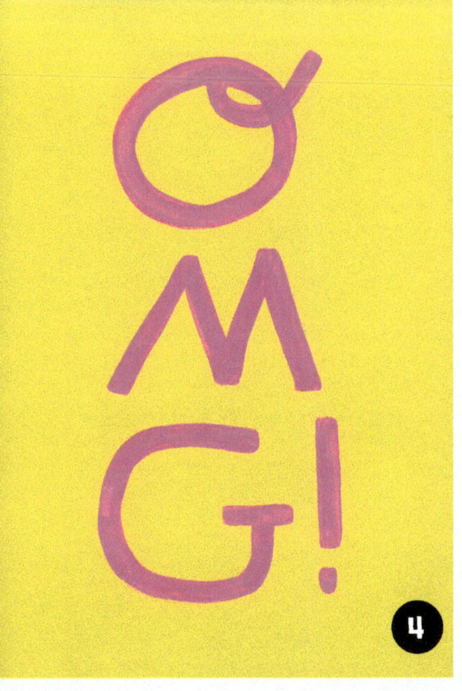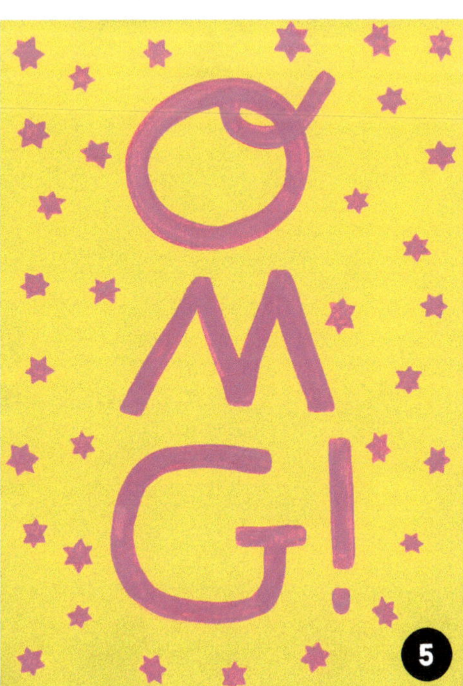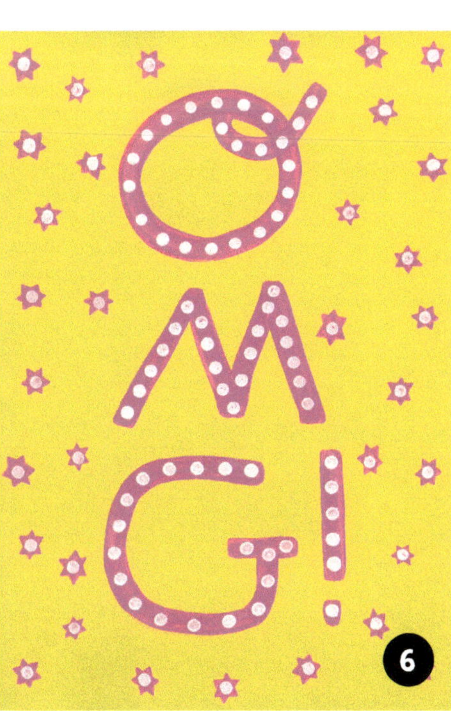

Letters three ways

1. Cut letter shapes out of painted paper and make a collage of your name.

2. Look at existing letterforms and paint each letter of the alphabet in a different way to experiment with shapes, lines and forms. Utilize your skills from the line exercise (see Techniques: Line Work).

3. Use your brush to draw some letters or words to get a feel for how the paint moves and to better understand the consistency that you need. If you're feeling confident, why not try lettering a quote that inspires you?

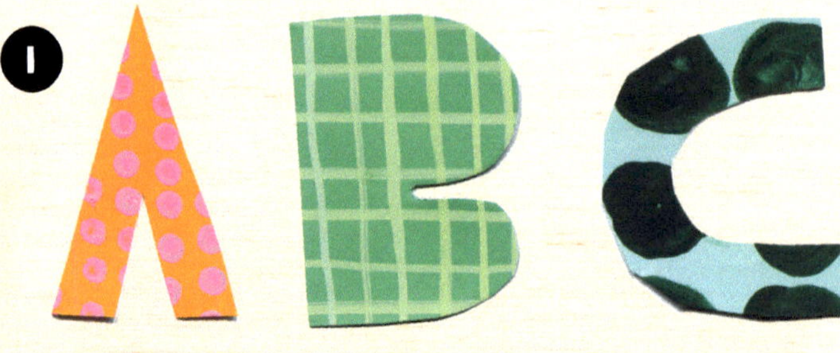

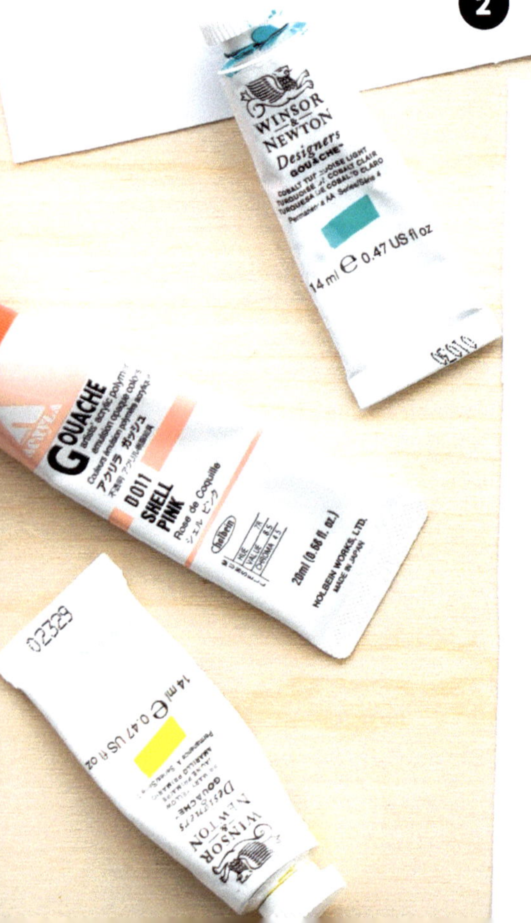

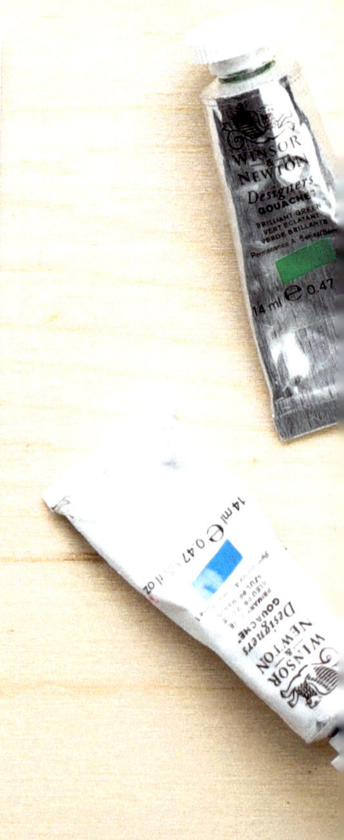

Faux calligraphy

In hand lettering, you can imitate calligraphy created with pen and ink to create a faux calligraphy style with paint. The general rule is that the downstrokes are thicker than the upward strokes. You can sketch out the letter shapes before you begin to paint or try it freehand.

LOOPY LETTERS

Think about how the letters would link together if they were handwritten, and add tails or loops for maximum calligraphic style.

Overlaying

The opaque nature of the paint makes gouache – and especially acrylic gouache – the perfect medium for overlaying. You can create beautiful textures and details easily by adding layer upon layer to gradually build a faux texture or pattern or to add depth to a landscape.

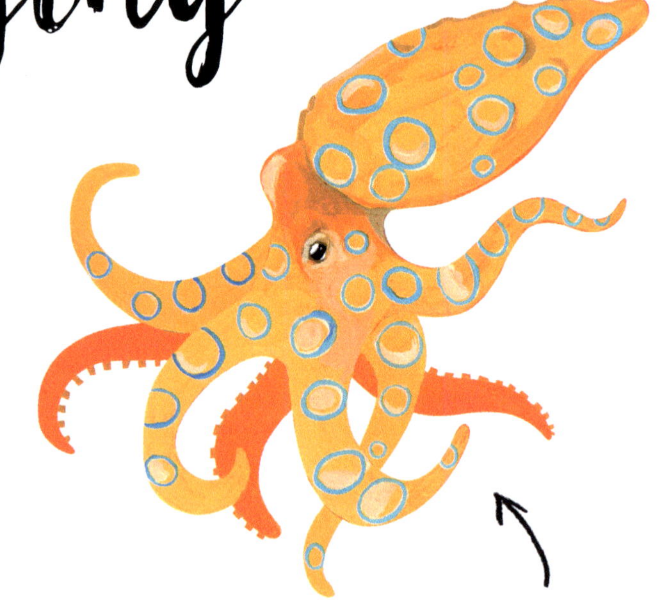

THIS ARMADILLO PAINTING SHOWS A LIGHTER CREAMY COLOUR ON TOP OF A DARKER GREY/ BROWN COLOUR. ONE OF THE BENEFITS OF GOUACHE IS ITS OPACITY.

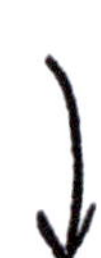

ON THIS PAINTING, I'VE CONTRASTED THE ORANGE BASE COLOUR WITH THE BRIGHT BLUE RINGS THAT ARE CHARACTERISTIC OF THIS TYPE OF OCTOPUS. THERE ARE ALSO SHADOWS AND HIGHLIGHTS AROUND THE BLUE RINGS AND EYES TO GIVE A FEELING OF DIMENSION.

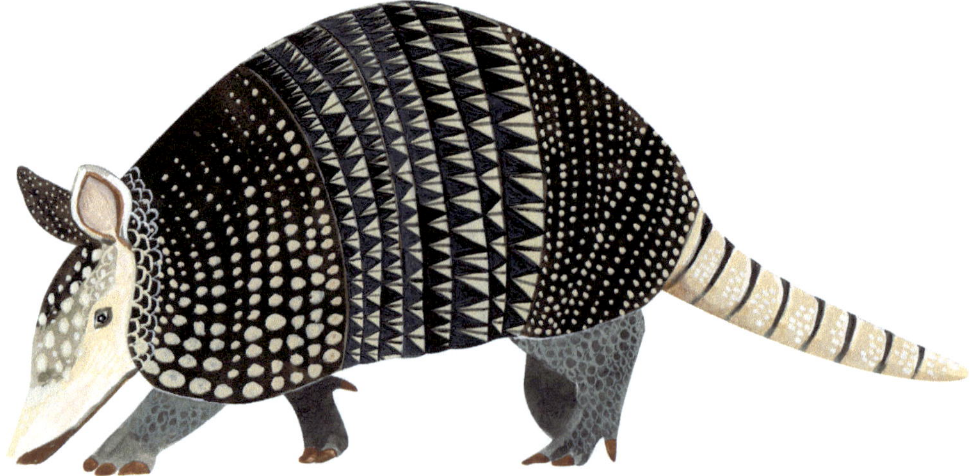

A wooden performance

1. With this wood texture, I began by roughly covering the page with a medium orange-brown colour, leaving visible brush marks.

2. Next, I drew on some wood grain lines in dark brown.

3. Then I took a slightly lighter brown and followed some of those darker lines to pick out highlights and to give dimension.

4. Lastly, with a just off-white brown, I repeated Step 3 to give more dimension. You can use this same technique for other textures such as fur, feathers, hair, water and anything else that is detailed, such as an elaborate vase with a floral or geometric pattern.

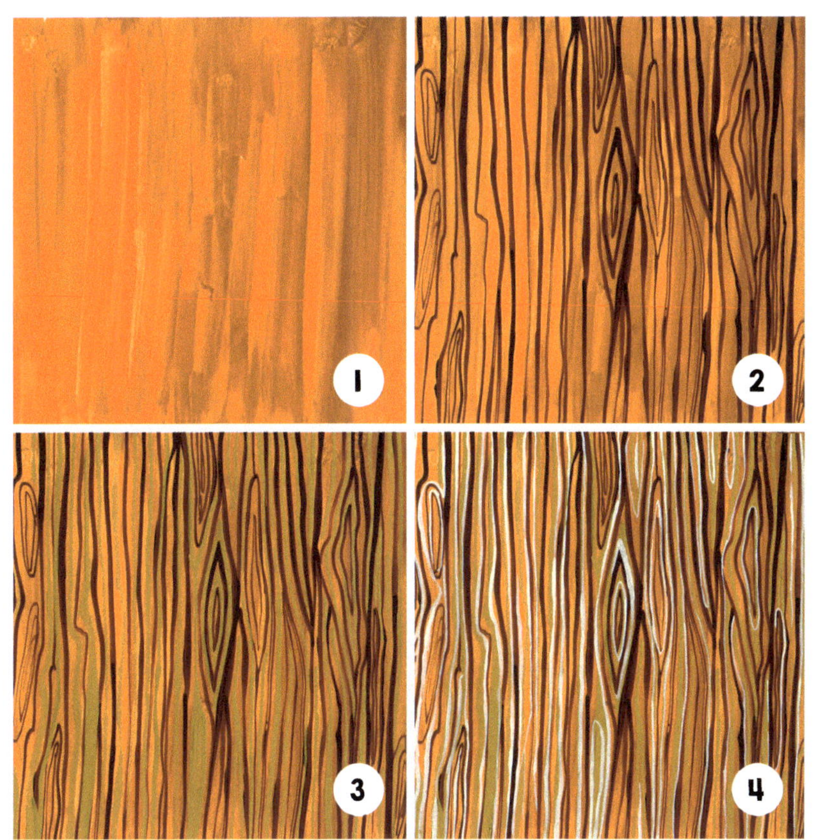

Rough it up

Look for different textures and patterns around you and try to replicate the patterns by building layers. This could be grass, water, tree bark, animal fur and so on. As you add layers, you'll notice that you're hiding parts of the previous layer – make sure that each new layer of paint is thick enough so it doesn't lift the underneath paint.

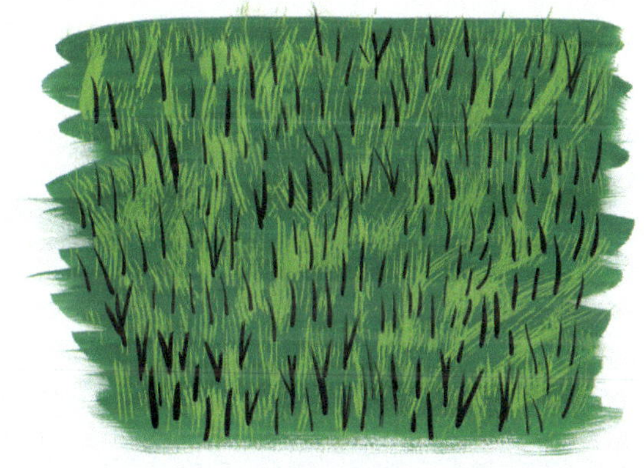

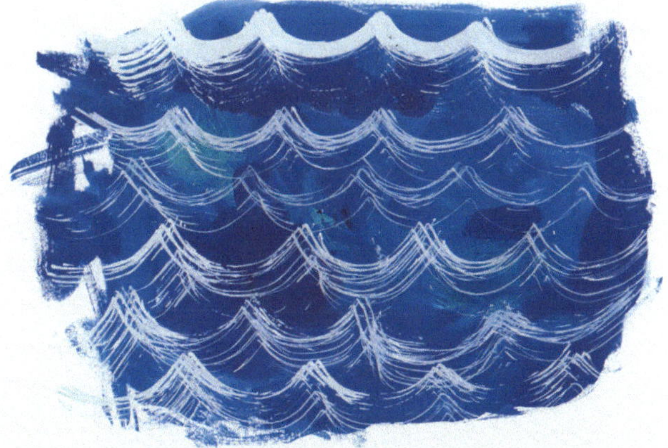

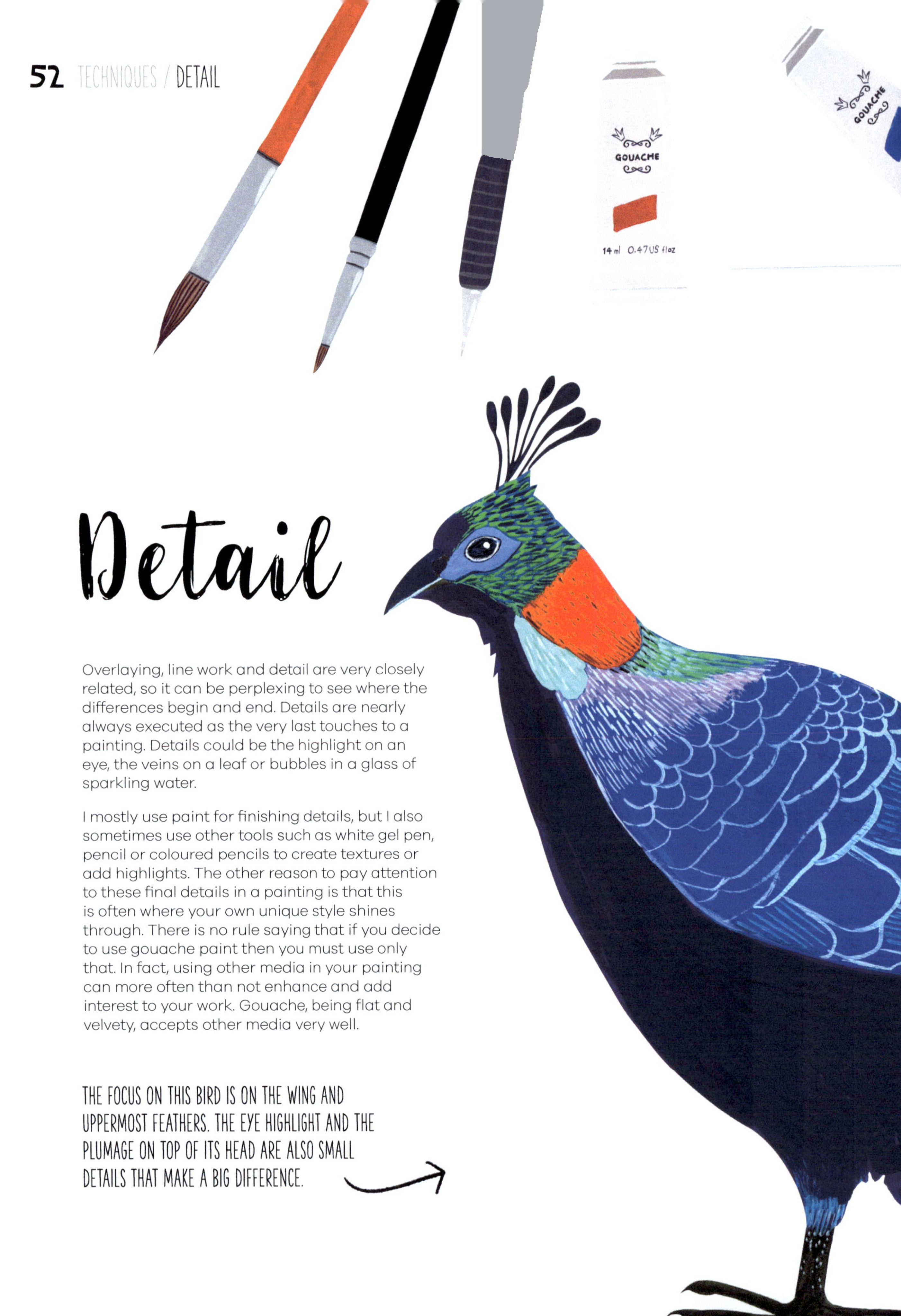

Detail

Overlaying, line work and detail are very closely related, so it can be perplexing to see where the differences begin and end. Details are nearly always executed as the very last touches to a painting. Details could be the highlight on an eye, the veins on a leaf or bubbles in a glass of sparkling water.

I mostly use paint for finishing details, but I also sometimes use other tools such as white gel pen, pencil or coloured pencils to create textures or add highlights. The other reason to pay attention to these final details in a painting is that this is often where your own unique style shines through. There is no rule saying that if you decide to use gouache paint then you must use only that. In fact, using other media in your painting can more often than not enhance and add interest to your work. Gouache, being flat and velvety, accepts other media very well.

THE FOCUS ON THIS BIRD IS ON THE WING AND UPPERMOST FEATHERS. THE EYE HIGHLIGHT AND THE PLUMAGE ON TOP OF ITS HEAD ARE ALSO SMALL DETAILS THAT MAKE A BIG DIFFERENCE.

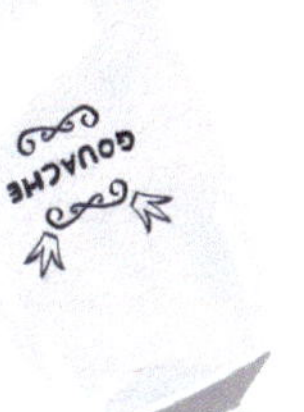

A leaf out of my book

Paint some leaf shapes and, once dried, finish them off by adding the vein details. Try looking at different leaves, as they all have different visible vein structures. You can use anything for the detail, but some ideas to try are gouache paint, coloured pencil, white gel pen, china markers, pastels, pencil or even collage.

THE DETAILS IN THIS PAINTING ARE MADE WITH PENCIL. I WANTED TO KEEP EVERYTHING QUITE SIMPLE AND JUST PICK OUT THE SMALLEST OF DETAILS - THE PERFORATION ON THE TISSUE ROLL, THE LETTERING ON THE HAND WASH AND MEDICINE PACKAGING AS WELL AS THE LITTLE TABLETS.

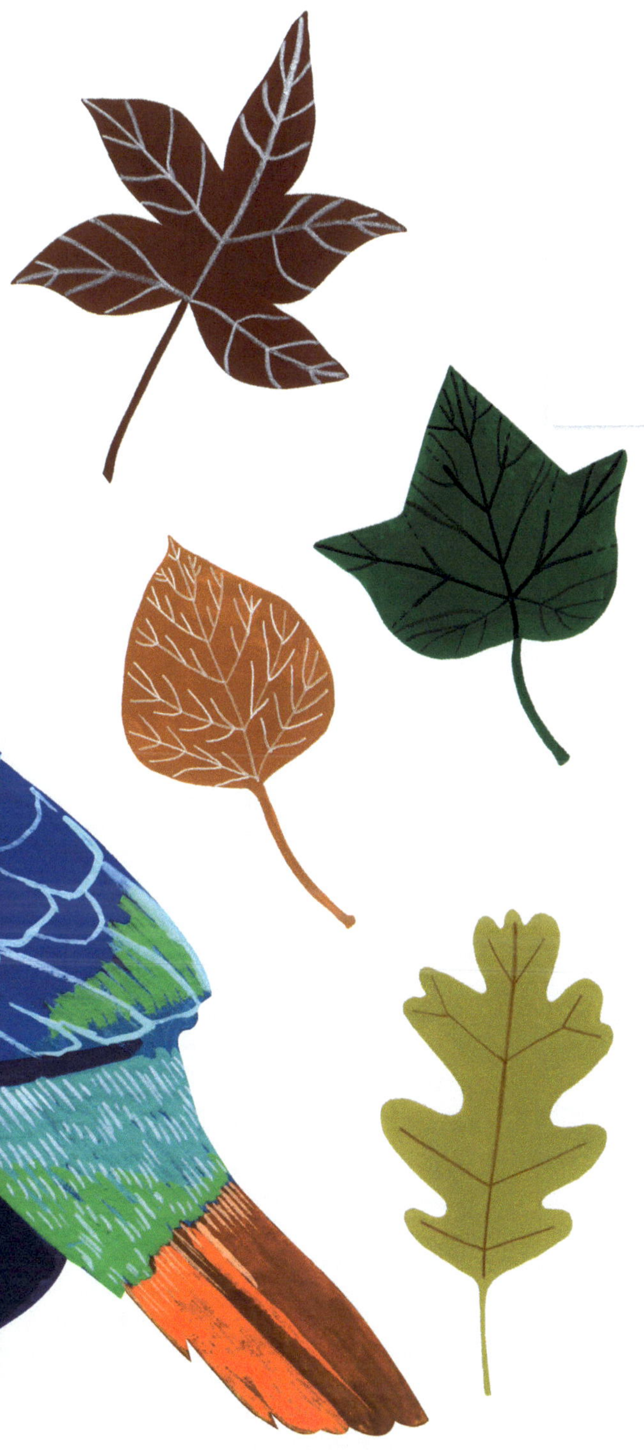

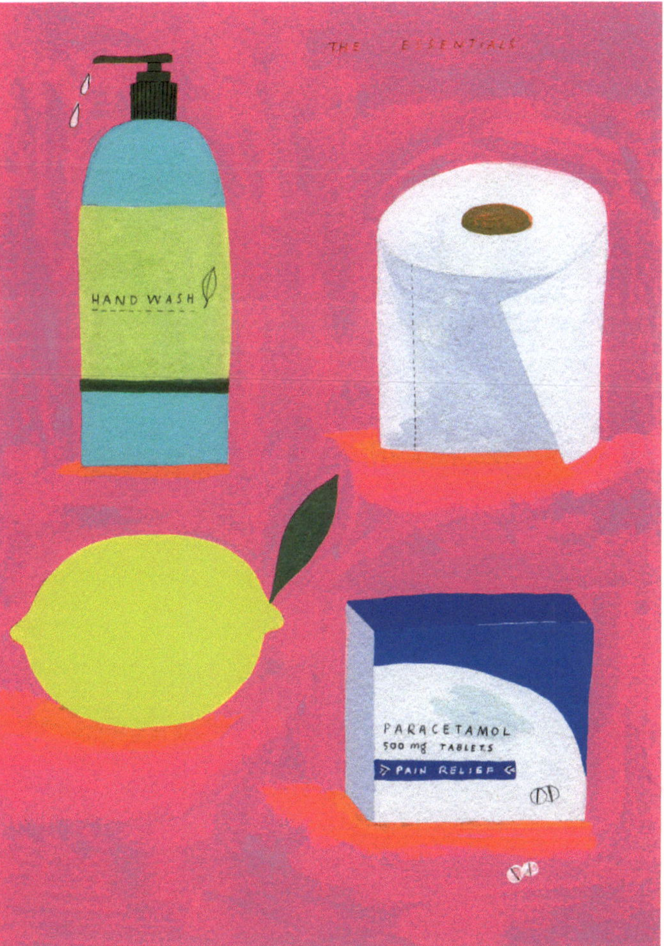

Dark Backgrounds

Gouache is really great for painting on dark backgrounds. Unlike watercolour, which is very transparent, the opaqueness of gouache means that there's very little show-through of the paper and the effects can be quite dramatic. You can paint straight onto black paper, off-the-shelf coloured paper, experiment with kraft paper or, if you want a specific colour, create your own painted paper.

Mix your paint a little thicker or use more layers if you don't want any show-through at all, or add a little more water for a more transparent finish. Be careful not to overload the paper as it will buckle if it's a loose sheet rather than a gummed block. For more resistant paper, you can buy black watercolour paper pads or stretch your paper onto a board (see Materials and Tools: Paper).

If you're going to sketch guidelines onto black or very dark paper, use a lighter or white pencil. If you like to sketch with the tracing technique, use a regular pencil, then go over the traced lines with something lighter so that you don't have to strain your eyes to see them. Generally, it's better to use lighter-coloured paint on black or dark backgrounds.

The examples opposite are all little experiments and explorations from my sketchbook, where I was specifically choosing to paint on a darker background. These are studies and, although they aren't finished pieces, they help to inform my work, looking at colour, marks and composition. You can see how the paint opacity works here. I painted the backgrounds in advance with gouache and left them to dry before adding more paint on top.

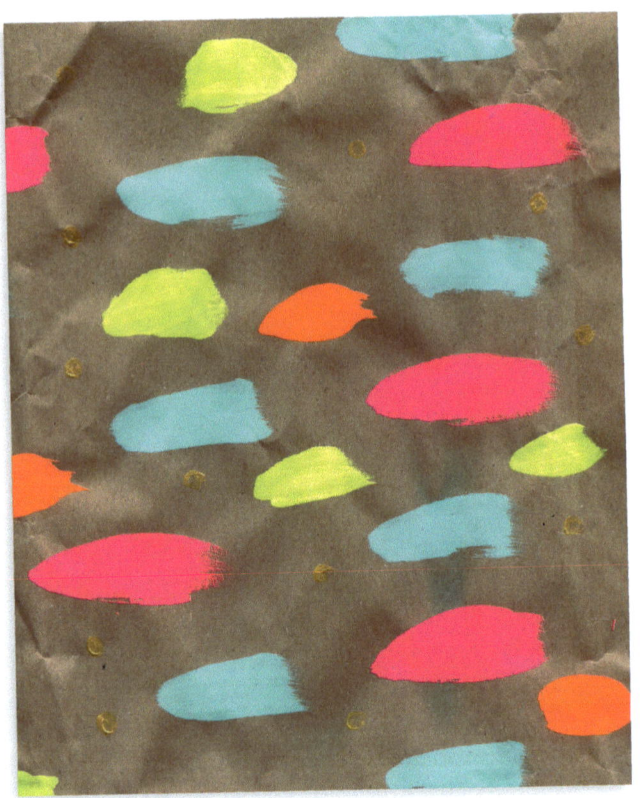

BRIGHT COLOURS CAN LOOK BEAUTIFUL ON BROWN KRAFT PAPER - LIKE THIS GIFT-WRAPPING PAPER I MADE FOR MY DAUGHTER'S BIRTHDAY. I CHOSE FOUR REALLY VIBRANT COLOURS THAT WOULD WORK WELL ON THE NEUTRAL BACKGROUND AND LAY DOWN BRUSH MARKS IN A PATTERN. I ADDED SOME GOLD GOUACHE DOTS, TOO, AS A LOVELY FINISHING TOUCH. AFTER THE GIFTS WERE UNWRAPPED, I KEPT THE PAPER TO ADD TO MY COLLAGE PAPER STASH.

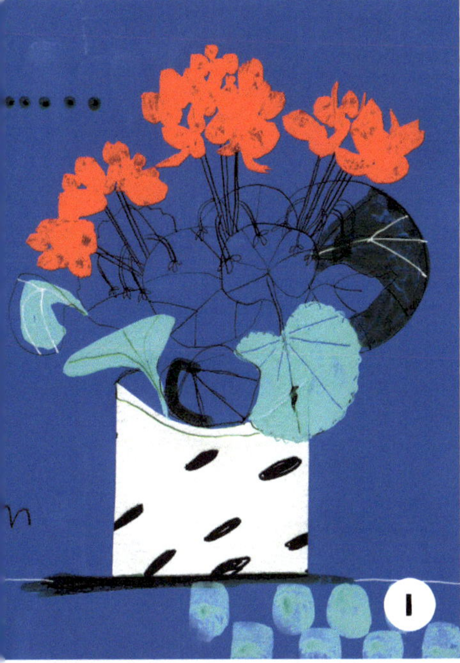

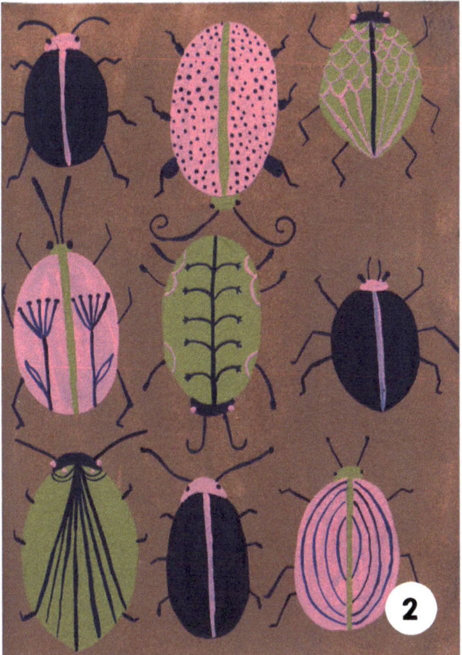

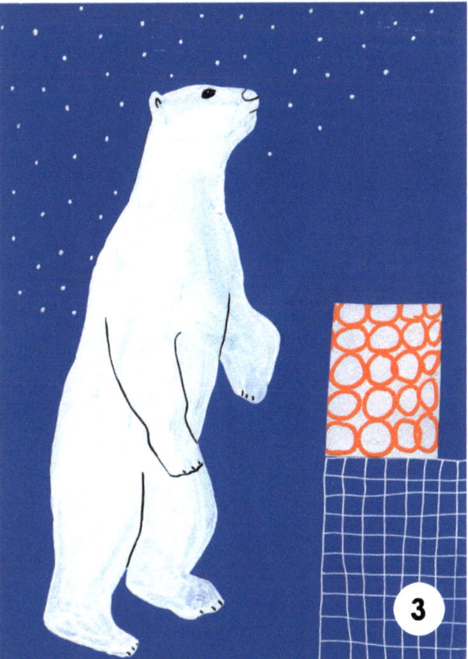

1. In the pieces above, I've combined various media. I used gouache on the petals and leaves. The vase is cut paper and the stems are drawn with ink.

2. In this example, the pattern basically started off as blobs on the page and I just kept adding to them with gouache, ending up with lots of little beetles.

3. Here's a good example of how white works over a dark background. It's a very quick, sketchy painting, but I love the contrast between the blue and white with an element of collage on the right.

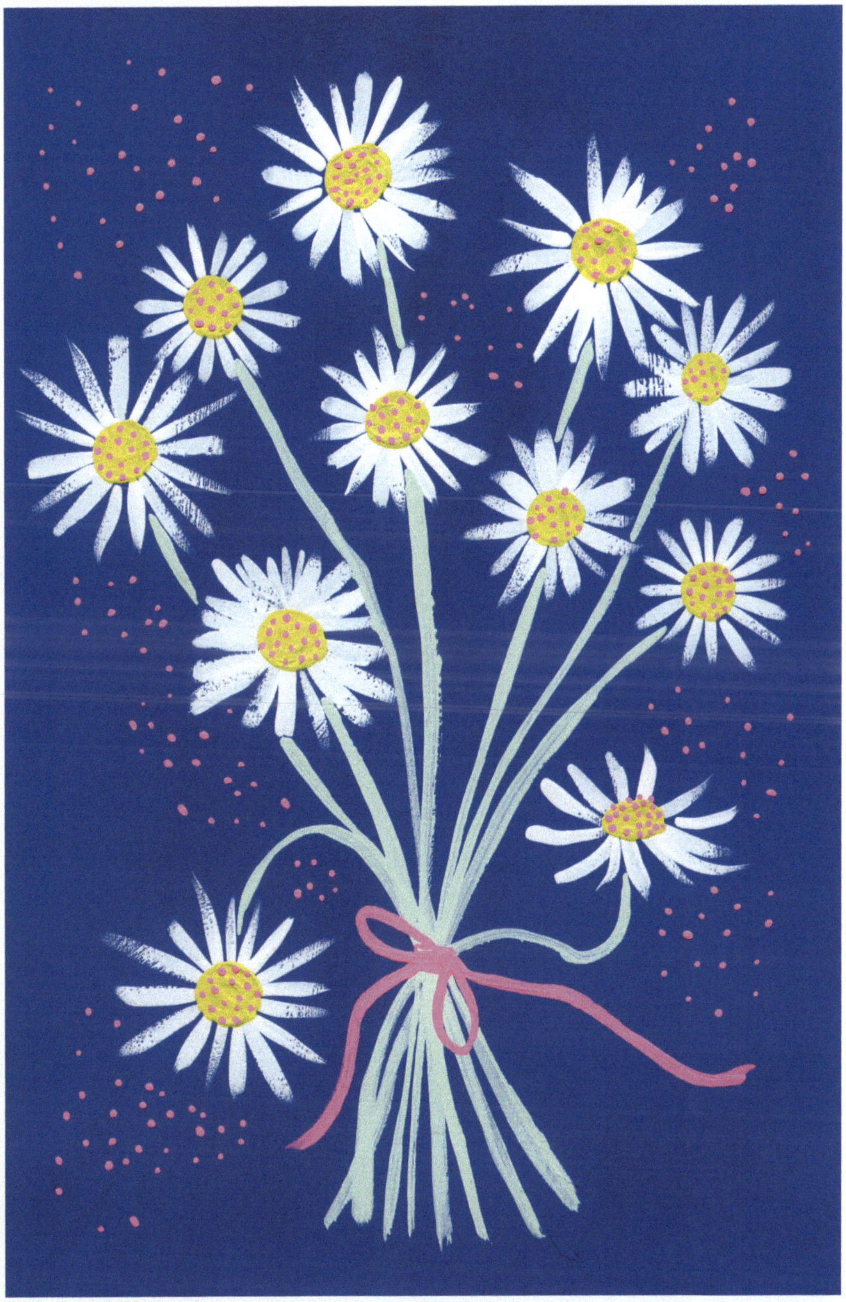

Layer up

Grab some black or dark paper or make your own painted sheets and paint some white flowers, or a white bird or animal. Pay attention to paint thickness and how the paint creates an opaque layer over the dark background.

Collage

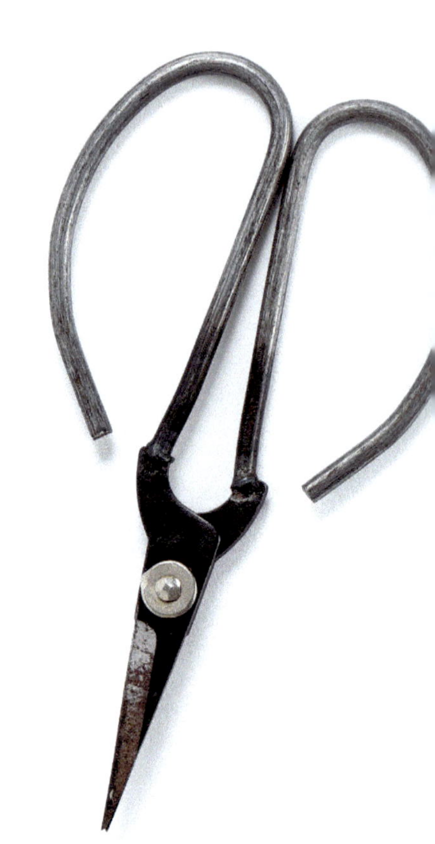

Collage is a lovely way to express your personal style, and it's a wonderful technique for making literal or abstract creations. I have a huge box full of papers from all over the place that I collect to play with – papers that I've made myself as well as found papers such as gift wrap, envelopes and newspapers.

To begin with, you could try something fairly abstract and decorative, like this example. I've used some of the sheets I painted in the mark-making exercise we looked at earlier (see Techniques: Mark Making), cutting them into little hill shapes and layering them to create a bright, colourful abstract pattern. With multiple layers like this, you'll need a sturdy board or a wood panel to work on to avoid buckling.

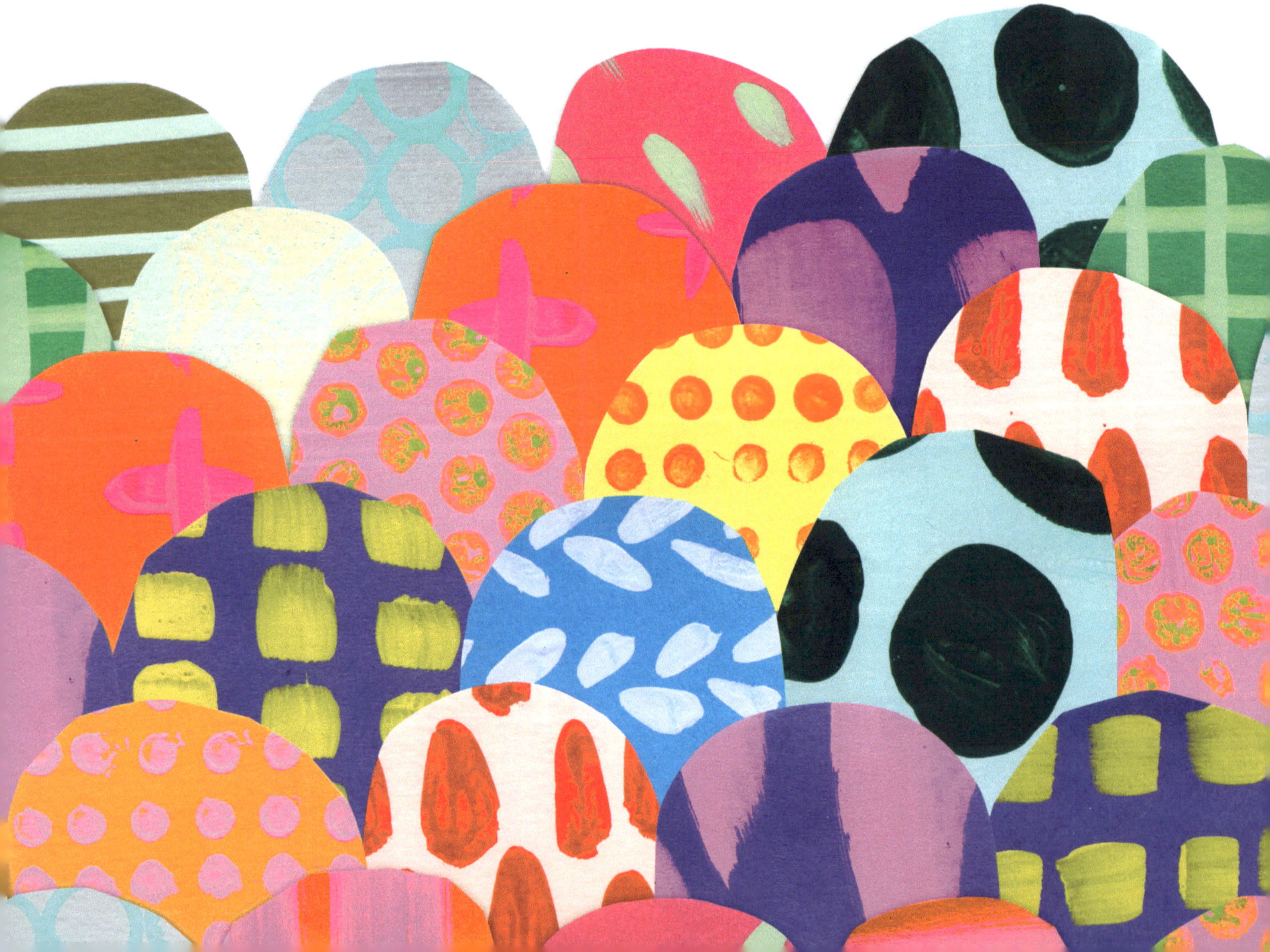

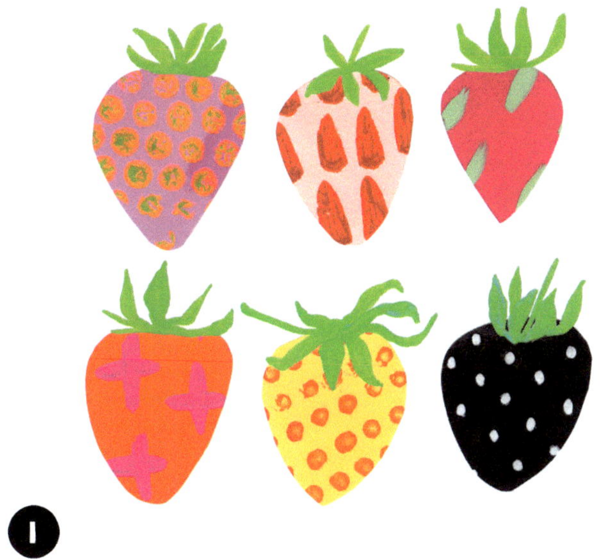

A simple abstract collage

To get started, all you need is your painted papers, scissors or a sharp cutting knife, a cutting mat and some PVA glue or, if you have it, gloss medium. I like to lay everything out first , and take a photo when I'm happy with the arrangement so that I remember how I want it to look. Then it's time to start sticking.

With something like the abstract hill pattern (left), it's best to start at the top as that's the layer that is furthermost in the background. Then gradually work down and forwards, adding more layers. Once everything is stuck down and dry, you can either scan it as a whole finished piece so that you can digitally reproduce it or frame it behind glass for protection. This is a traditional collage method, but, if you're comfortable working digitally, you could do it on your computer, too, scanning the individual pieces and assembling them in Photoshop (see Techniques: Digitizing).

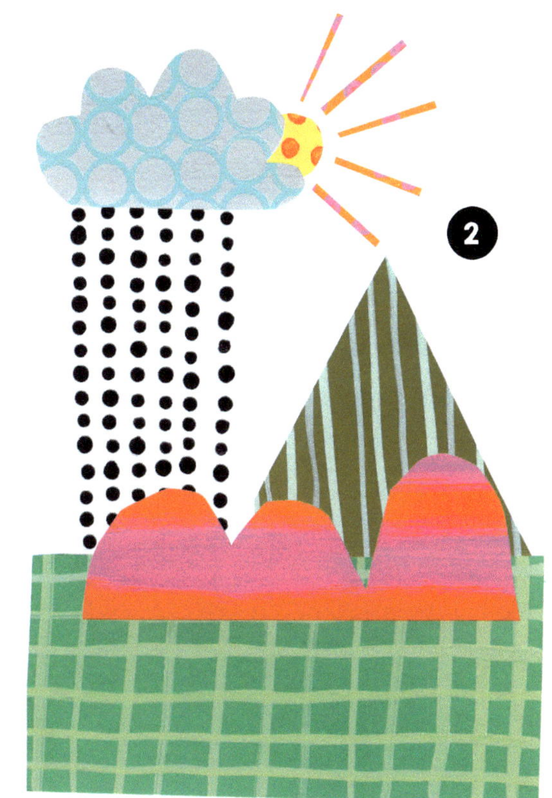

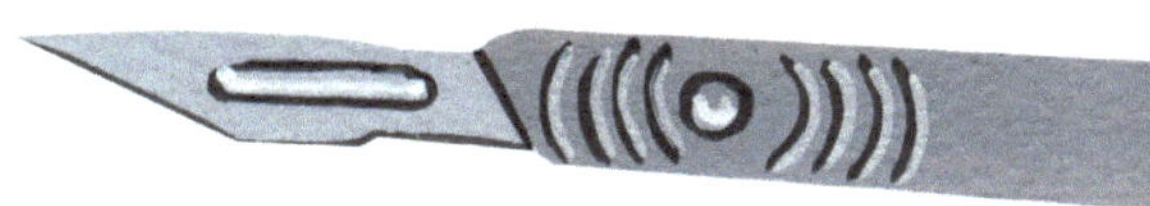

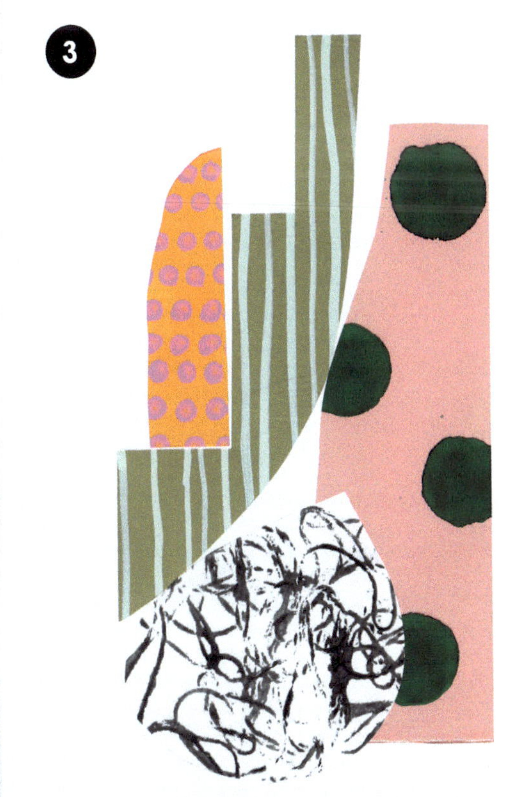

1. I used scissors to cut out some strawberry shapes from the same papers and then, after sticking them down, I painted on green leaves. This is a nice way to combine collage with painted elements.

2. The landscape depicts a field in front of some hills and a mountain, with the sun peeking out from behind a rain cloud. These are very simple shapes, but it makes a charming scene.

3. I love making abstract collages, focusing on the interplay between colours, shapes and patterns without worrying about making it look like a figurative piece. Here I played around with shapes, contrasting colours, marks and placement to find a pleasing composition before committing to sticking anything down.

Digitizing

To digitize your paintings, you'll need a computer with photo-editing software, such as Adobe Photoshop, and a scanner.

When I paint, I generally create individual, 'floating' images or icons rather than full scenes, so that when I scan them into my computer, I can cut them out in Photoshop using the pen tool. Then I can arrange everything that way. This technique could be described as 'digital collage'. This is how I like to work because if I need to change something (say, for example, that the layout of part of the design isn't quite working), I can remove just that part and replace it easily without having to begin the whole thing again from scratch.

While this book is not a guide on how to digitize your artwork, the technique is an important part of my process, so it's worth mentioning and might give you a little insight into taking your painting further. If you want to create and sell prints of your work, it can be useful to know how to tidy everything up digitally. Scanning your paintings is also an efficient way of storing and archiving all of your work on your computer.

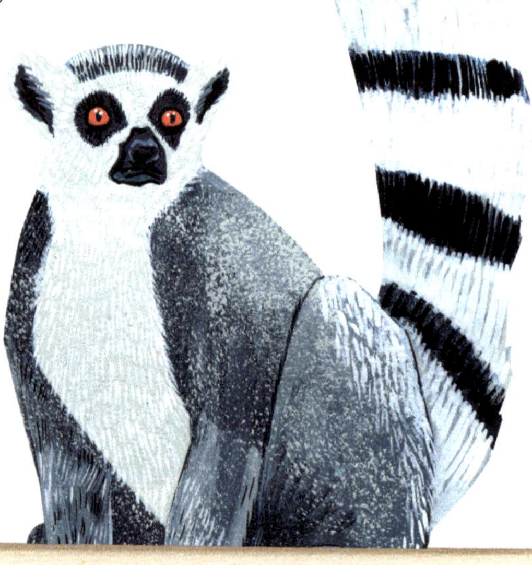

THIS IS A PATTERN I CREATED DIGITALLY USING
A LOT OF 'ICONS' THAT YOU'LL RECOGNIZE FROM
THE PAGES OF THIS BOOK.

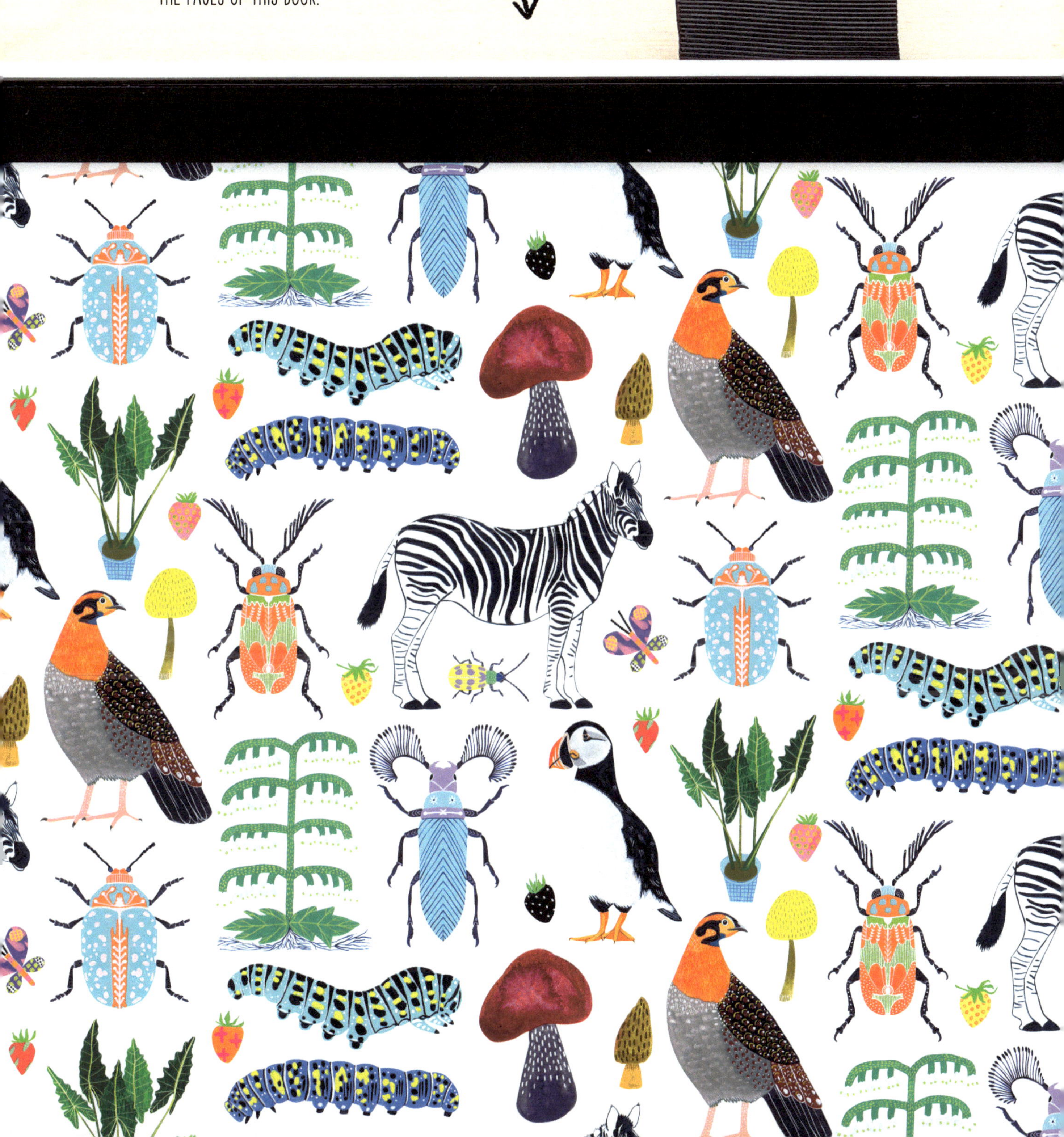

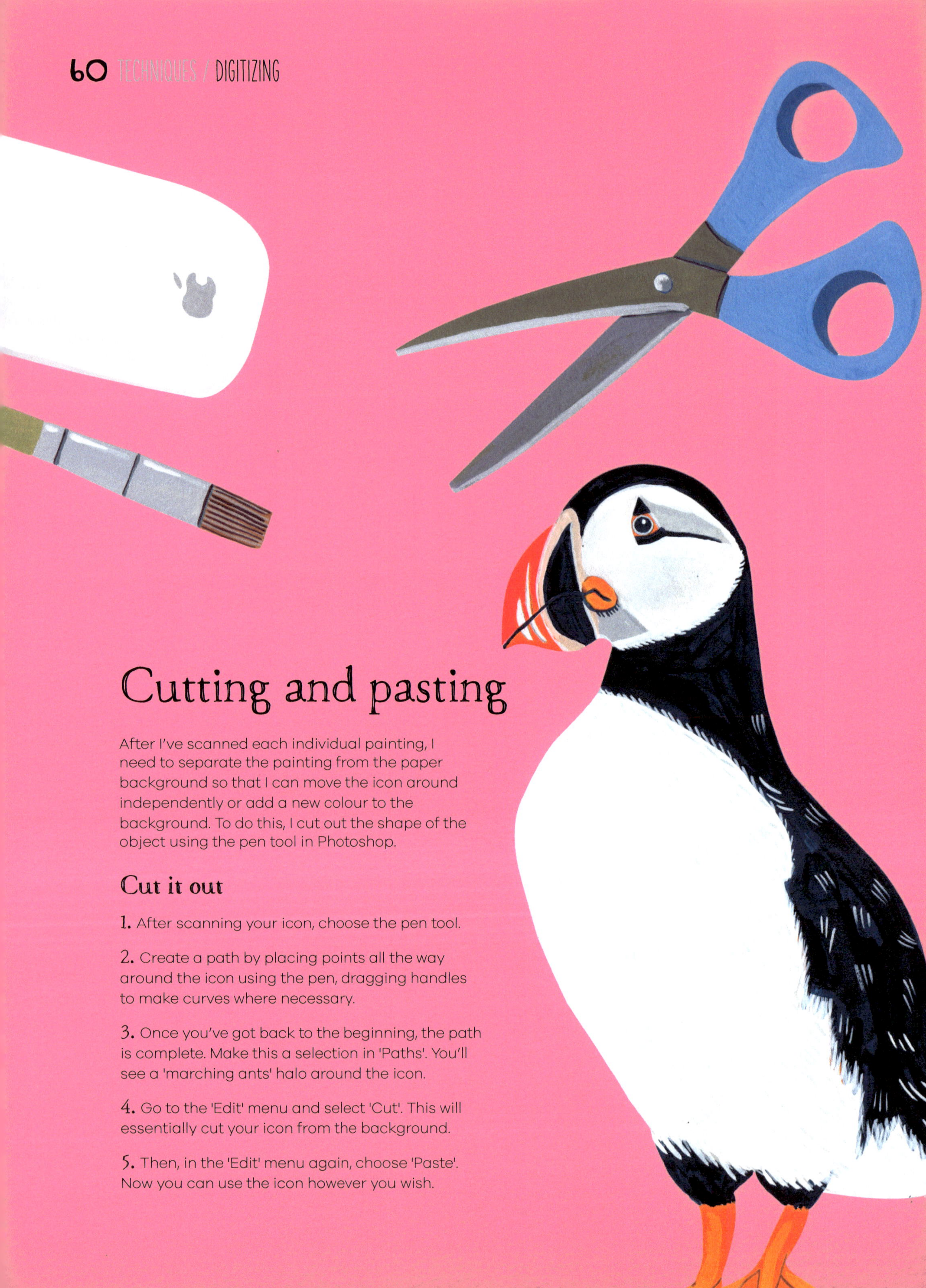

Cutting and pasting

After I've scanned each individual painting, I need to separate the painting from the paper background so that I can move the icon around independently or add a new colour to the background. To do this, I cut out the shape of the object using the pen tool in Photoshop.

Cut it out

1. After scanning your icon, choose the pen tool.

2. Create a path by placing points all the way around the icon using the pen, dragging handles to make curves where necessary.

3. Once you've got back to the beginning, the path is complete. Make this a selection in 'Paths'. You'll see a 'marching ants' halo around the icon.

4. Go to the 'Edit' menu and select 'Cut'. This will essentially cut your icon from the background.

5. Then, in the 'Edit' menu again, choose 'Paste'. Now you can use the icon however you wish.

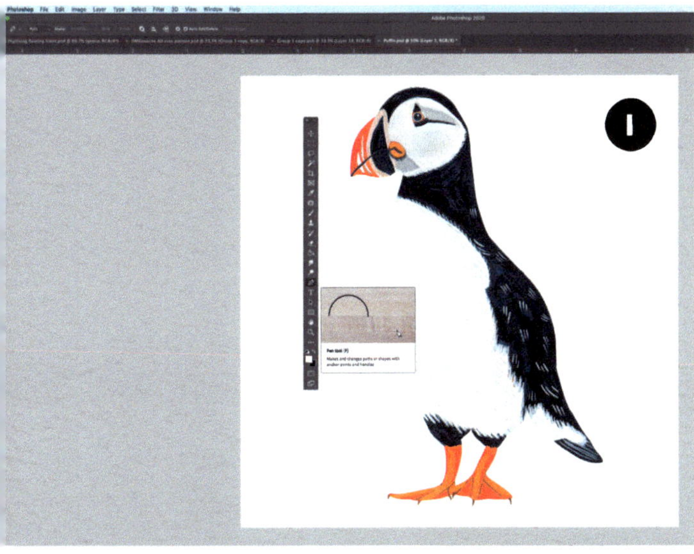

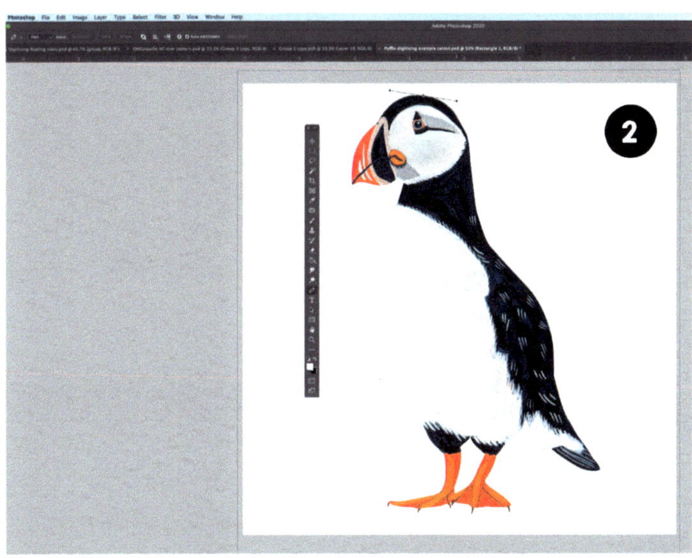

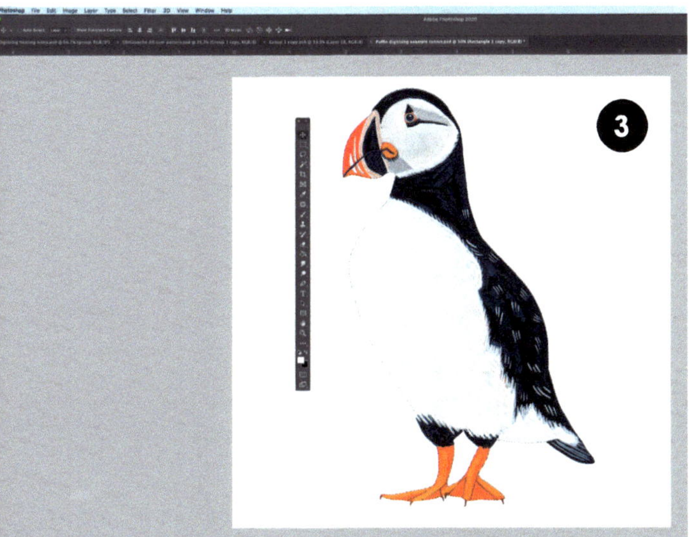

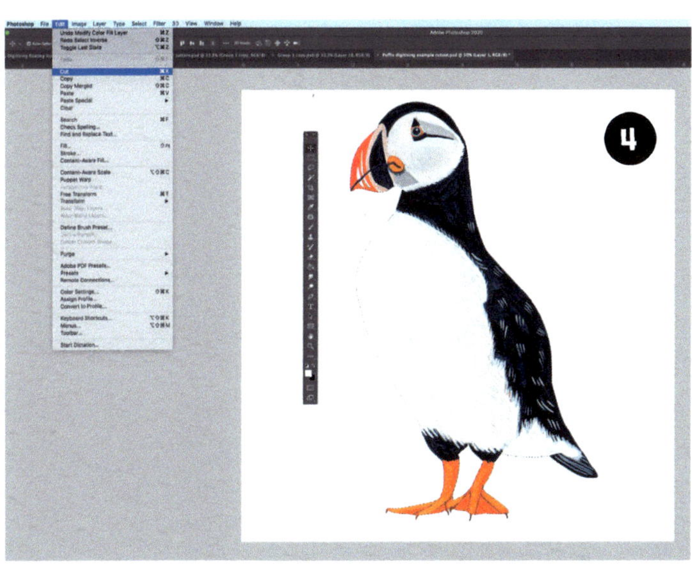

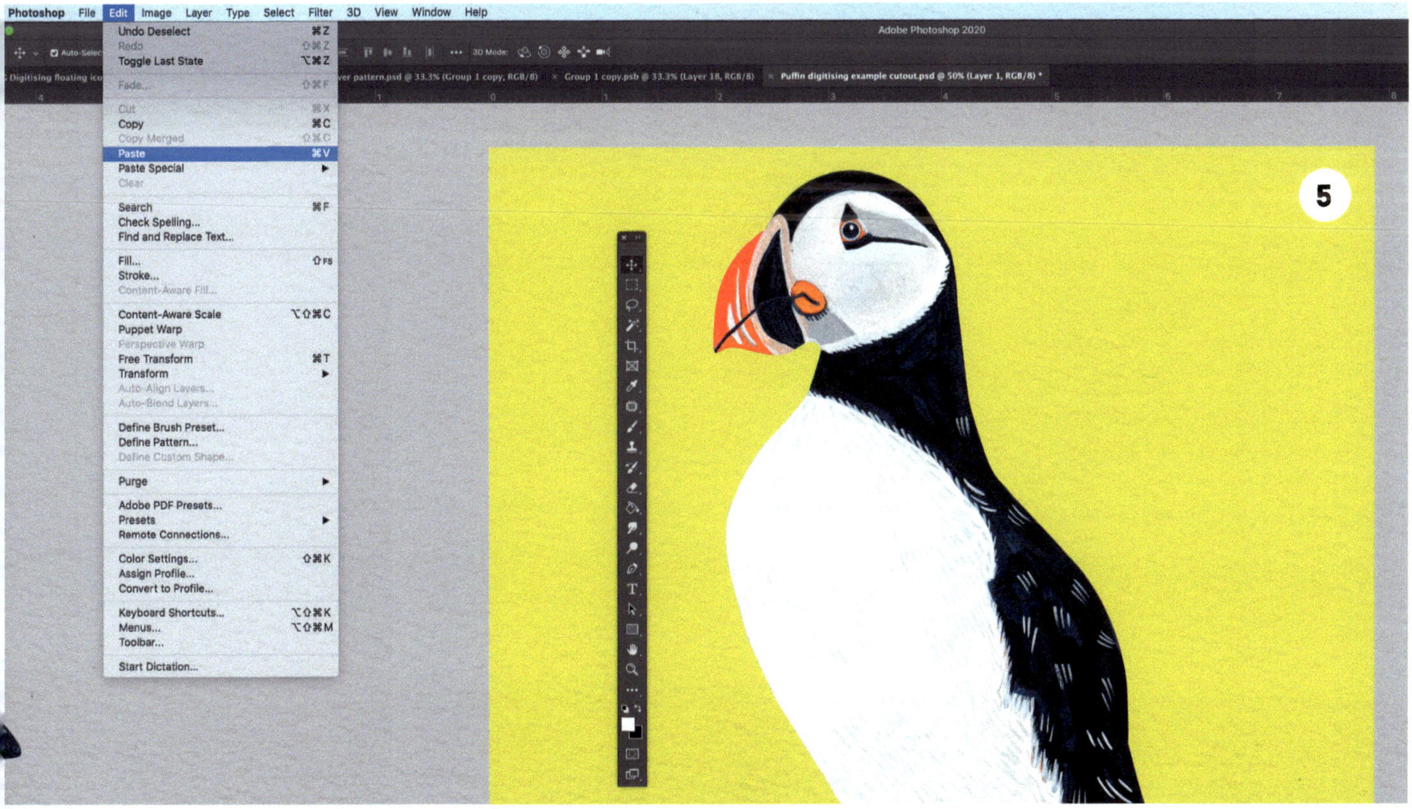

Putting them all together

After you've scanned and cut out the icons you've painted, you can place them all in the same file and begin to lay them out in a pattern. It's really helpful when thinking about how to put a layout for a pattern together to consider the scale, direction and shapes of icons and how they'll fit together. Varying scales will create interest within your pattern.

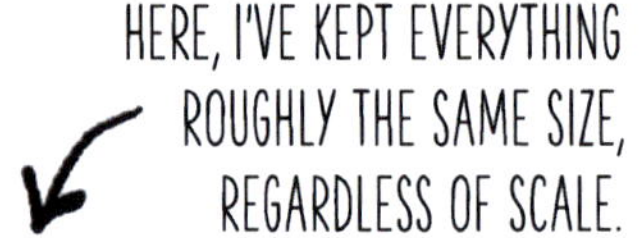

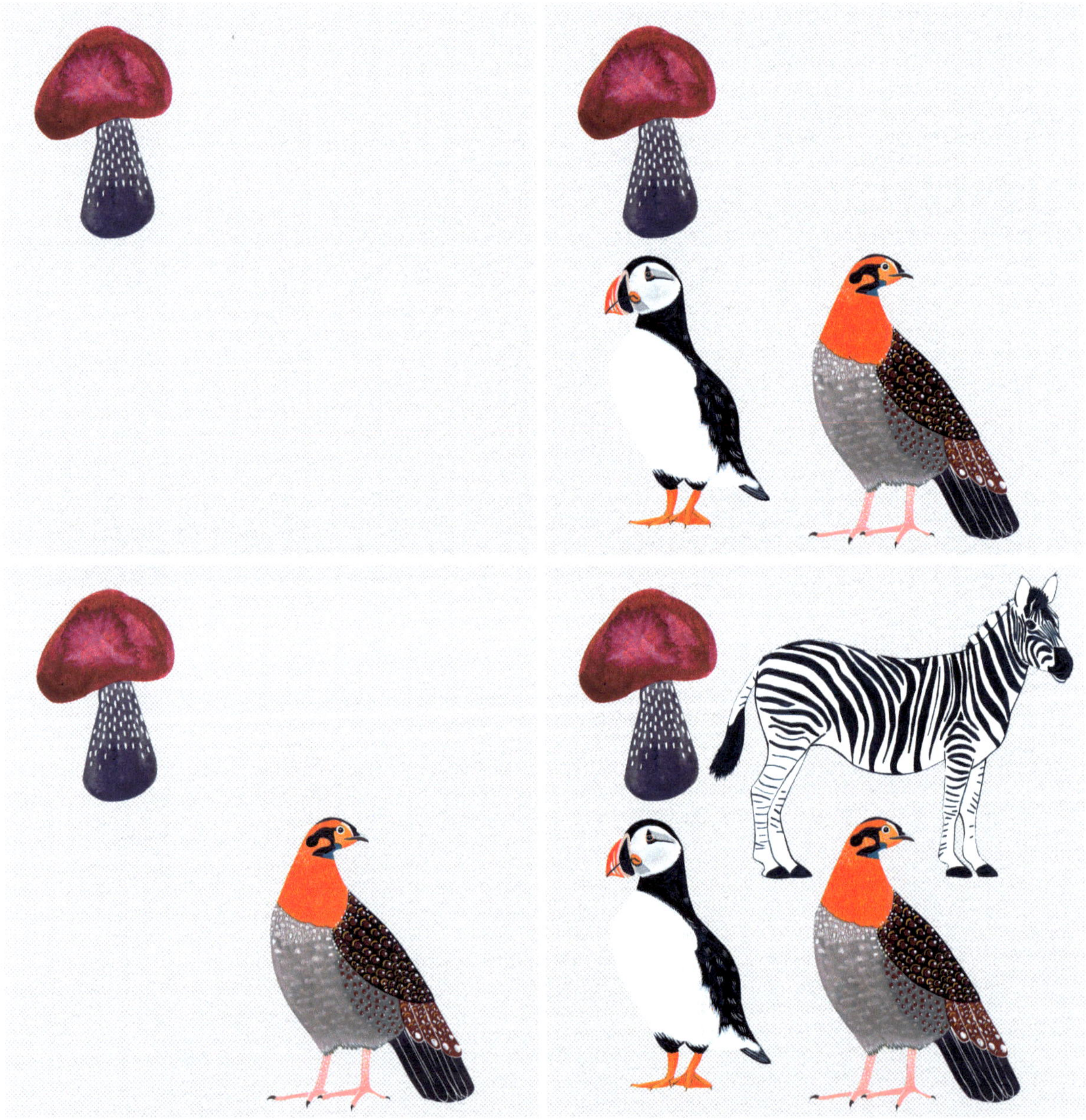

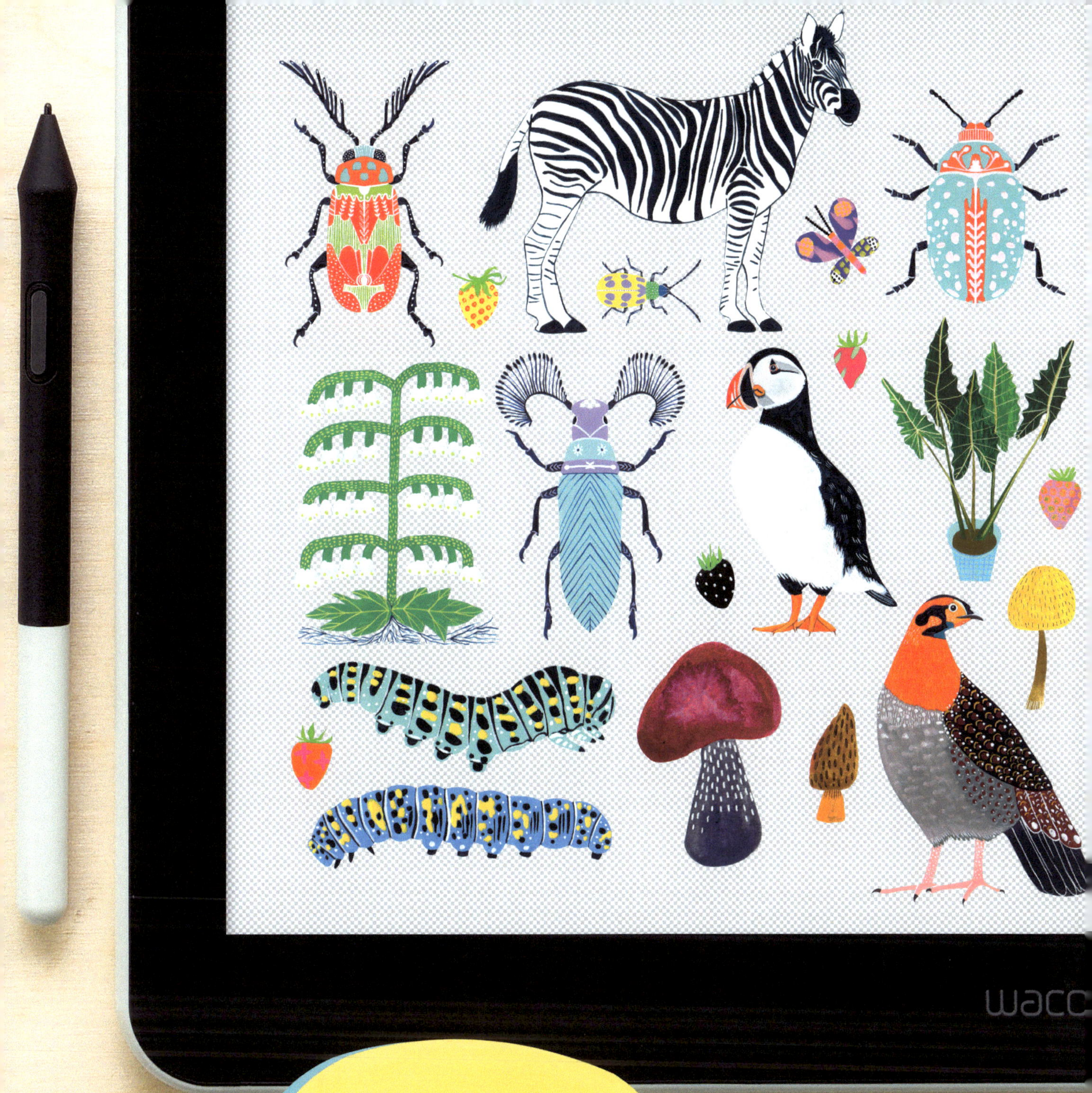

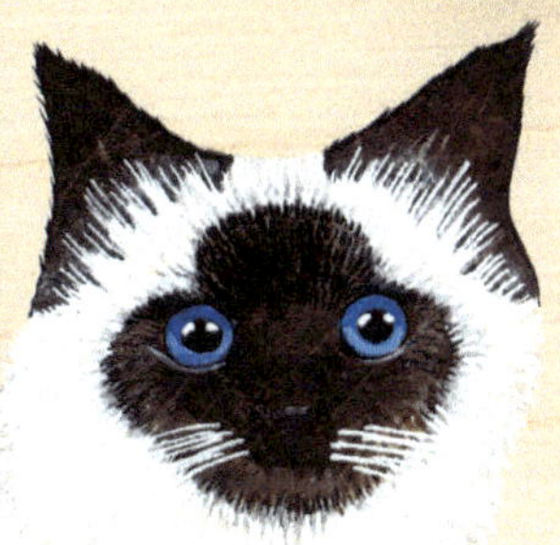

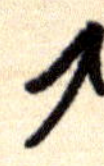

THIS SHOWS THE FINAL REPEAT WITH ALL THE INDIVIDUAL ICONS FOR THE OVERALL PATTERN.

PROJECTS

In this next section of the book, there are 11 fun projects with step-by-step directions for you to follow along with or try in your own way. I want you to have the confidence to explore your hand and style, so I encourage you to try these projects with your own spin on them. This is most definitely not a guide for you to paint like me, but rather a demonstration with examples of how layers are built up until a painting emerges. Don't be apprehensive – there are no mistakes, only lessons to learn.

Of course, you'll need your paint, palette, water, brushes, watercolour paper and other coloured paper and some of your previously painted mark-making collage papers. You'll need scissors or a craft knife as well, as there are a couple of projects that include collage elements. A white pencil will come in handy, too, for drawing on black paper.

All the colours and papers I used are included on each project page for reference. I've listed the tube colours I've used for my painting if you'd like a rough guide to work from, but do try to mix the colours intuitively to make each painting your own. You can jump around from project to project, and you don't need to complete each project consecutively – feel free to start anywhere that sparks your interest.

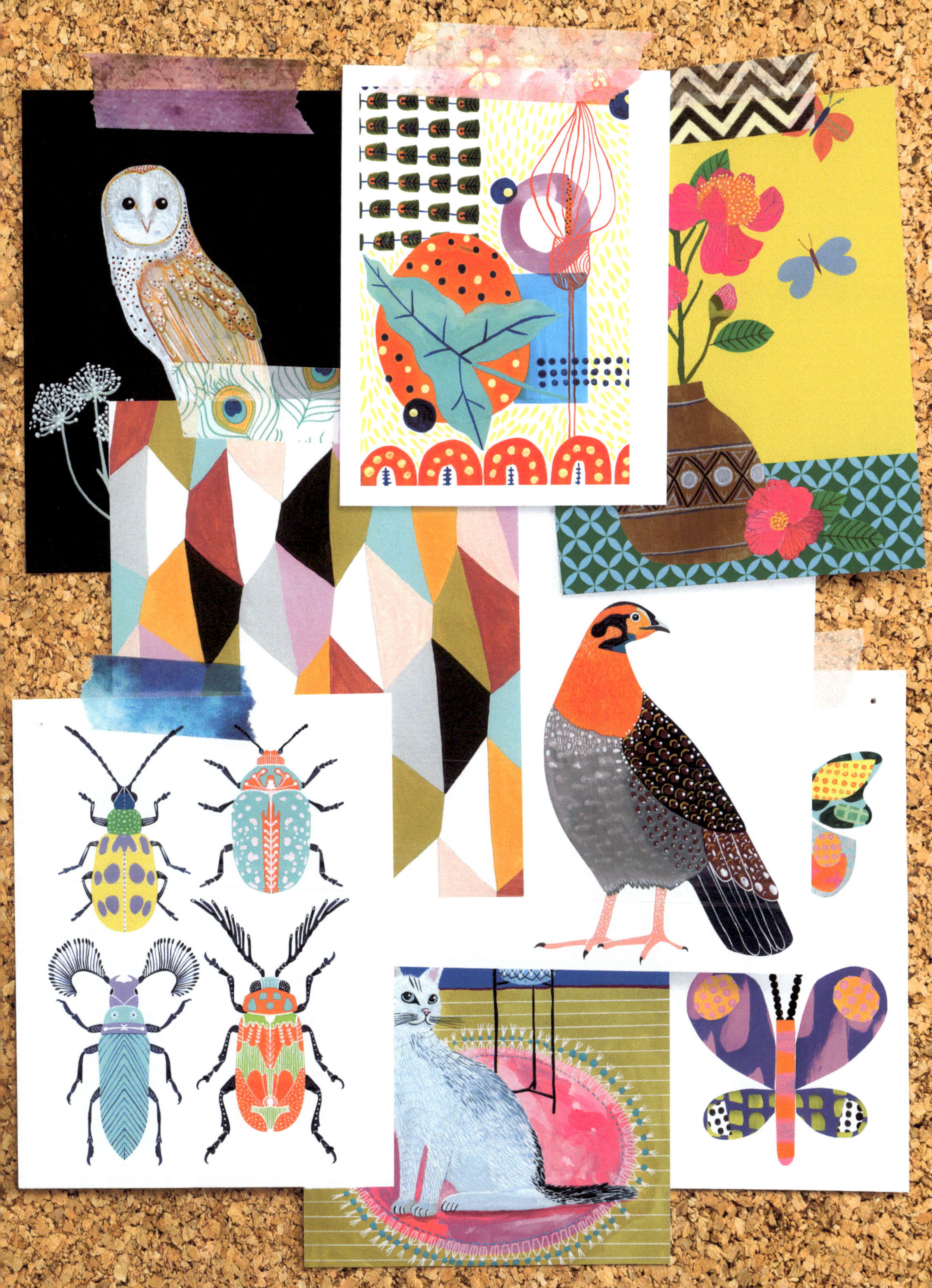

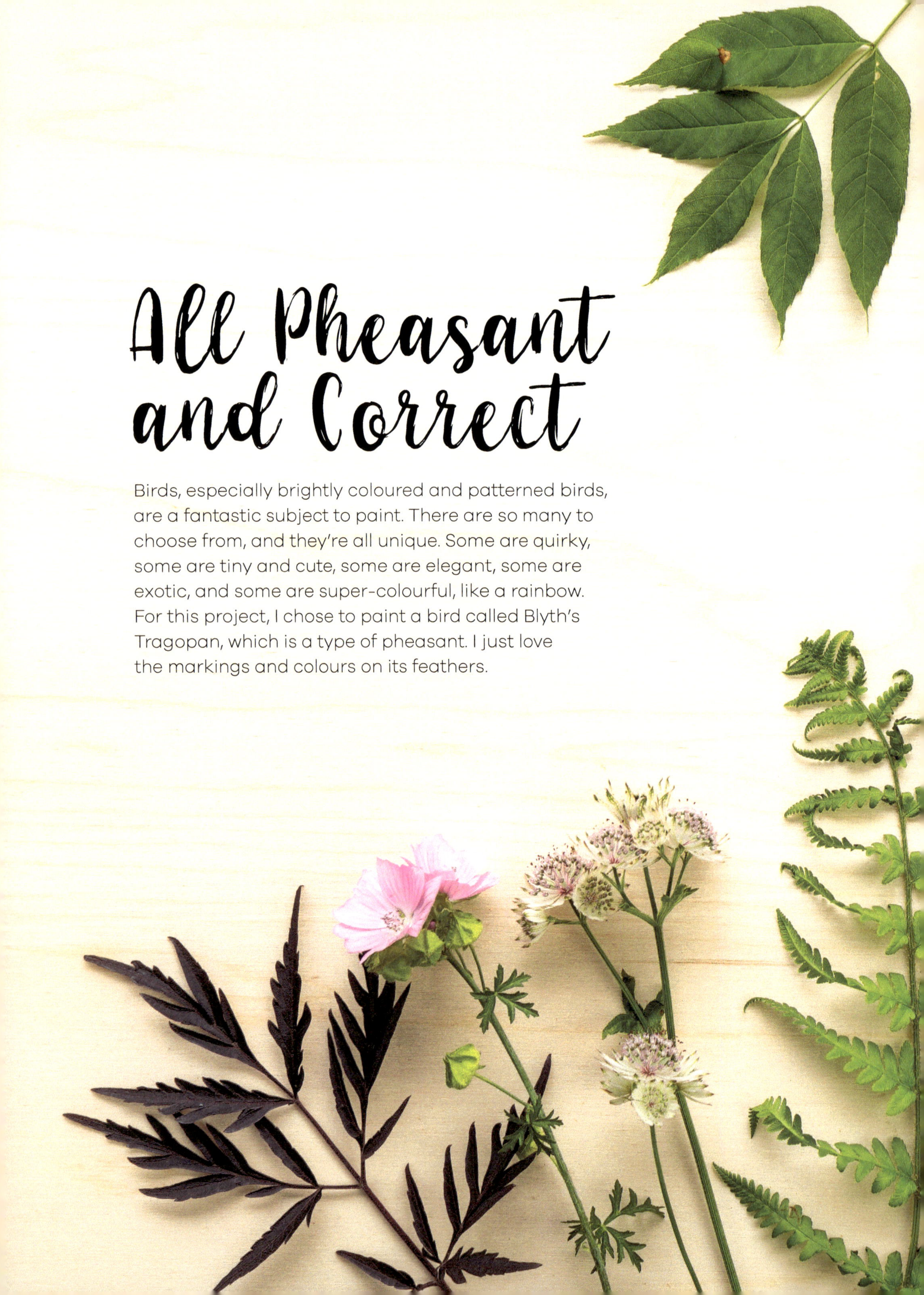

All Pheasant and Correct

Birds, especially brightly coloured and patterned birds, are a fantastic subject to paint. There are so many to choose from, and they're all unique. Some are quirky, some are tiny and cute, some are elegant, some are exotic, and some are super-colourful, like a rainbow. For this project, I chose to paint a bird called Blyth's Tragopan, which is a type of pheasant. I just love the markings and colours on its feathers.

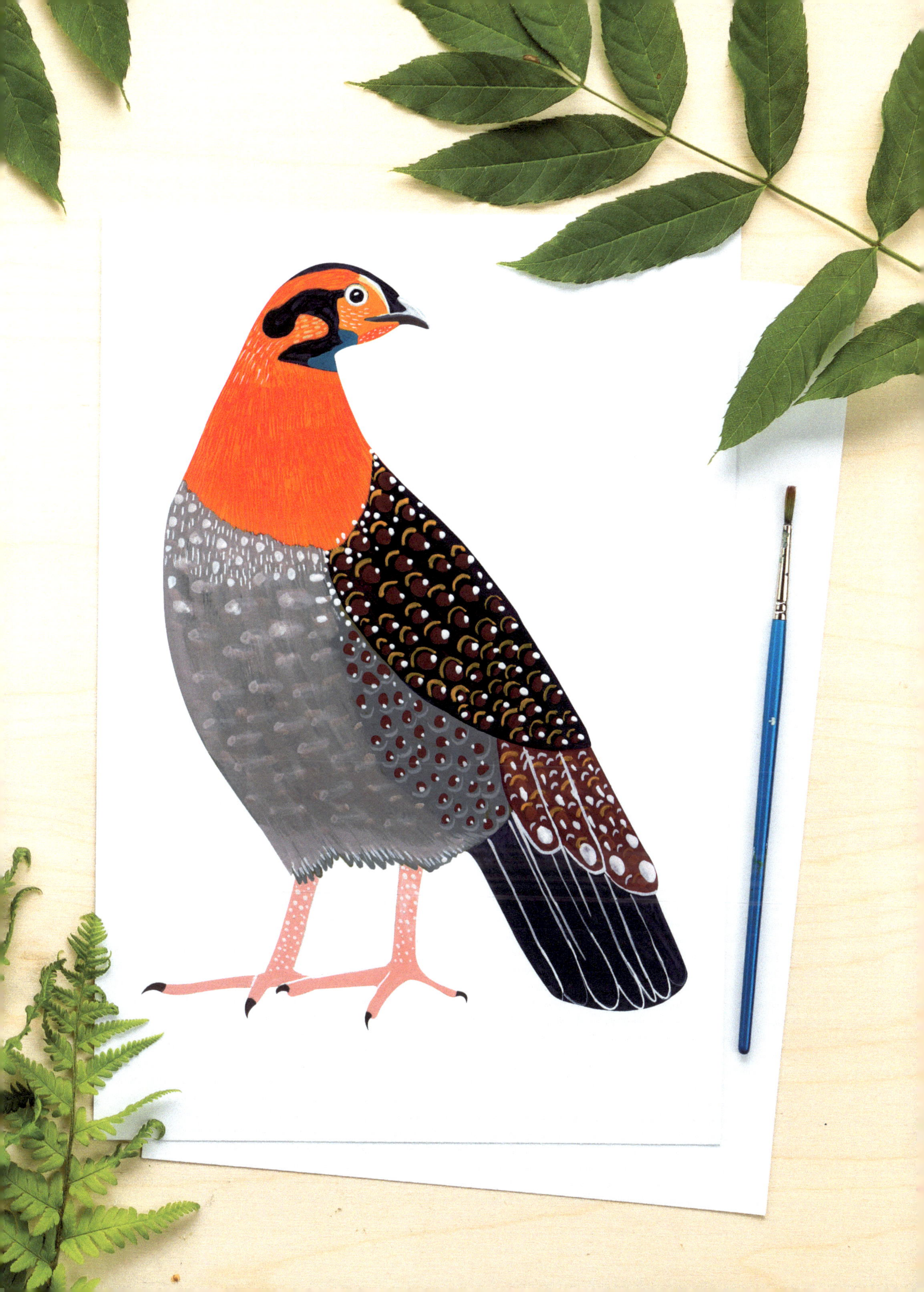

COLOURS

- Deep magenta
- Scarlet
- Orange
- Orange yellow
- White
- Mint green
- Turquoise blue

PAPER

Plain cartridge
or printer paper

Tracing paper

Watercolour
block paper

TECHNIQUES

Sketching

Washes

Mark Making

Overlaying

Detail

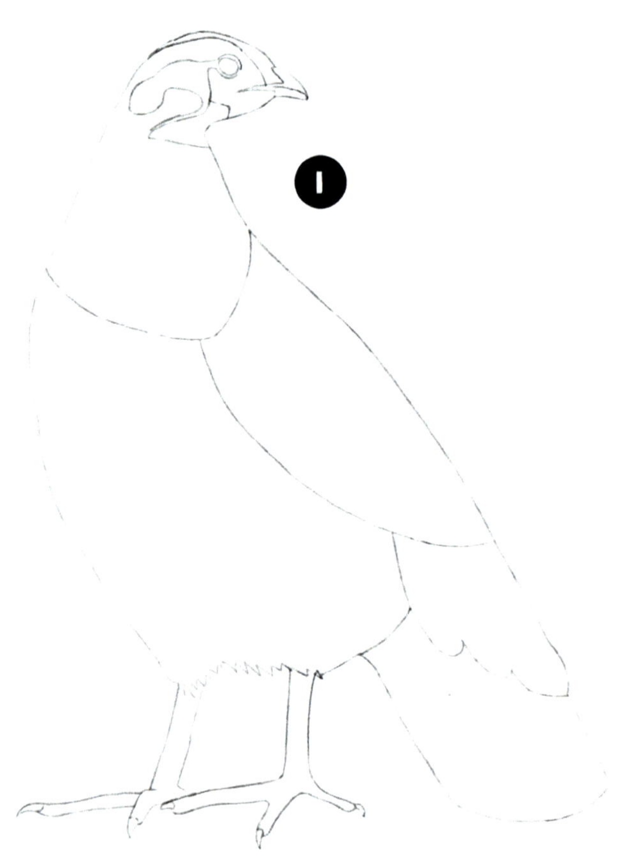

1. Begin by sketching out the bird shape using a photo for reference, or feel free to follow the shape that I've used here. Pay attention to the main areas such as the head, eye and beak. Try not to get too concerned about the details as these will come later in the painting. Mark in a rough line for the wing and tail feather areas. Once the sketch is finished, go ahead and transfer it using the tracing paper method if you haven't drawn directly onto the paper.

2. Now start to lay down some initial colours. We're not looking at details yet – this is just a base. You can use a fairly big brush for this. Leave to dry.

3. In my example, once the colours had dried, they didn't look quite right for me, so I added more grey to the breast area and darkened down the wing. I also added a little pop of turquoise under the neck. Everything is still fairly rough at this point, so it's a good time to make adjustments.

4. At this stage I started to overlay a little detail on the breast and wings. Try not to get bogged down with detail and simply focus on the patterns and colours that you see on the feathers, then make marks with your brush to try to replicate that. Remember, it doesn't have to be realistic – it's your own personal interpretation.

5. Now you can add the finishing details on the neck and face using a much smaller brush. Small, repetitive lines create the feather texture and white dots suggest the pattern on the bird. I like to leave any white and lighter details like this until the very end.

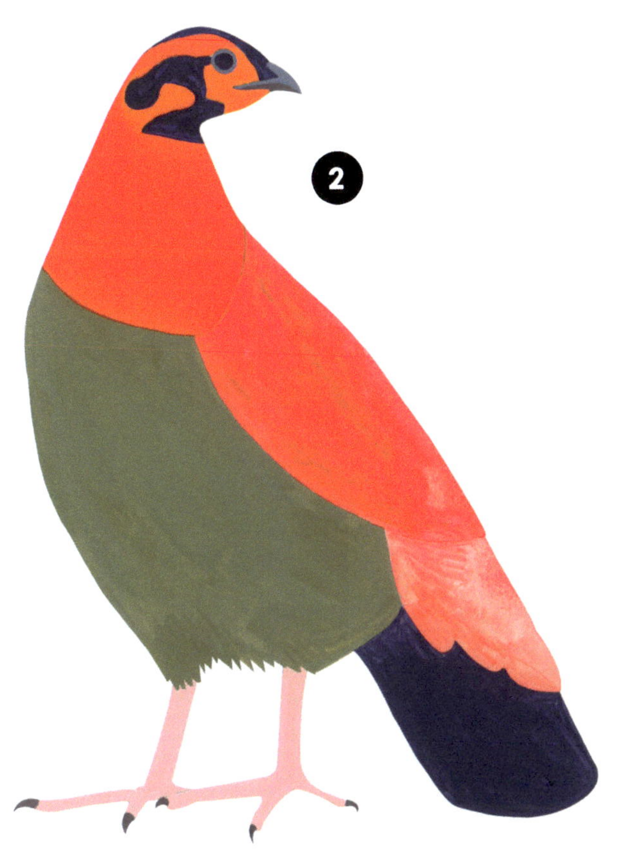
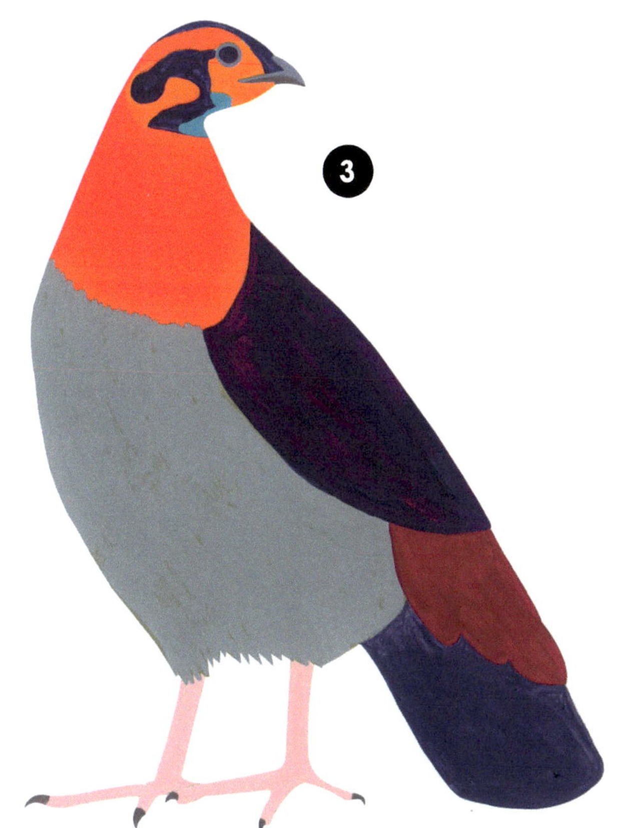
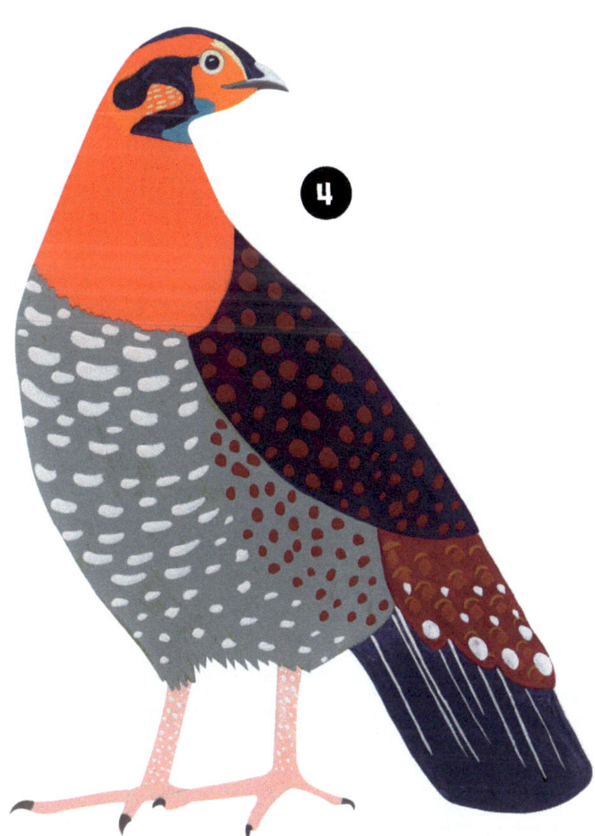
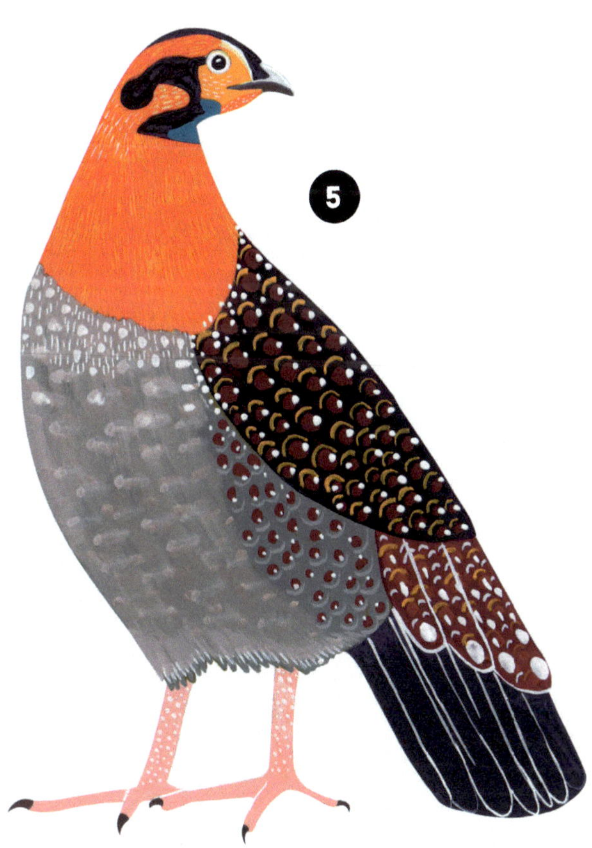

Beetle Mania

Beetles can be fun, vivid and decoratively dazzling. Be as fanciful as you like with their colours and patterns – there are no rules here. If you prefer to paint more realistically, search for photo inspiration online. You're free to skip the sketching step and go straight to paint if that's how you like to work. When you're finished, you'll have a bunch of beetles to create a pattern with or incorporate into your other designs.

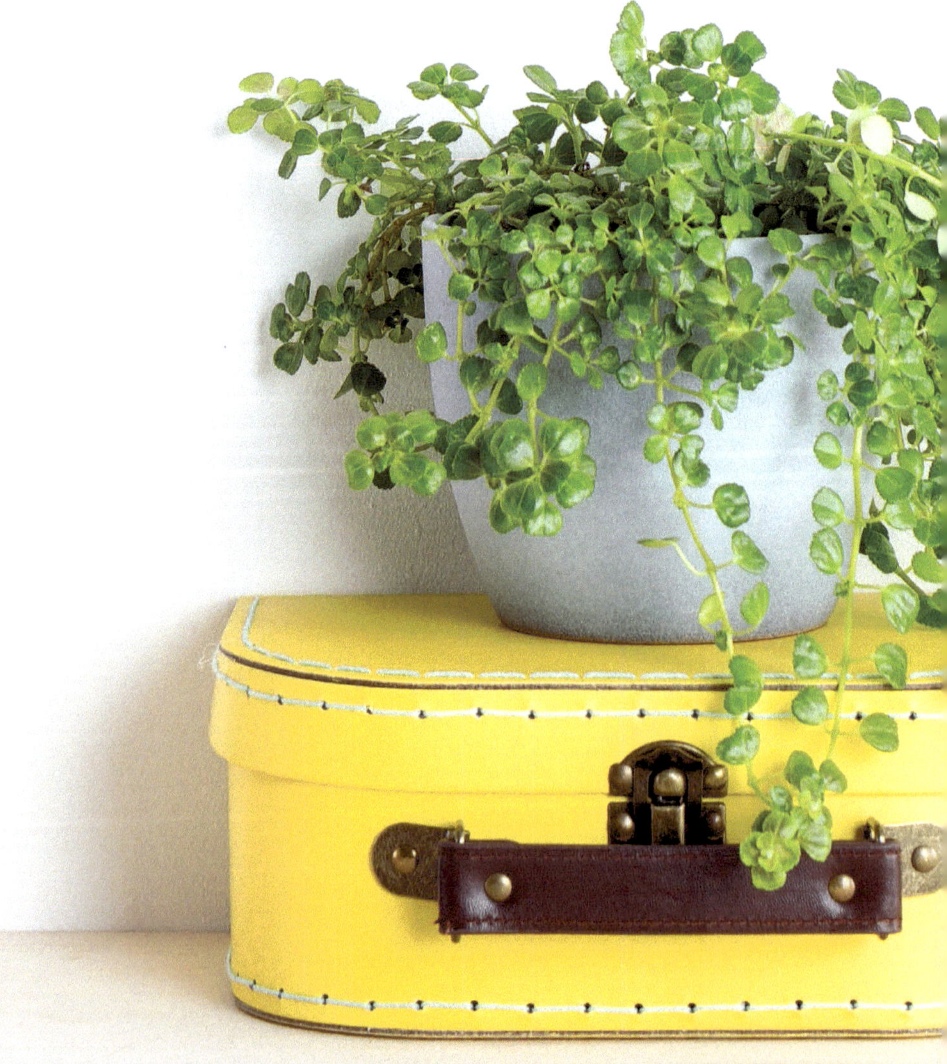

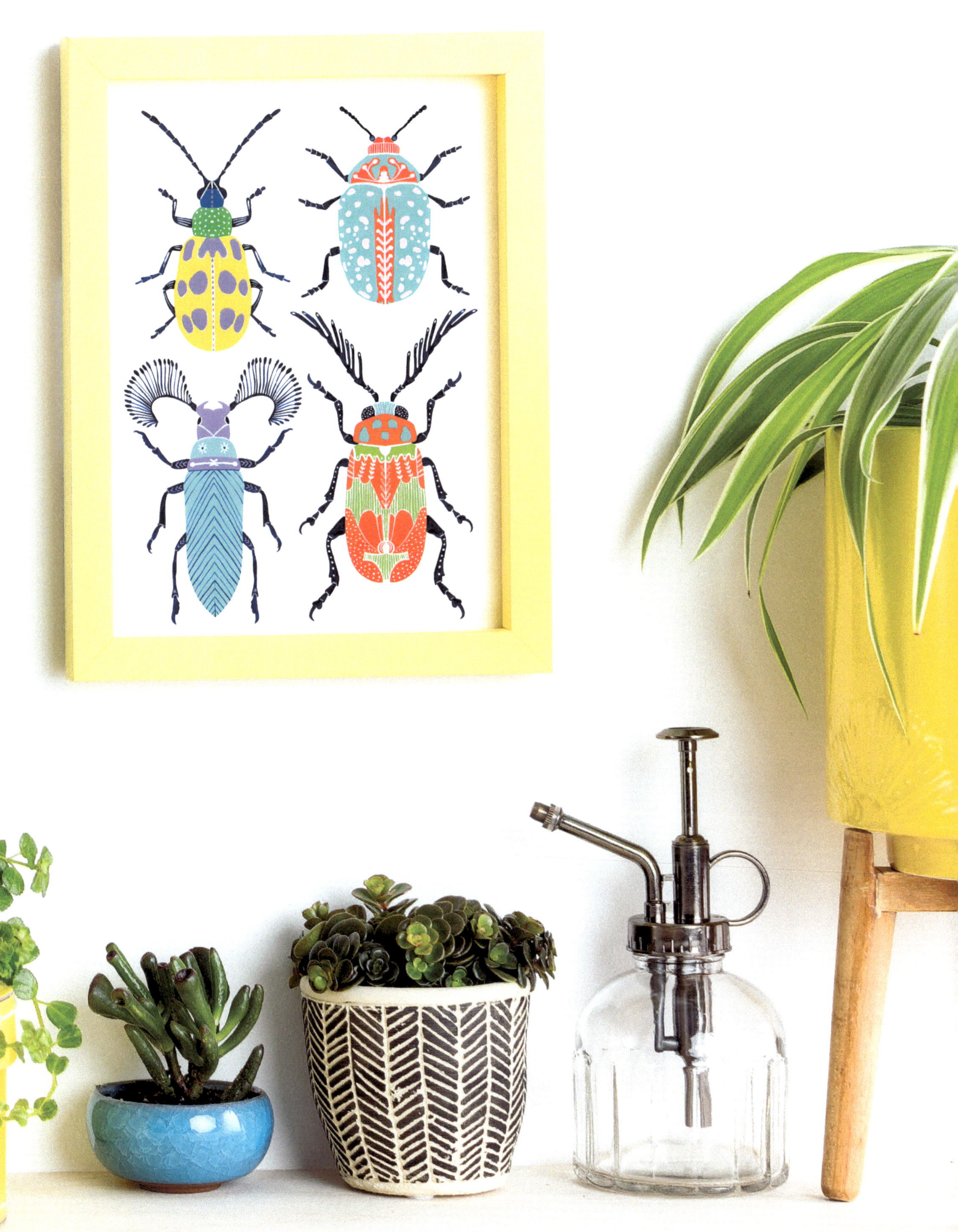

COLOURS

- Ice green
- Coral red
- Lilac
- Brilliant green
- Navy blue
- White
- Shell pink
- Spectrum yellow

PAPER

Plain cartridge
or printer paper

Tracing paper

Watercolour
block paper

TECHNIQUES

Sketching

Overlaying

Detail

Digitizing

---

1. Sketch out your beetles. Remember, we're only sketching the essentials. If you want to, add in the lines of the pattern on the body, or you can make that up as you go along.

2. Next, lay down some initial bright colours on the bodies of the beetles. I've used opaque colour here rather than washes.

3. Gradually add in more colour on the bodies. Also, add a darker colour for the legs, eyes and antennae.

4. Once the darker colours are dry, add the final details in lines and dots to finish off the paintings.

5. In this final step, I've scanned my beetle paintings and used Photoshop to mirror each one so that they're symmetrical. Although nothing in nature is perfectly symmetrical, I like to do this sometimes with my paintings for a very graphic feel.

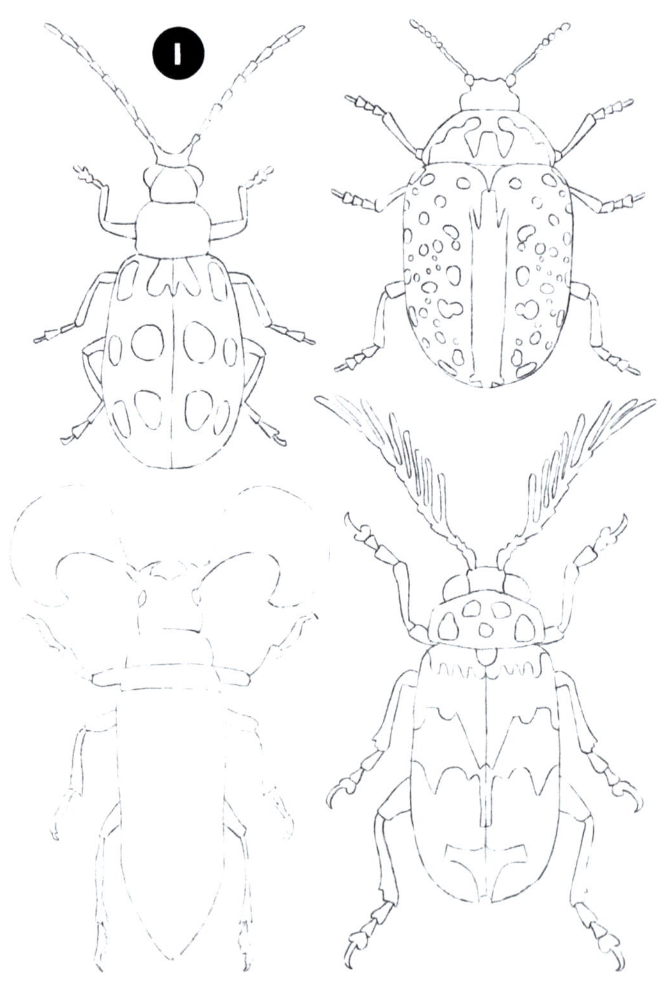

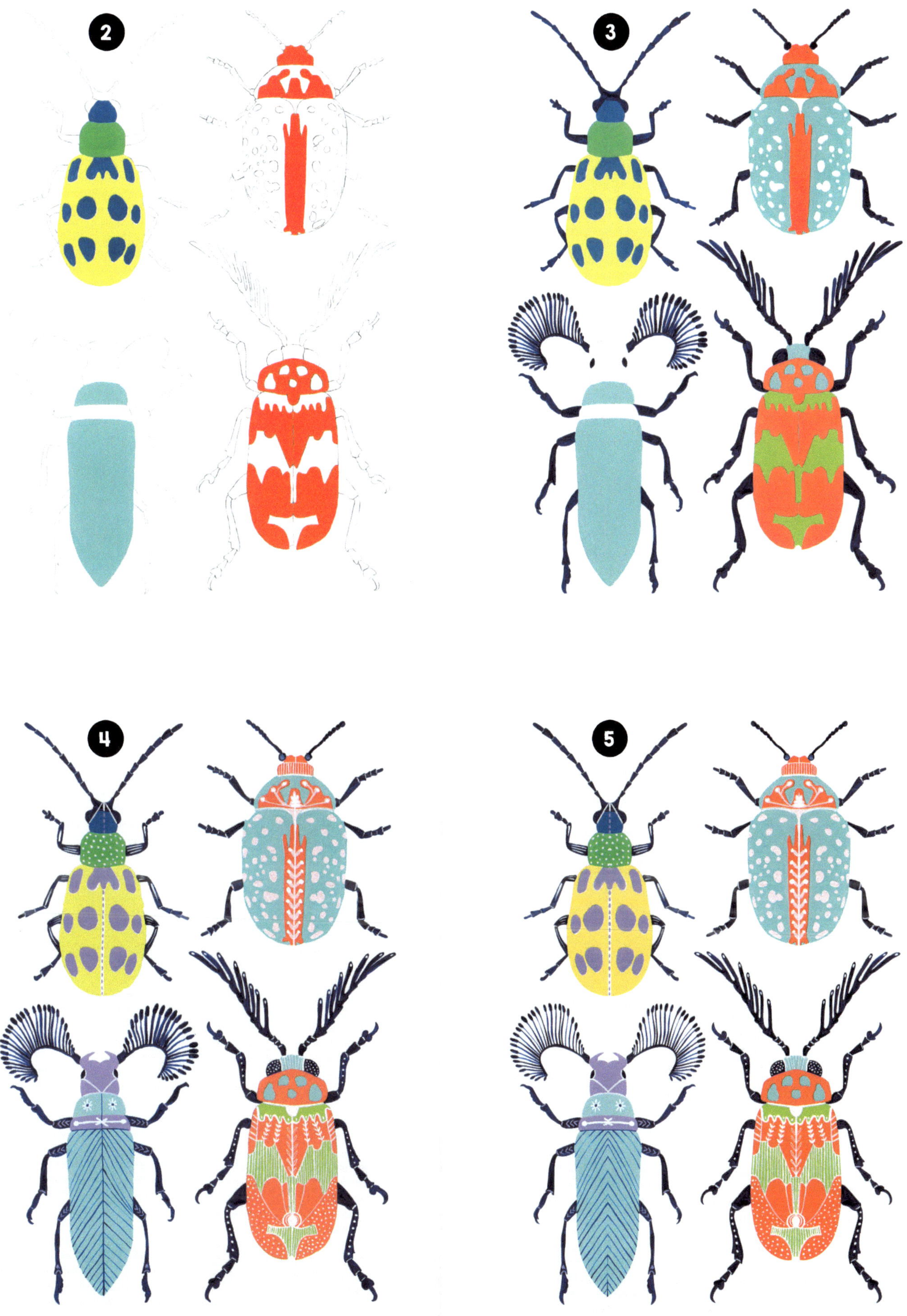

Plant One on Me

House plants are a hot trend right now, and it's no wonder, with all their beautiful foliage and air-purifying qualities. The plant in this example is just one of the many you could paint, so don't feel limited. There are palms, rubber plants, ferns and succulents to choose from, to name a few, some with incredible patterning on the leaves. Painting plants is so satisfying, and they can be quite visually impactful individually or grouped together.

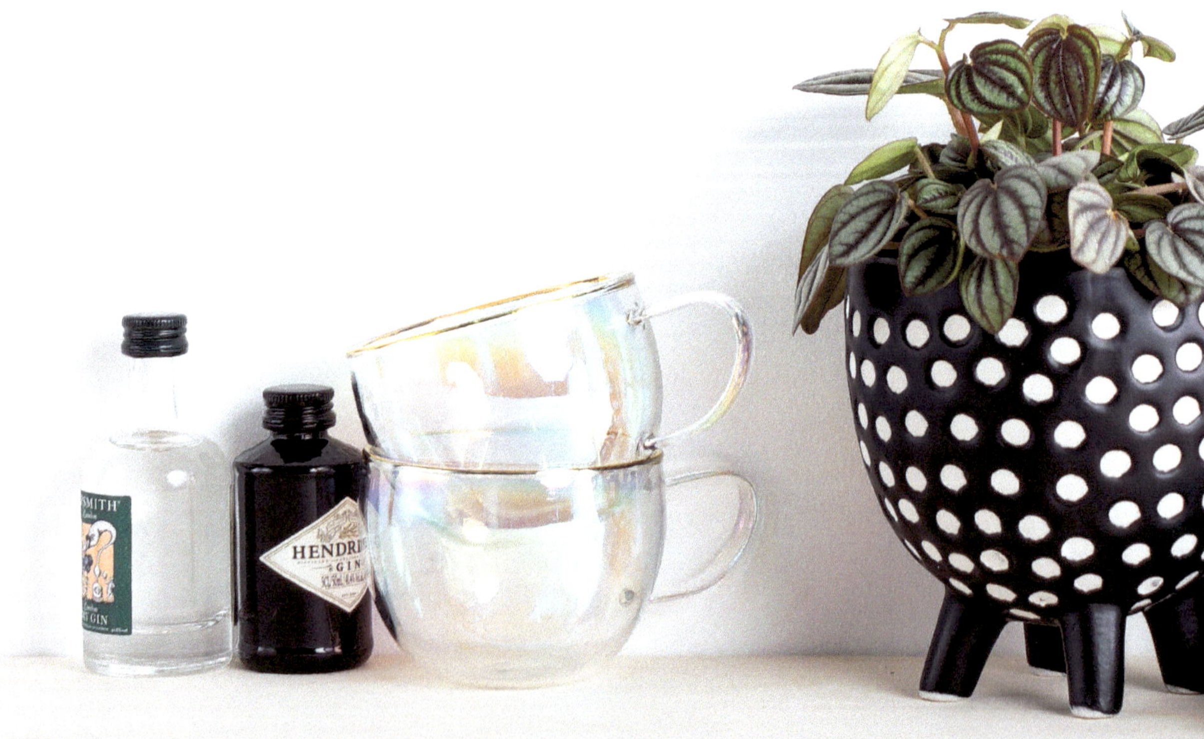

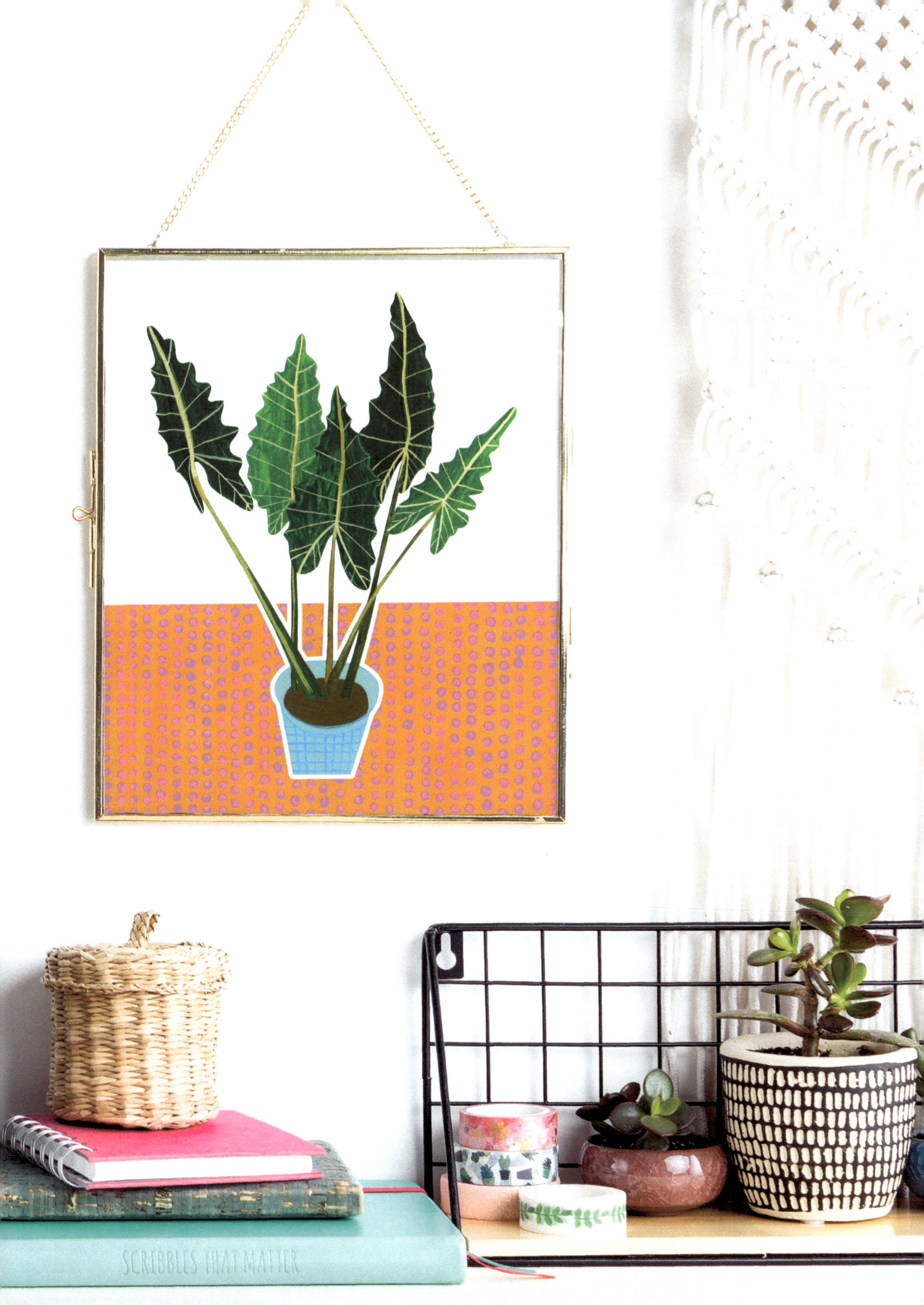
SCRIBBLES THAT MATTER

COLOURS

- Deep green
- Burnt umber
- Spectrum yellow
- Ice green
- Turquoise blue

PAPER

Plain cartridge
or printer paper

Tracing paper

Watercolour
block paper

Collage papers
made previously

TECHNIQUES

Sketching

Line Work

Shapes and Edges

Overlaying

Detail

Collage

---

1. Start with a sketch to get the proportions and shape of the plant right. Pay close attention to the leaf shapes and the overall scale. Once you're happy with your sketch, you can move on to the next step.

2. Block in the main shape of the leaves and stems. I used various shades of green, but left a line down the middle of each leaf blank to fill in when I overlay the veins later.

3. Choose a different colour (in this case I have used an ice green) and block in the rim and outside of the plant pot. To keep all the colours crisp, block in the pot colour by painting along the edges of the stems rather than painting over them.

4. Now use another block of colour for the earth inside the plant pot. We won't add texture here so that the focus is on the leaves and the pot.

5. Once everything is blocked in and the paint is dry, add some details and lines to the leaves. Give the outside of the plant pot a pattern, using the paintbrush as a drawing tool.

6. Finally, add some collage around the plant pot to give the effect that the plant is sitting on a table or rug. My version is created digitally. I used a solid patterned paper that I had painted and scanned previously, and placed it behind the plant layer in Photoshop. I then added a thick, white stroke to the plant to give it this white cut-out effect. This could be done in a similar way with scissors by cutting the shapes from painted patterned paper.

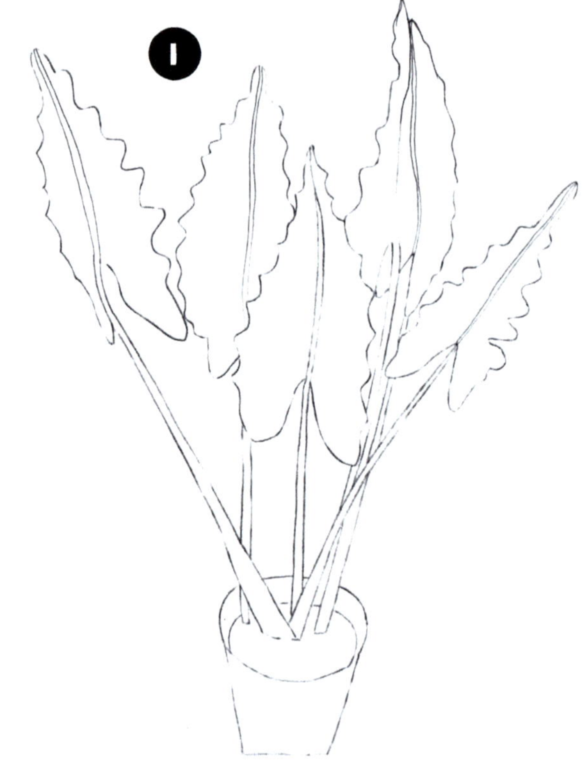

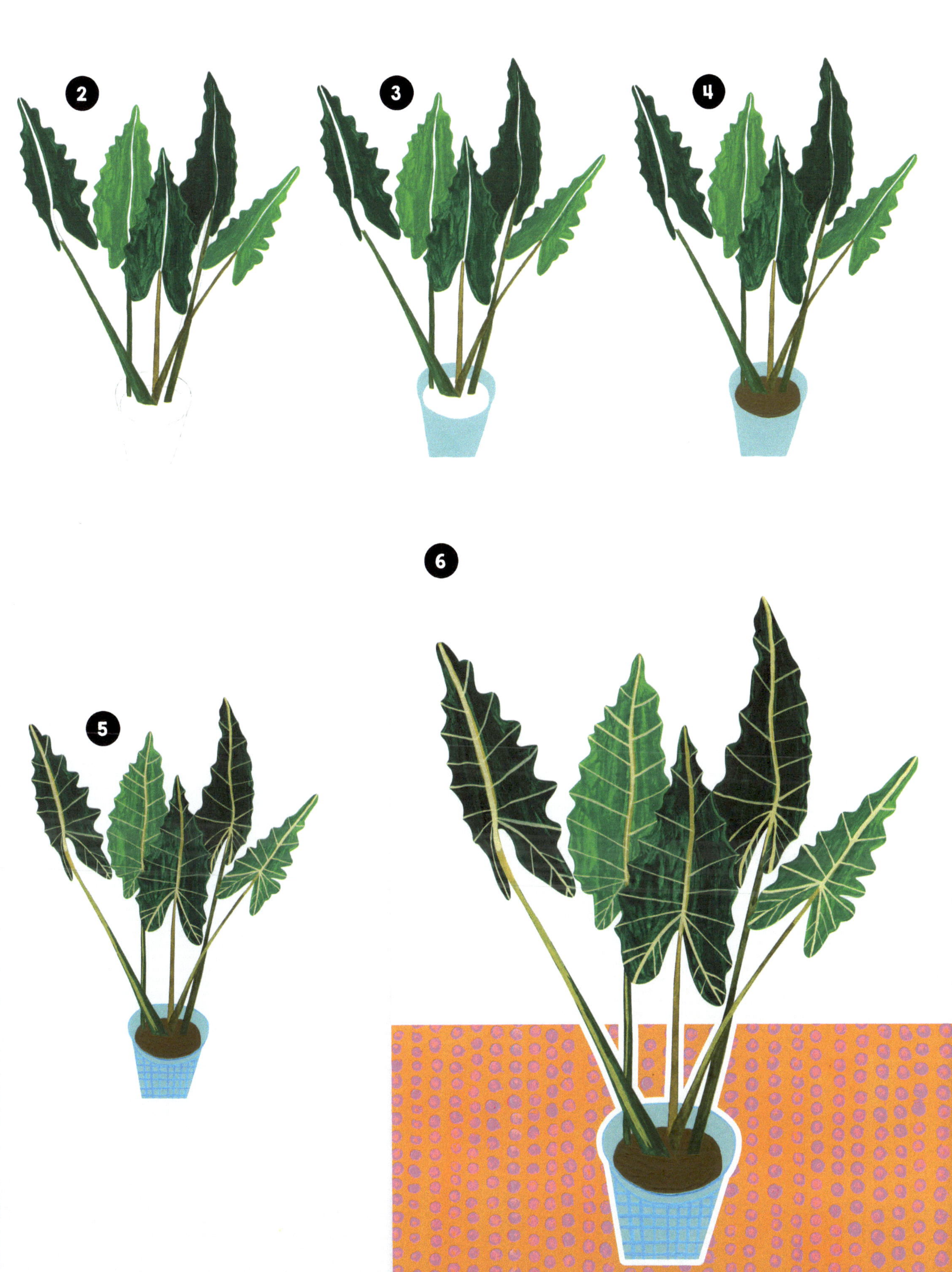

Whoo Are Yoou?

I'm always drawn to creatures with beautiful markings, be it a bird or a butterfly, a cheetah or a caterpillar. Nature is truly amazing, and there is endless inspiration everywhere within our world. I love how these caterpillars seem to have segmented bodies and the way they ripple when they move along. They also remind me of the caterpillar in *Alice in Wonderland*, especially the blue one!

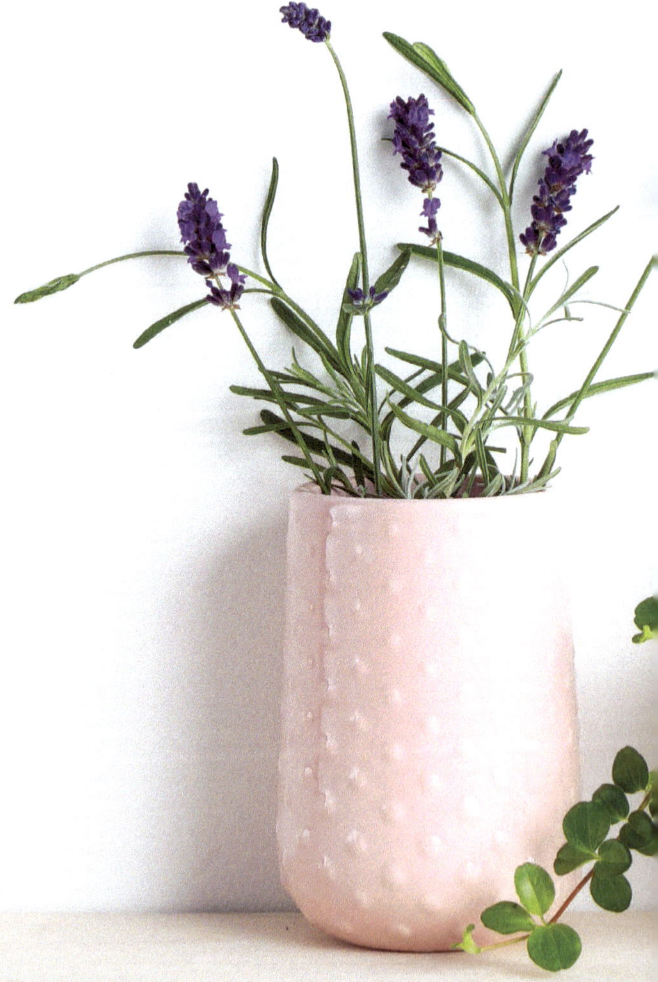

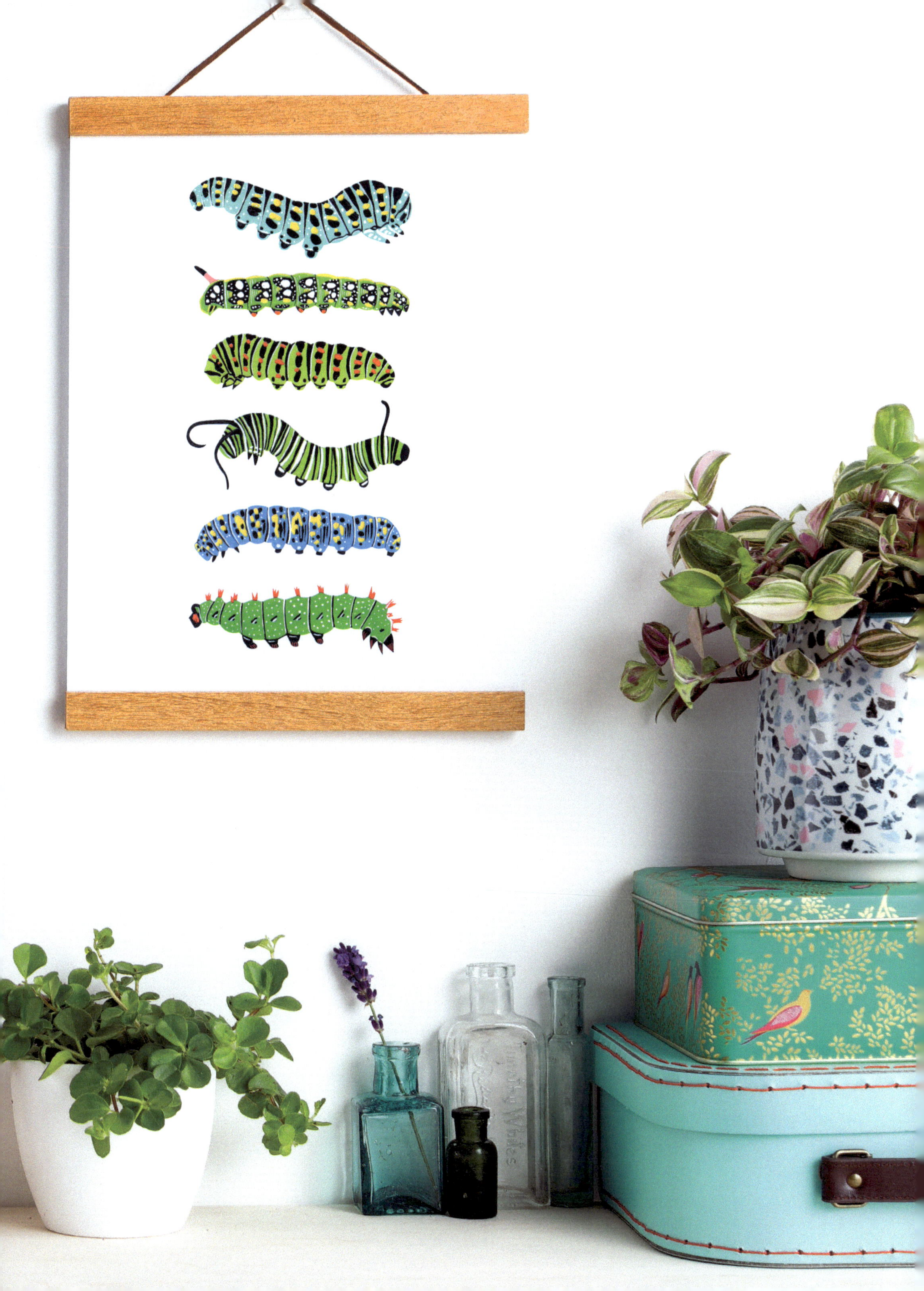

COLOURS

- Ice green
- White
- Smalt blue
- Scarlet
- Spectrum yellow
- Prussian blue
- Brilliant green

PAPER

Plain cartridge
or printer paper

Watercolour
block paper

Tracing paper

TECHNIQUES

Sketching

Line Work

Overlaying

Detail

1. Sketch out your caterpillars on plain paper. It doesn't have to be fancy paper – computer paper or a page in your sketchbook will do. I tend to use the tracing paper technique for this type of sketch, as it makes it easy to simplify the lines.

2. Choose your main colours and begin by blocking in the body shapes. I've used a variety of greens and blues for my caterpillars, but they don't have to be realistic. Go for hot pink or purple if you feel like it! Allow this layer to dry before moving on to the next layer.

3. Begin to add in some details to build up the layers. I used a dark navy colour across all of my caterpillars to give them a cohesive feel, even though the colours underneath are all slightly different. Look at photos as a reference for distinguishing marks, and replicate those in your own way on the caterpillars' bodies.

4. Continue with the next layer of detail, adding little pops of colour so that your caterpillars come to life! Again, refer to your photographs for ideas on colours and markings. Of course, you can choose completely unrealistic colours or stick more closely to the real thing: it's entirely up to you!

5. In this final step, the addition of fine white details completes the little group of caterpillars. I overlaid dots and lines to add to the markings.

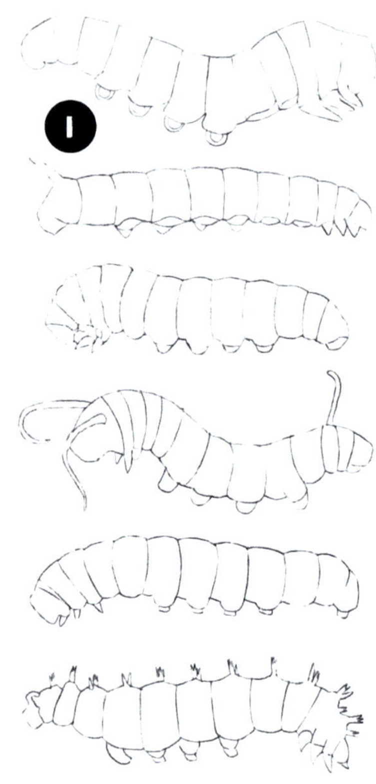

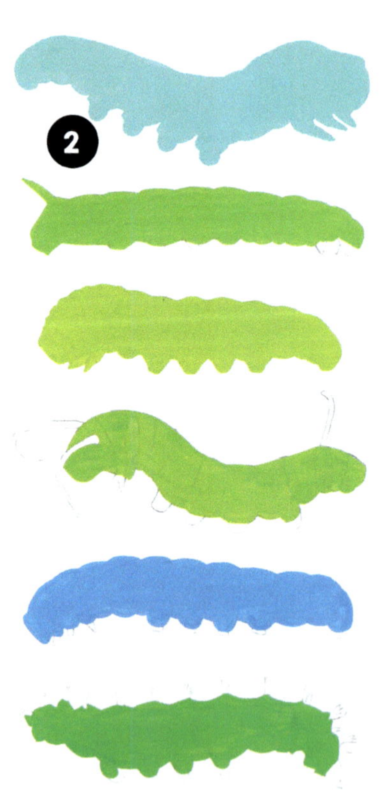

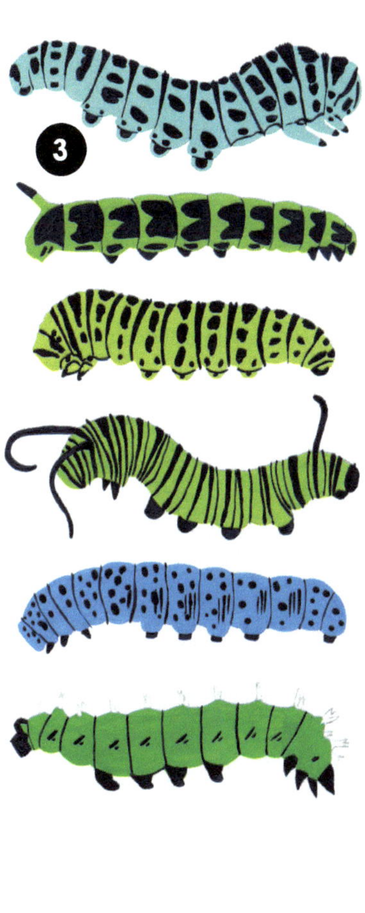

3

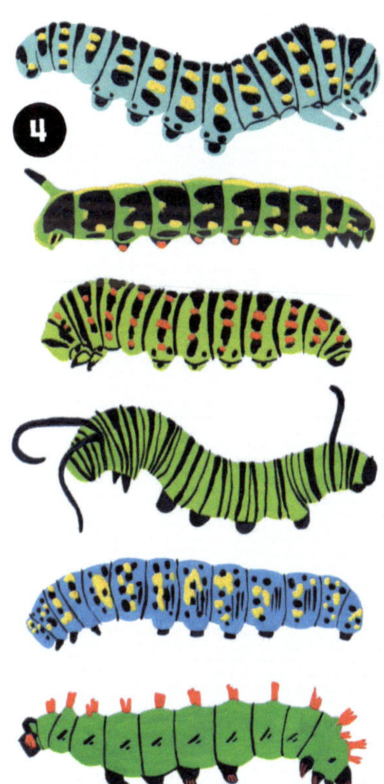

4

5

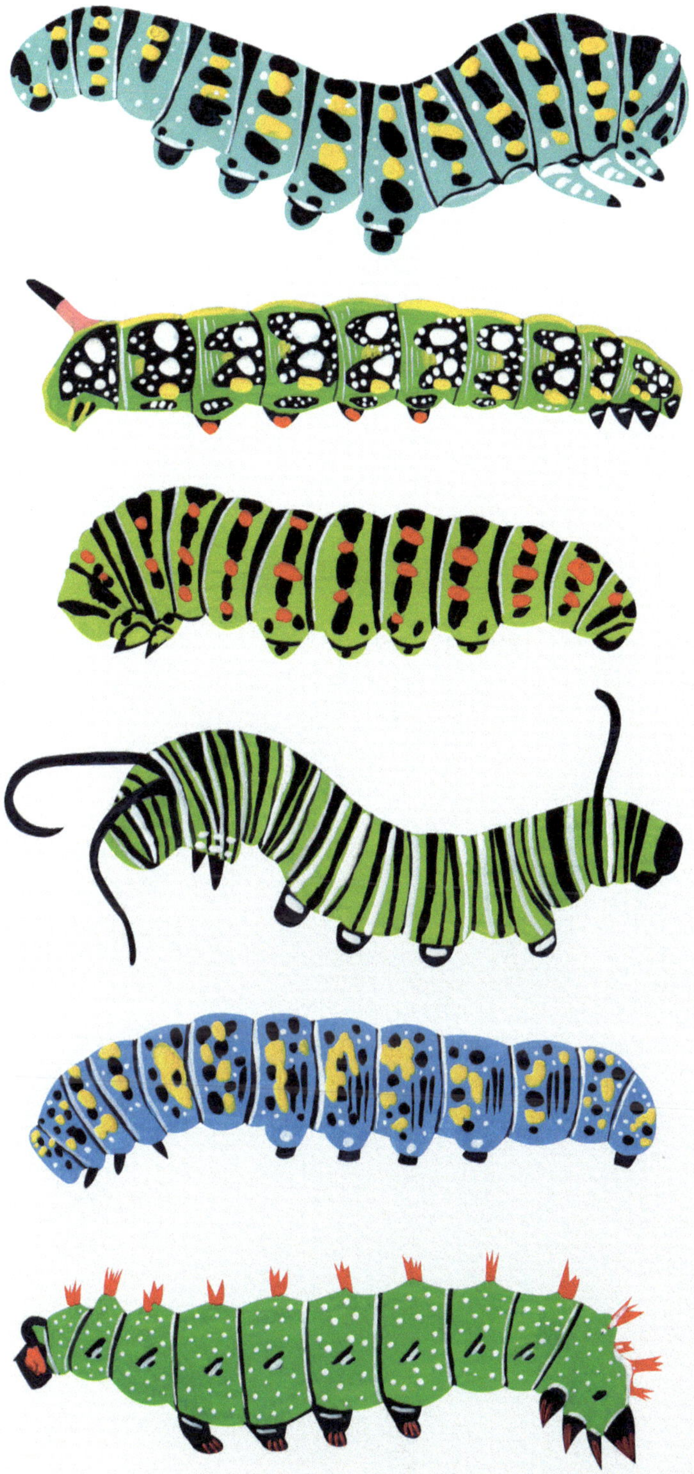

All of a Flutter

In this project, I used a lot of papers that I'd previously painted and decorated with patterns. If you'd like to do the same, use coloured card or paint a solid background on paper, then get busy with your mark making. The more contrast and pattern you introduce, the better! Once your patterned papers are dry, you can start cutting...

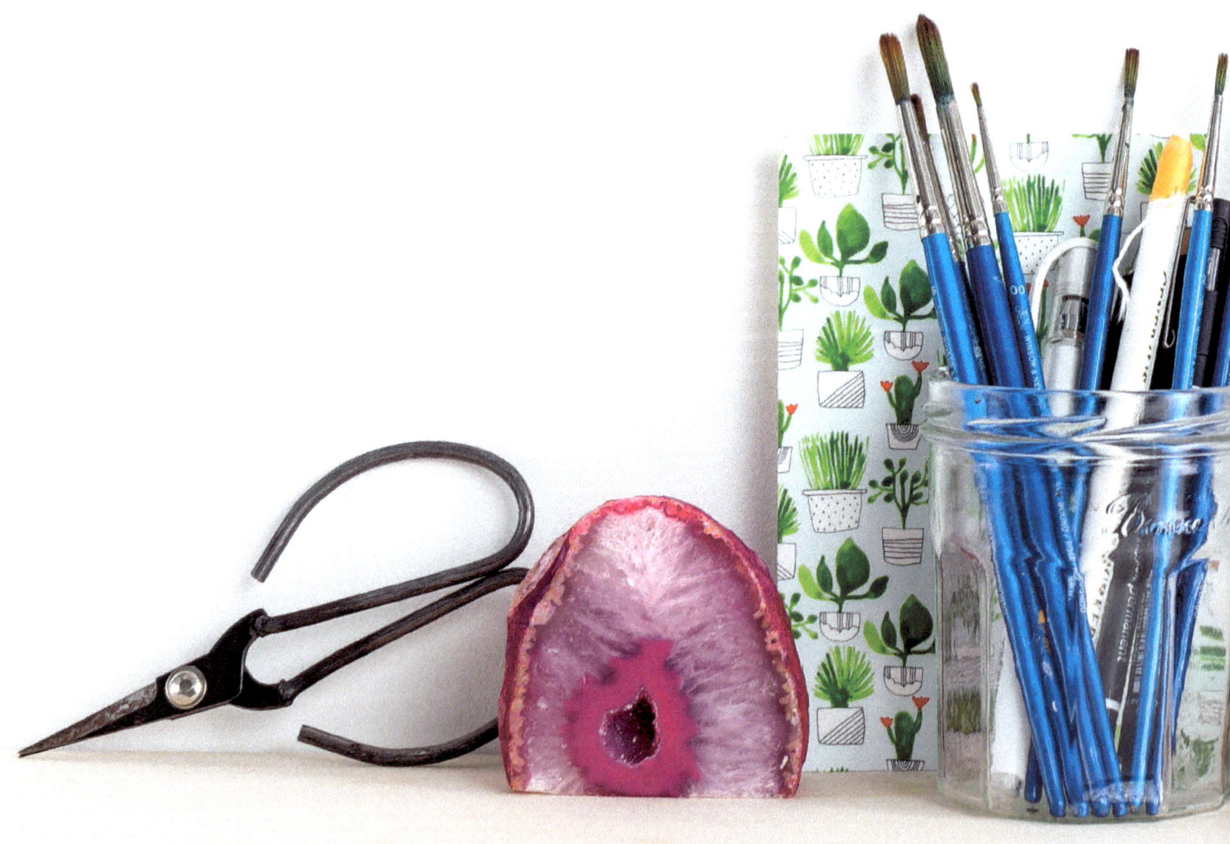

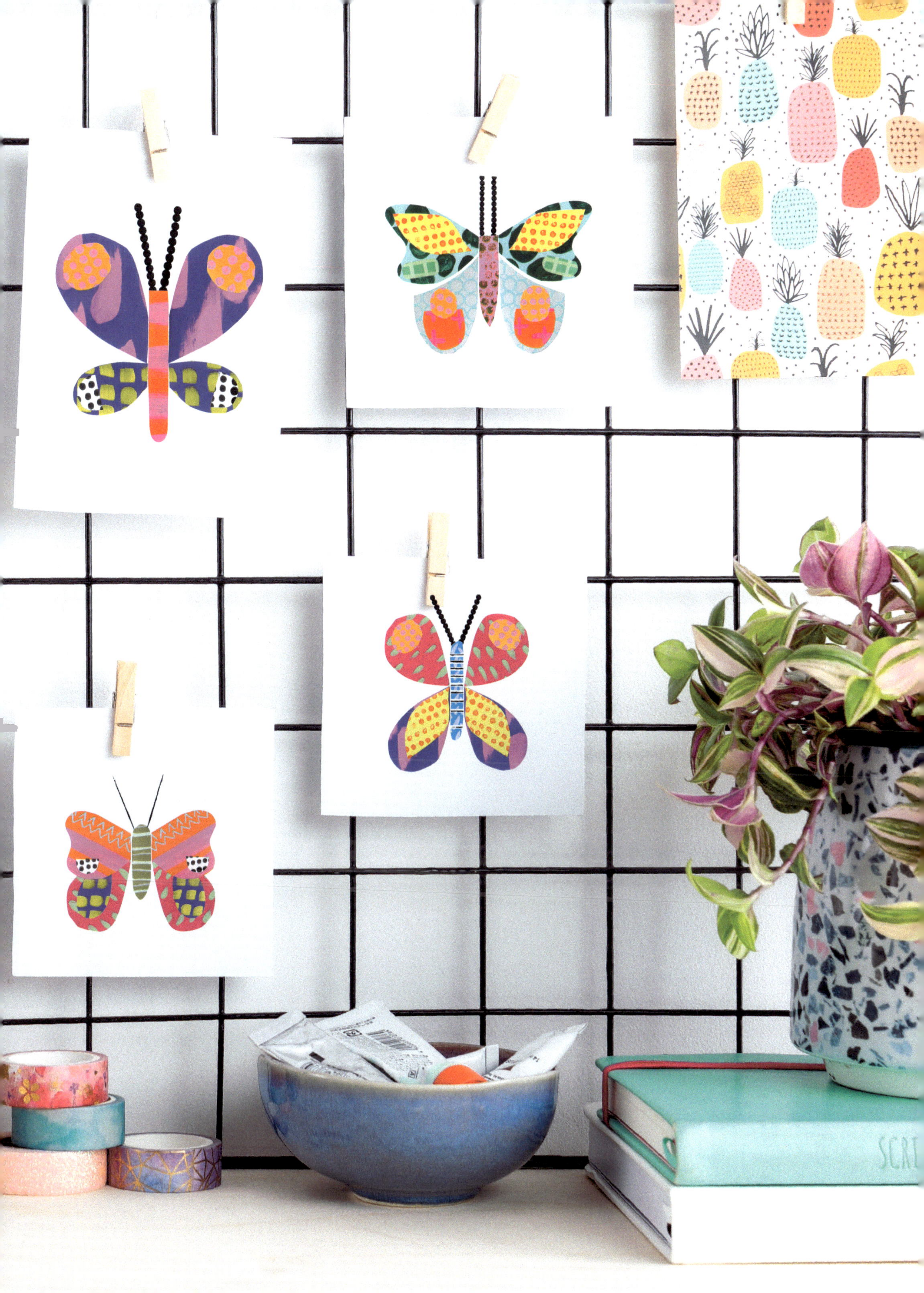

PAPER

Previously painted
collage papers

Thick card
or board

TECHNIQUES

Mark Making

Collage

Digitizing

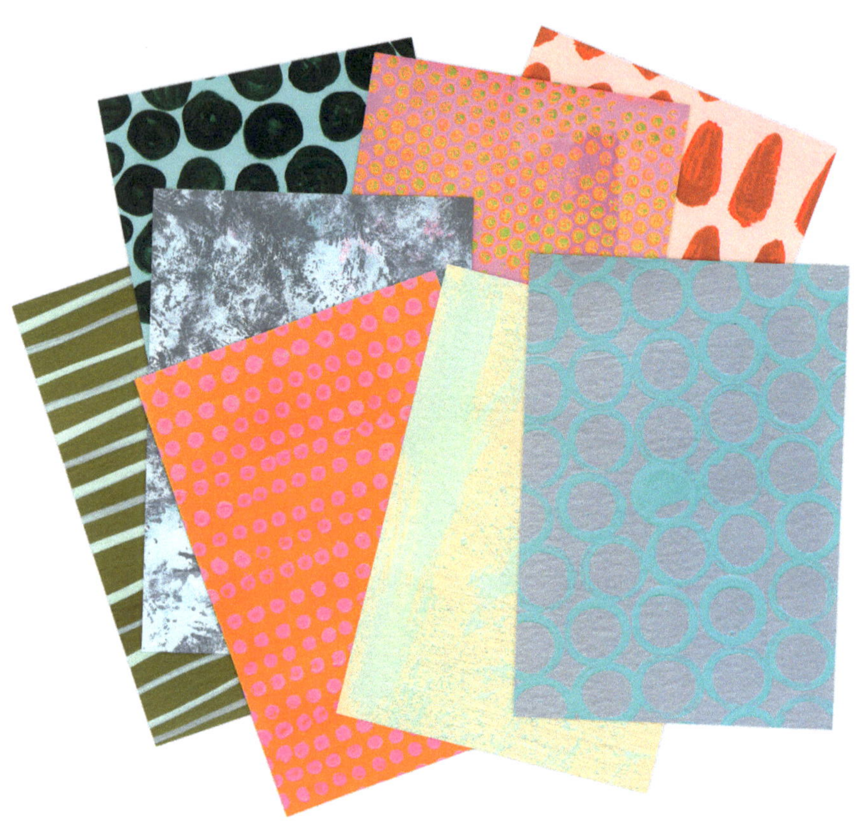

1. To begin, cut out some dot marks for the antennae. I made these ones with the tip of a cotton bud. Lay them down on a sheet of thick card or board, gluing them in place with PVA or a gloss medium.

2. Next, cut out the body shape. I've used a bright, chunky stripe pattern. Refer to photos to get the general idea of how a butterfly body looks – a long, thin lozenge shape is a good starting point. Glue the body shape down, slightly overlapping the antennae.

3. Butterflies generally have four wing parts, two on each side. Cut out the top wing parts by folding a patterned paper in half and then cutting two wings at the same time. The pattern doesn't have to be identical on each side, but this will make them almost perfectly the same shape and size. Stick the wings down close to the sides of the body, placing them towards the top so that you have space to add the lower pair.

4. Follow the same process for the bottom wings, using a different patterned paper. These wings can be bigger or smaller than the top wings – use your intuition and go with your own preference.

5. Here, I cut a pair of small black-and-white pieces to add to the tips of the lower wings. Add as many additional pieces as you like to build up interesting details.

6. Add detail to the top set of wings in yet another contrasting pattern. Again, carry on adding more details to your butterfly if you'd like to make it more intricately patterned.

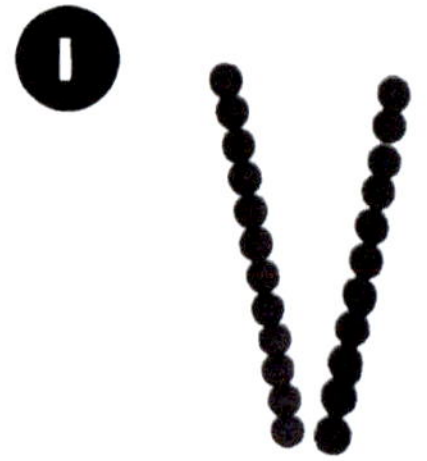

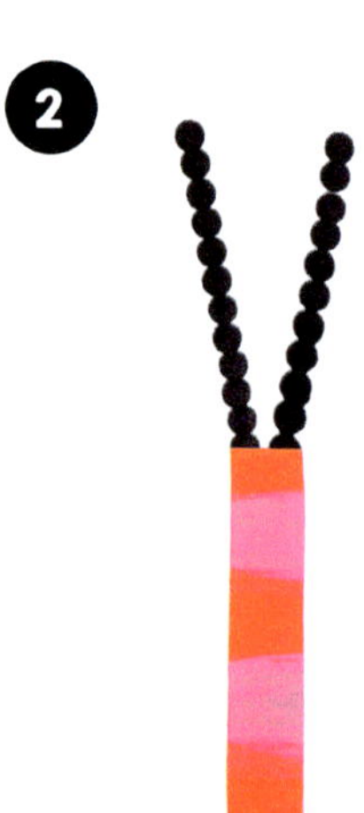

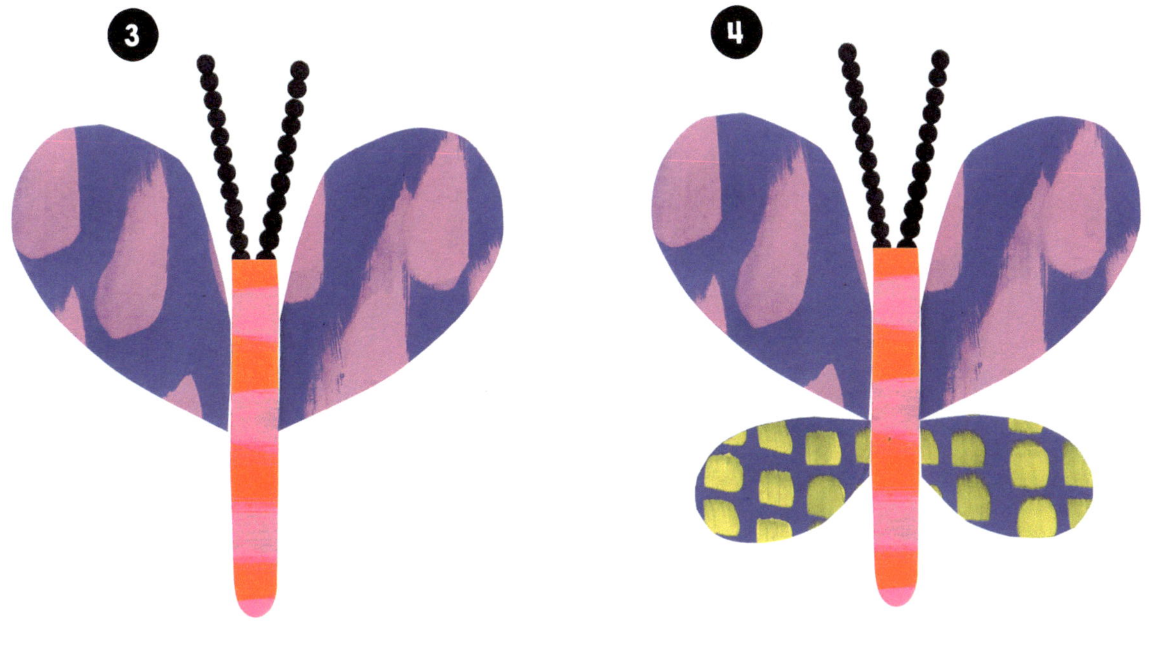

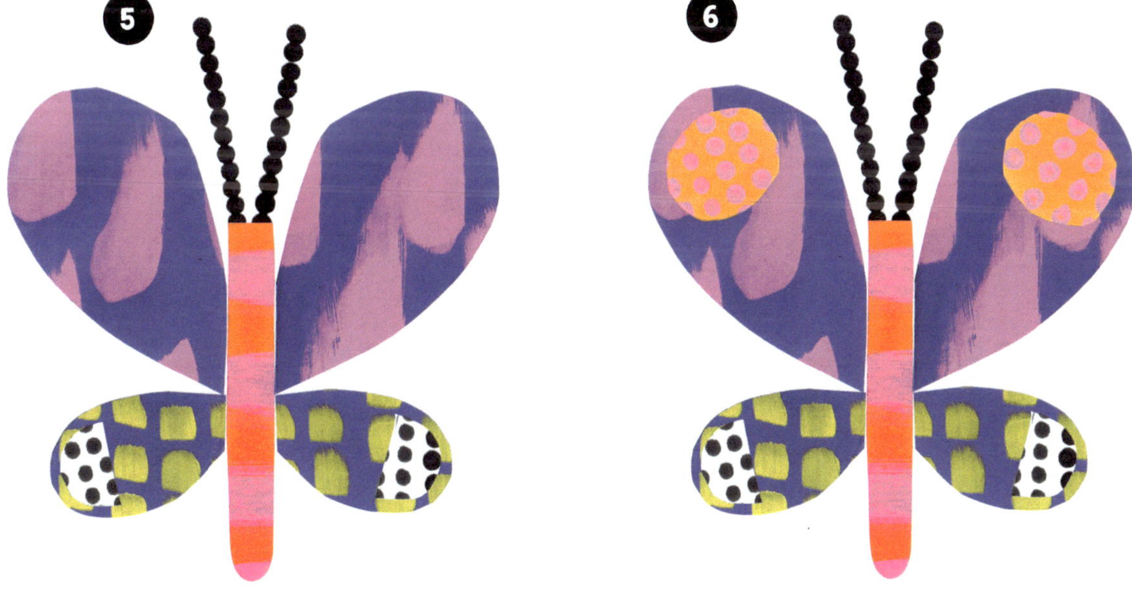

7. Make some more butterflies in the same way, mixing up the patterns and shapes each time. You could use three or four different butterflies to make a wall art print or card by laying them out in a group.

8. If you want to take it further, you can create lots of different butterflies. Lay them out as an analogue pattern or scan them to your computer and create a beautiful, bright butterfly display. Clashing colours and patterns are a fun way to go with this, but a more realistic rendition or a colour theme could be interesting too – perhaps you want to use all blues, for example, but keep all the patterns different. This pattern could be used as an all-over repeat on fabric.

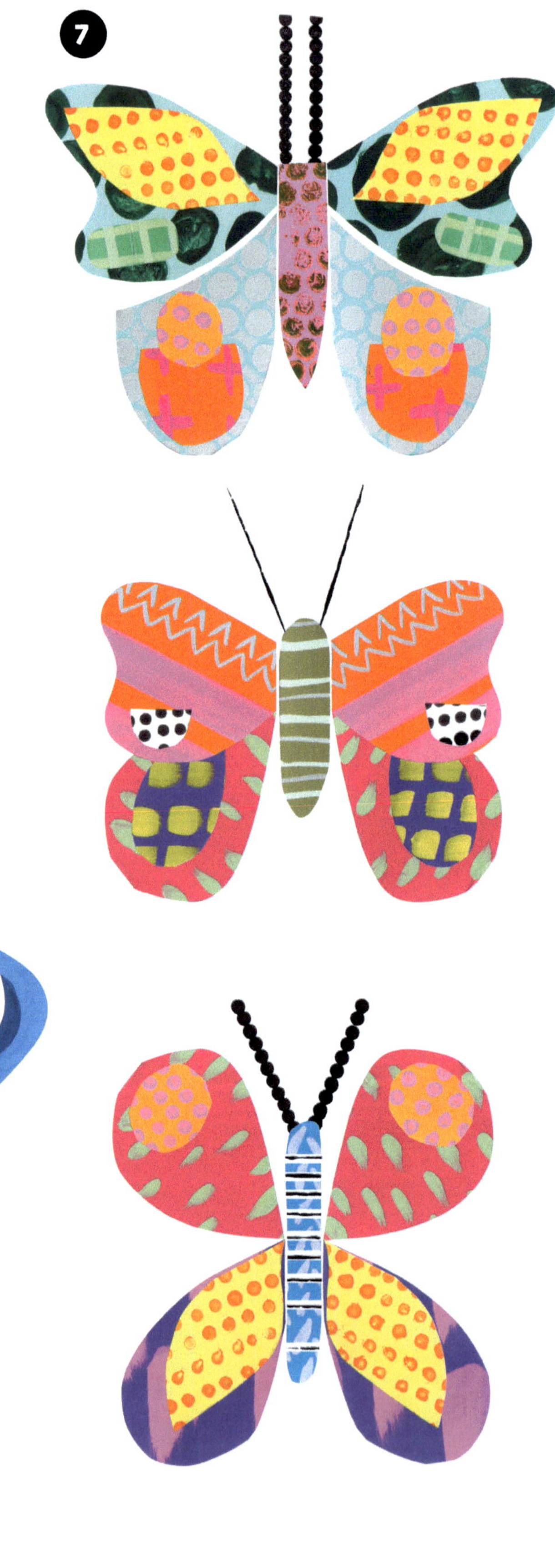

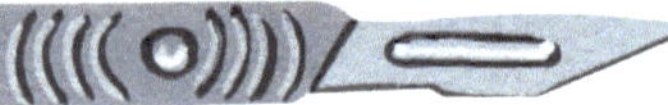

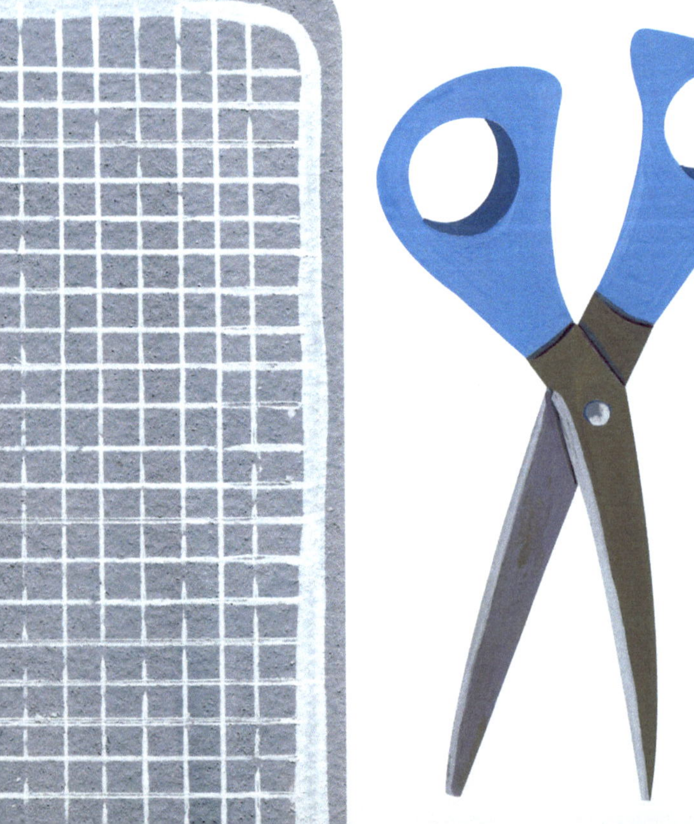

MY FINAL PATTERN IS FAIRLY REGIMENTED,
BUT I'VE FLIPPED AND ROTATED SOME OF THE
BUTTERFLIES SO THAT THEY AREN'T ALL FACING
IN THE SAME DIRECTION. I FEEL THIS ADDS
SOME INTEREST TO THE PIECE.

8

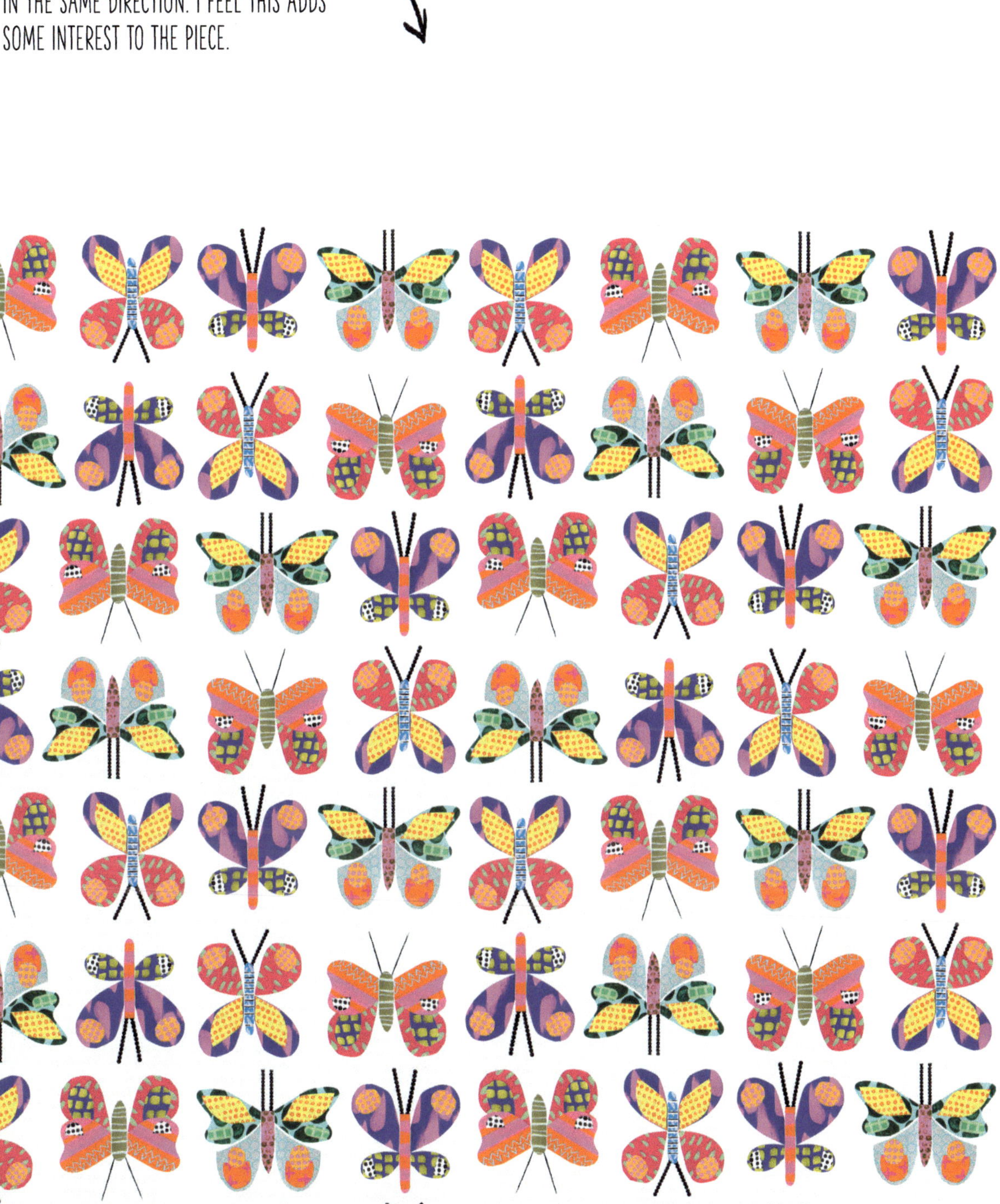

Jumbled Geometry

Painting a geometric pattern like this is such a relaxing thing to do. It gives me a great sense of calm. I love seeing the pattern develop and change with each new colour that I add. Your design doesn't have to be perfect – the wobbly lines actually give it a lovely human touch rather than a computer-generated, pixel-perfect feel. Other shapes to try are diamonds, rectangles, ovals or triangles.

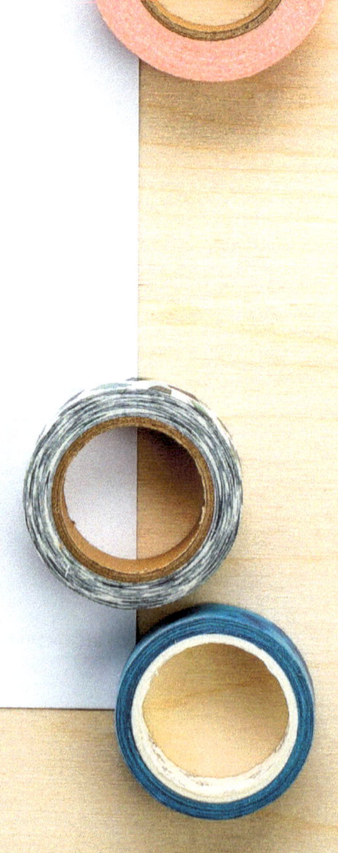

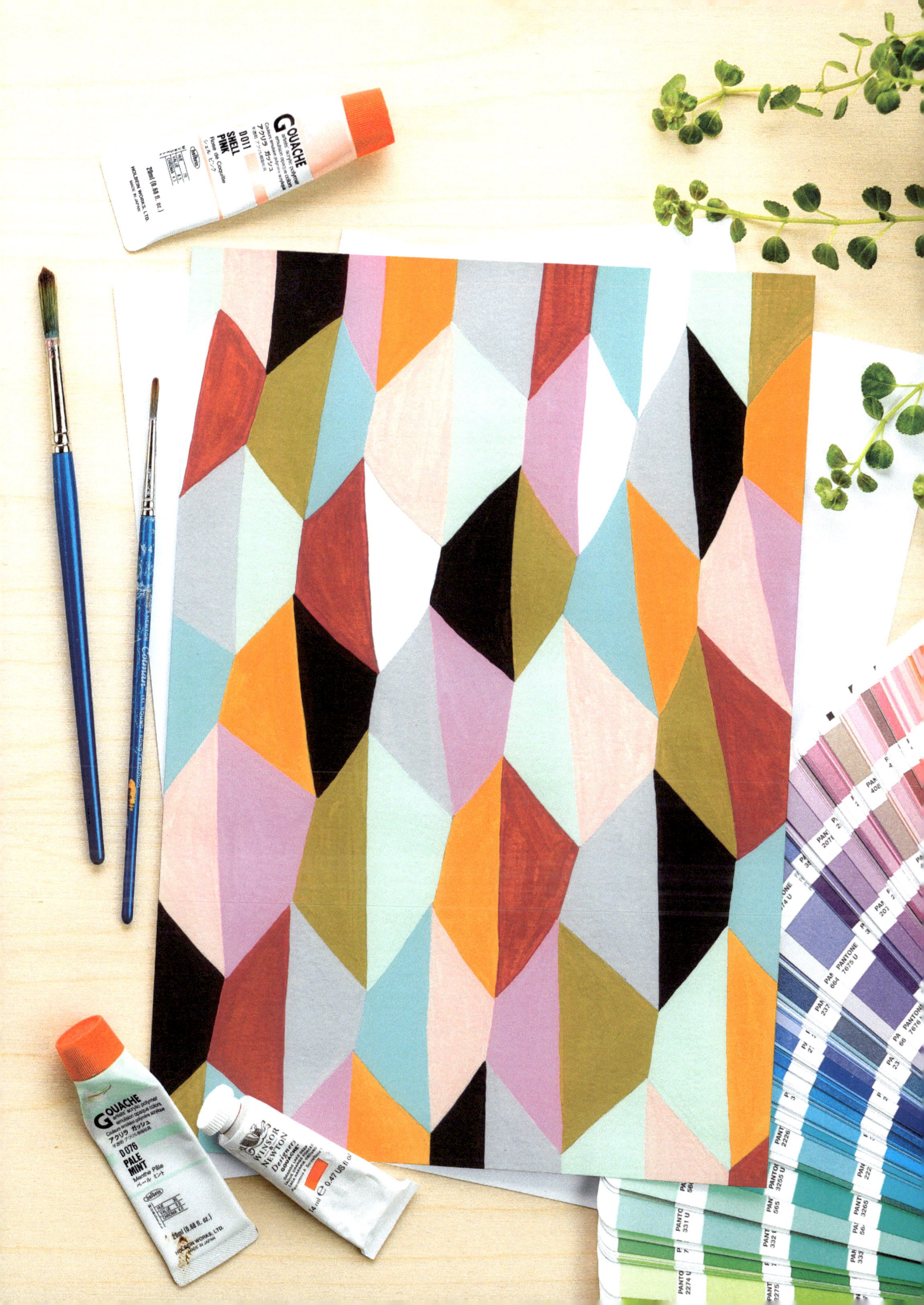

COLOURS

- Mint green
- Ice green
- Opera pink
- Yellow ochre
- Orange yellow
- Grey
- Burnt umber
- Scarlet
- Shell pink

PAPER

Plain cartridge
or printer paper

Tracing paper

Watercolour
block paper

TECHNIQUES

Sketching

Shapes and Edges

1. Begin by roughly sketching your geometric pattern in pencil straight onto your watercolour paper. It doesn't have to be precise or mathematically accurate – we're having fun here and creating a dynamic and interesting geometric pattern.

2. Now lay down the first colour – I've used a lovely pale pink, adding it to one shape on each row to make sure that the colours will be evenly spread out.

3. Continue to do the same with the next colour, keeping everything balanced by adding one block of colour to each row.

4. Next up is a bright orange. Following the same method as before, block out a shape in each row with colour. I've positioned my blocks randomly along the row to keep things interesting.

5. Add yet another colour, this time a raspberry red. As you add more colours and they start to touch within the pattern, it's best to let each layer dry before moving onto the next.

6. At this point I thought that maybe a little neutral will add some interest within the pattern and help the other colours to pop, so I added in some grey.

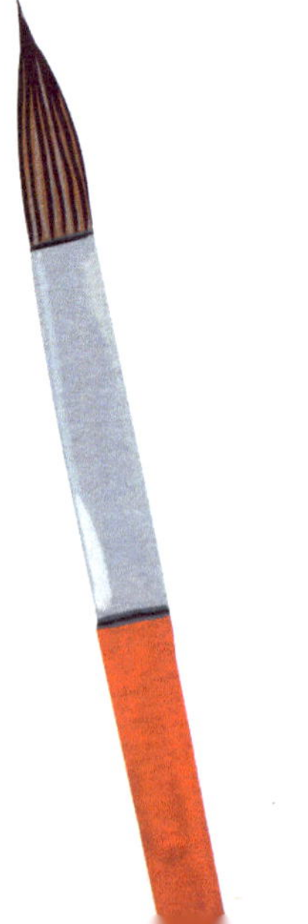

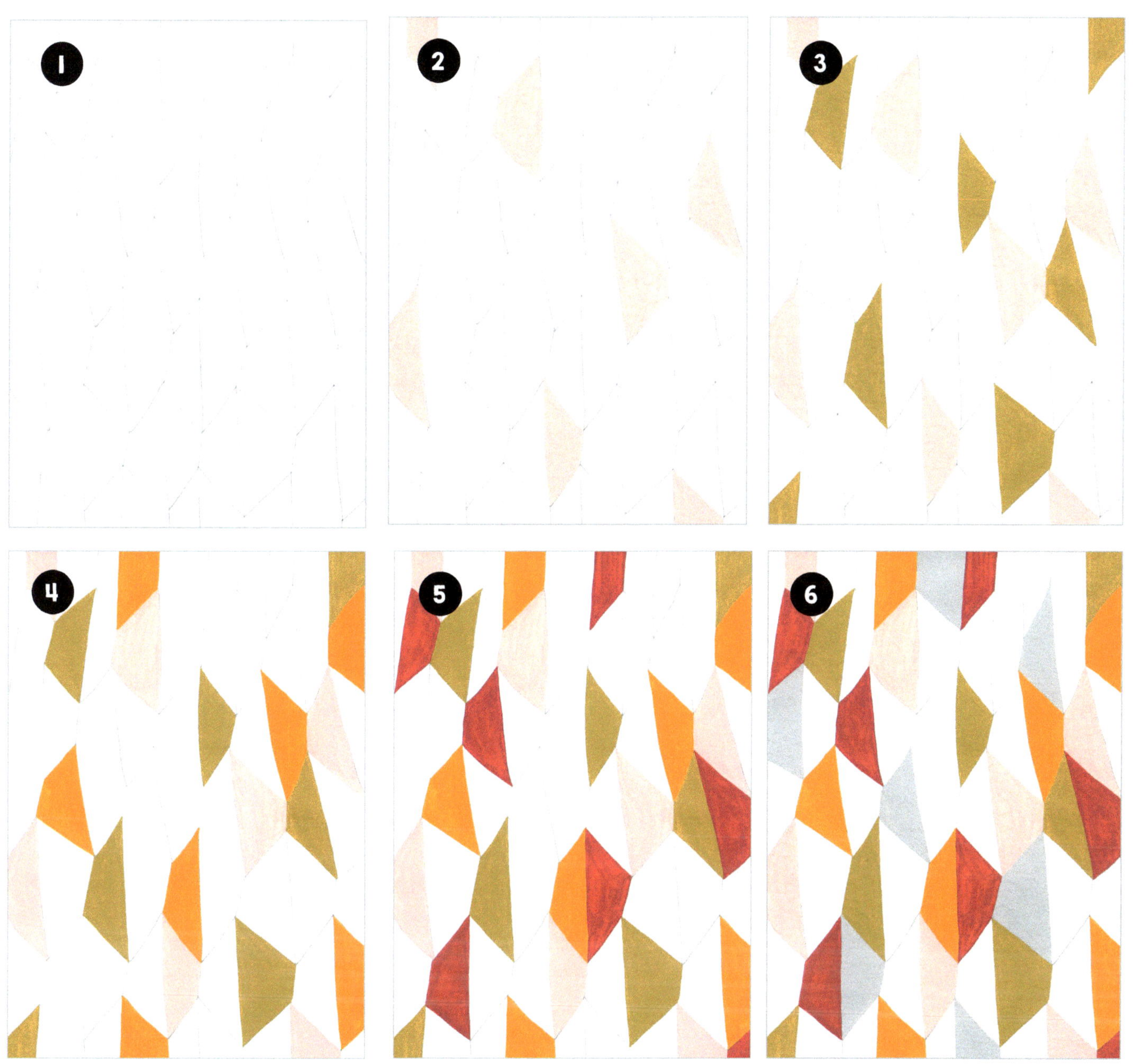

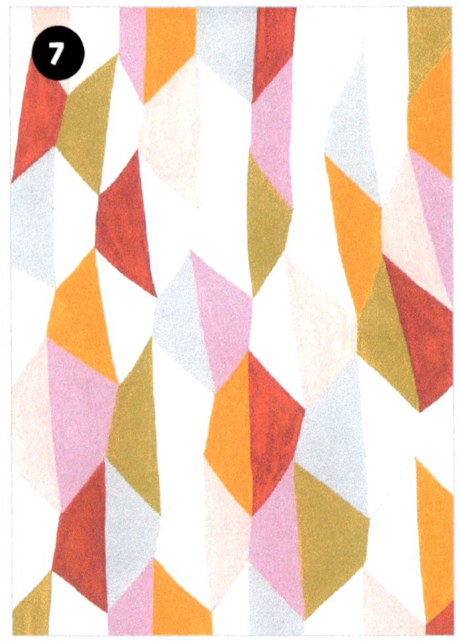

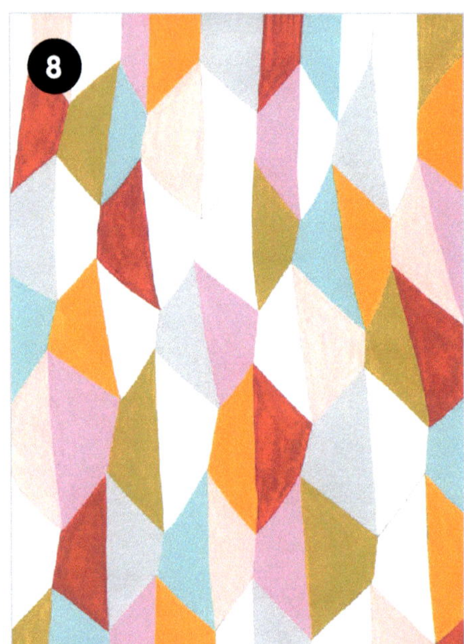

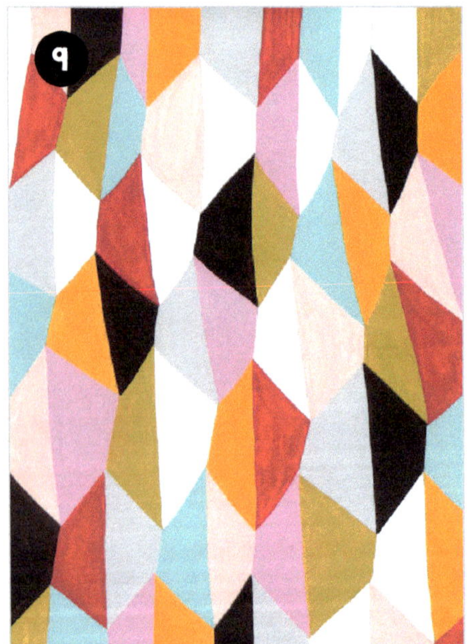

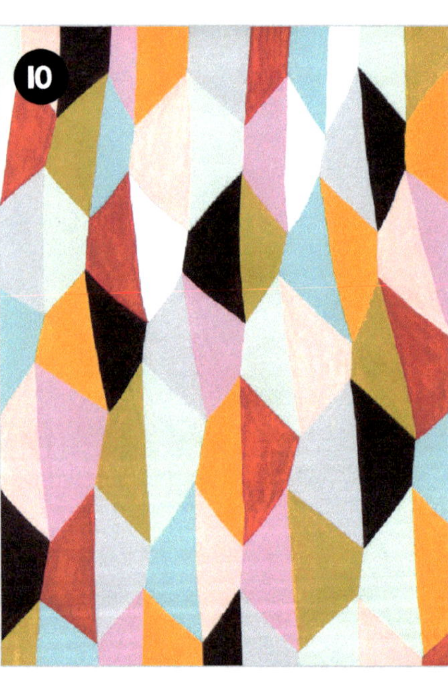

7. Next, a brighter pink is added to give the image some energy. You could achieve this by mixing a little of the shell pink with the opera pink.

8. Then I added a delicious fresh, icy green to contrast with the orange, adding another layer to this fun pattern.

9. For drama and more contrast, I added a darker colour. I love how it works with all the brighter colours. As a suggestion you could use prussian blue and burnt umber to make a dark colour.

10. To balance that out, I added a creamy, pale mint. Only a few more spaces left – we're almost done!

11. In this final step, I added another neutral so that the eye has somewhere to rest in between all that popping colour. I can see this pattern being applicable to fabric, fashion and interiors and possibly even gift wrap.

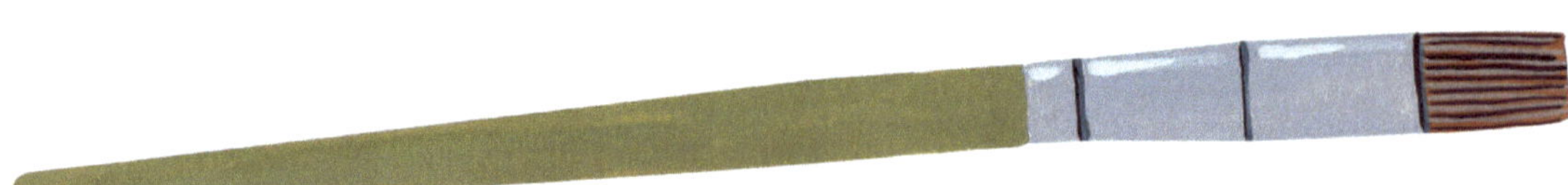

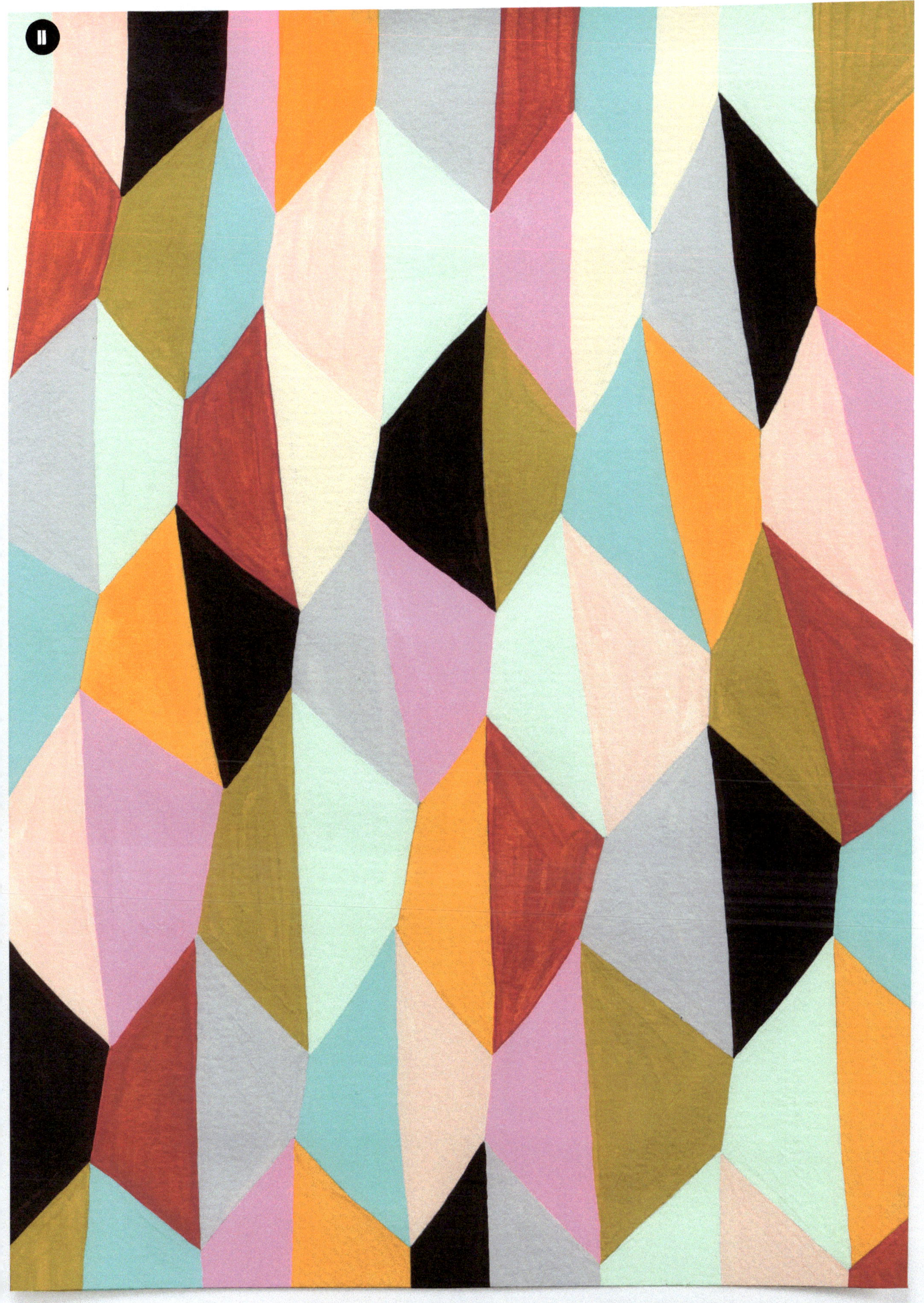

Owl Be Right Here

Painting onto dark backgrounds can produce some striking results. Using very light-coloured paints for a nocturnal bird, as I've done with this owl, contrasts quite powerfully with the dark backdrop of the black paper. The colours I've used to represent the feathers and markings on the owl and the seed heads are fairly neutral, with very subtle amounts of colour added.

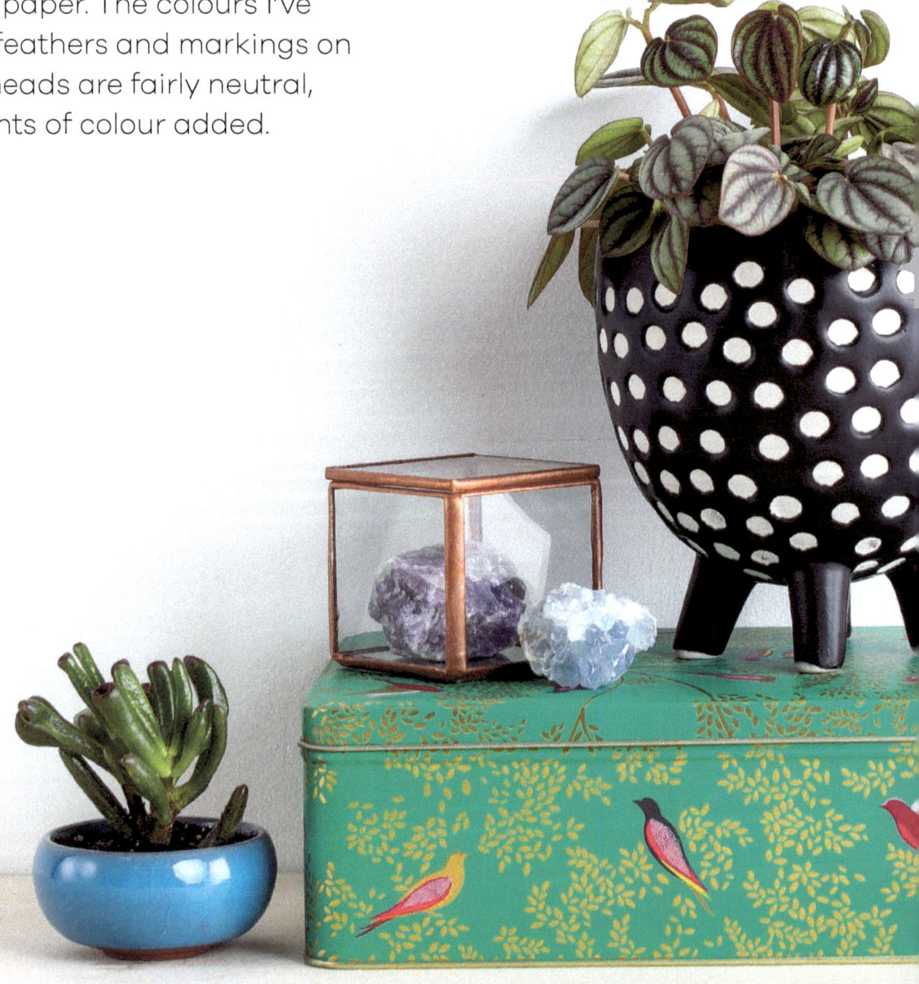

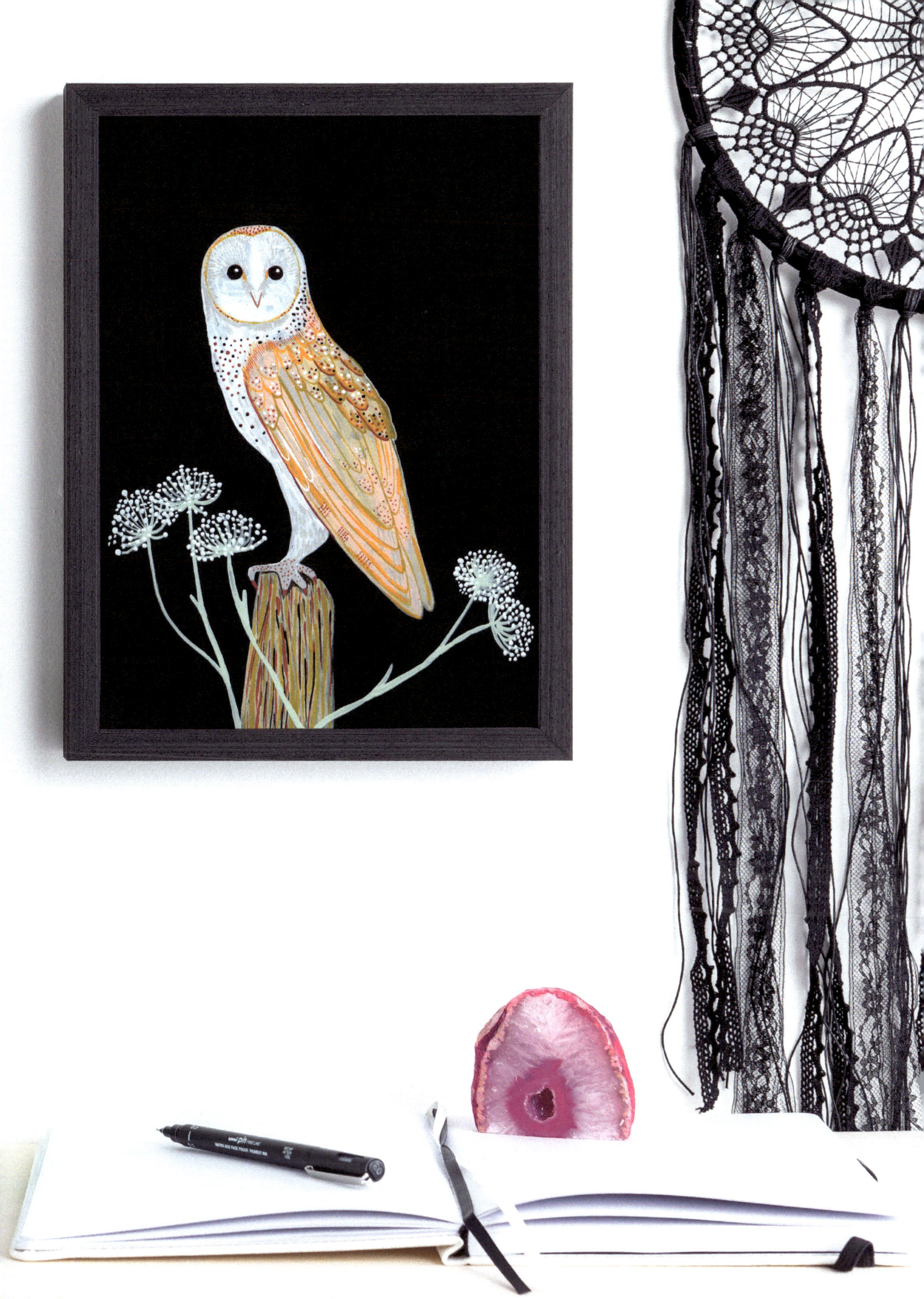

COLOURS

- White
- Orange
- Yellow ochre
- Shell pink
- Burnt umber
- Deep magenta
- Mint green
- Grey

PAPER

Black cartridge paper

TECHNIQUES

Sketching

Line Work

Overlaying

Detail

Dark Backgrounds

1. Sketch out your rough owl drawing on the black paper with a white china marker pencil so that you can see the outline clearly. You could also use a light-coloured pencil or pastel.

2. Lay down some initial colour to map out the wing, head, body and tree stump. The head and breast are a lot lighter than the wing. Leave two circular spaces unpainted for the eyes. There's a little translucency here with the paint, and the black paper shows through, but that's ok – it adds an interesting texture.

3. Next, I added a little warm pink colour to the wing to define it more. I used the same colour to mark out the shape of the face with a circular line.

4. At this stage, I drew in some rough feather shapes on the wing as well as the beak, eye details and a little texture on the tree stump.

5. Continue to add colour to the feathers, building up the layers. This time I used a brighter orange colour. I like the way the translucency is still visible underneath the linear markings of the feathers.

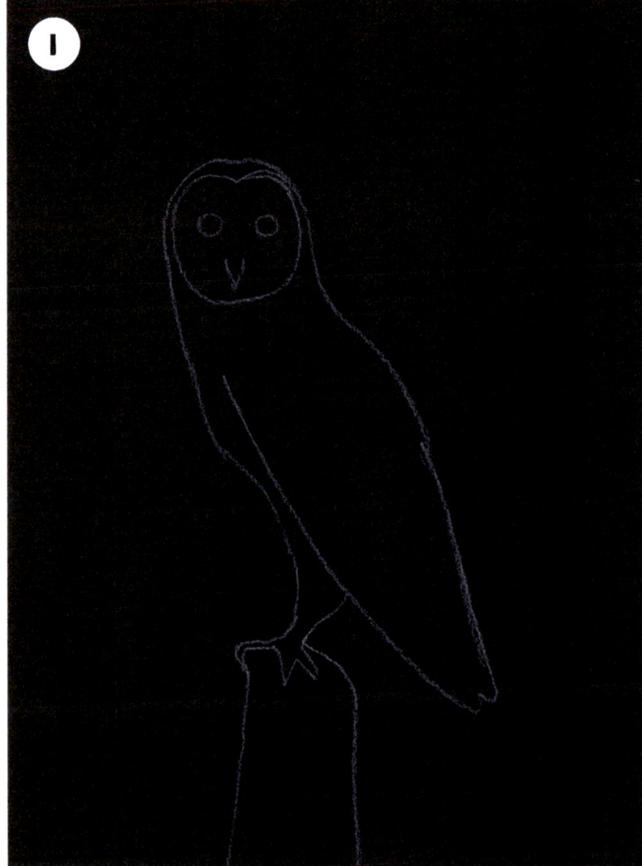

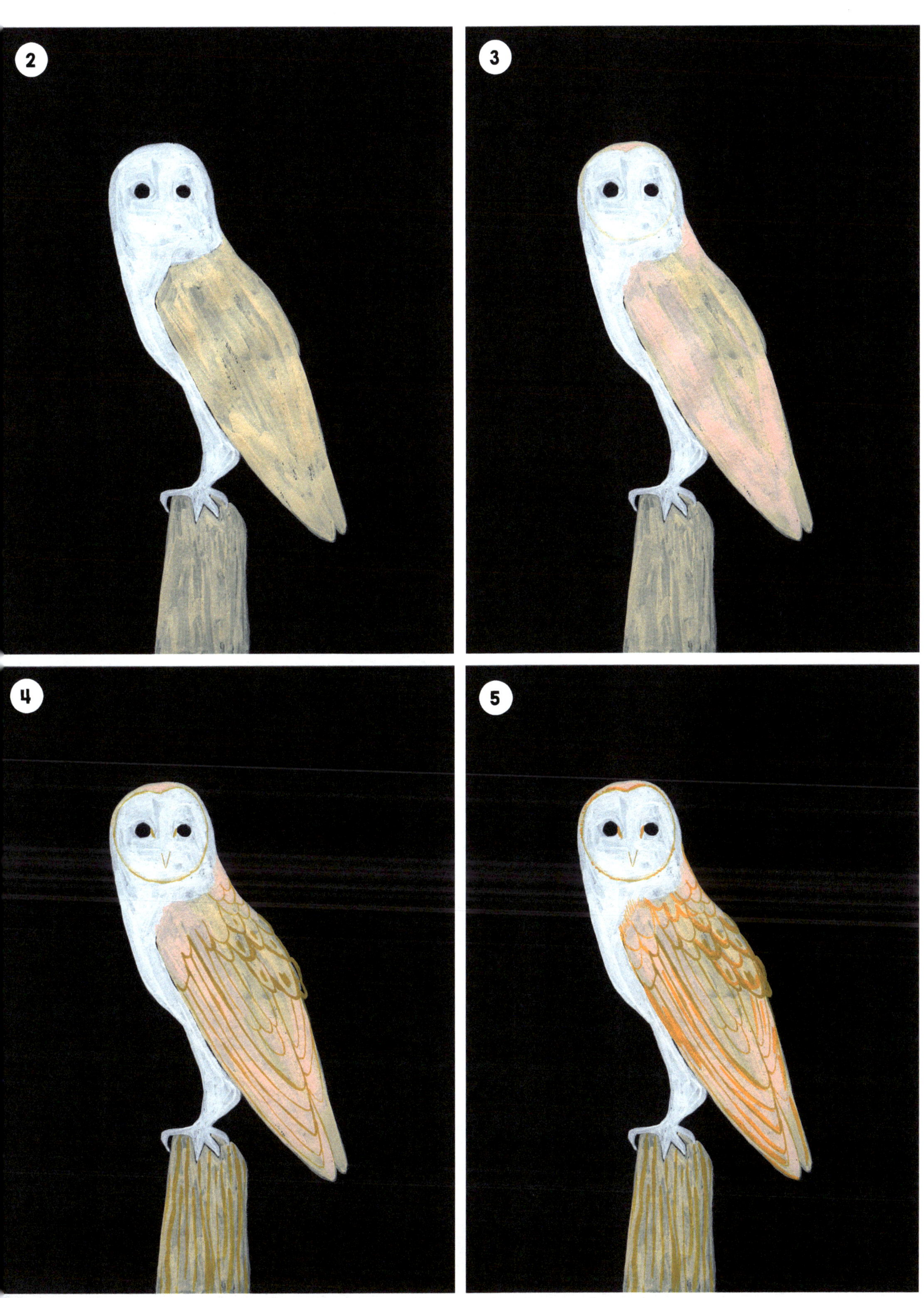

6. The addition of little dot textures to the head, neck, breast and feathers gives a little more interest and mimics the markings on the bird. Extra linear detail on the tree stump, beak and eyes are painted in at this stage, too.

7. I added some texture to the face in grey and some white dot highlights to the feathers. Don't forget to add the highlights for the eyes, too, as they really help to give life to the bird.

8. To finish, I drew in some Queen Anne's Lace in front of the tree stump to soften the overall feel and to add a little more interest to the scene. You could add more flowers or stars and moon to your piece to reinforce the night-time mood.

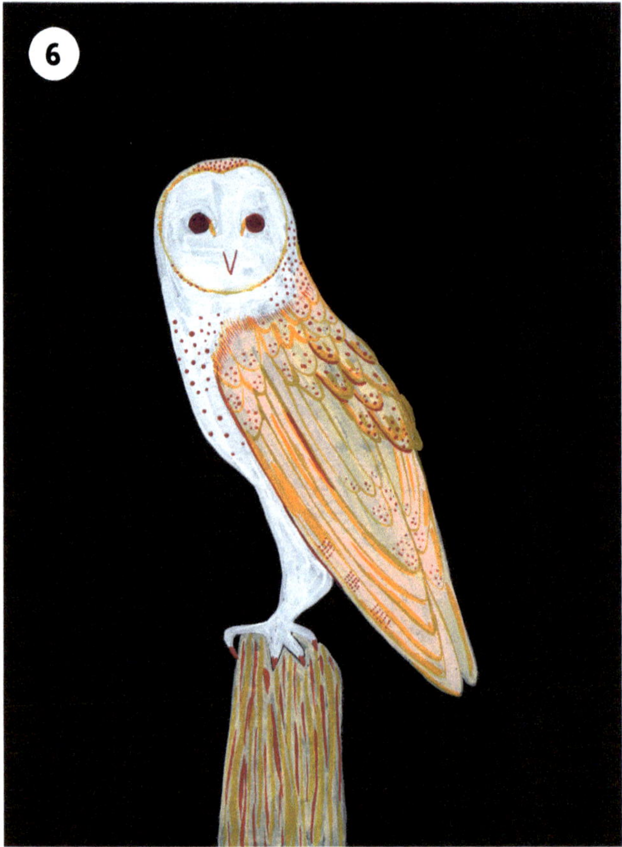

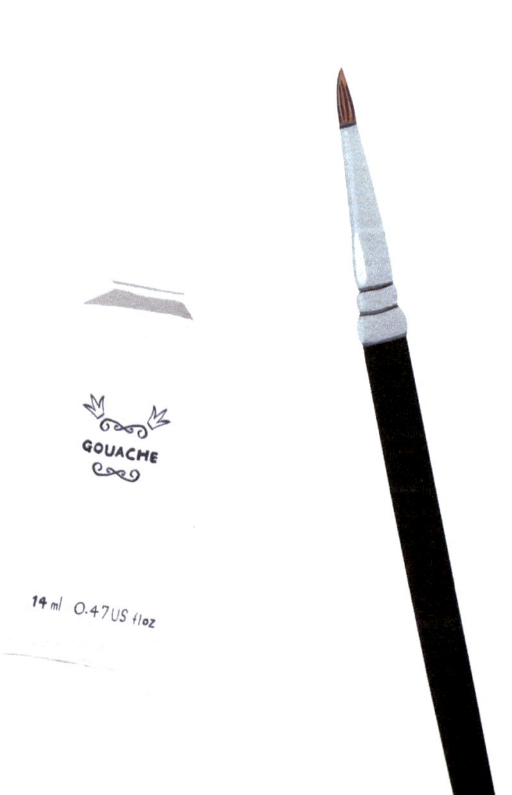

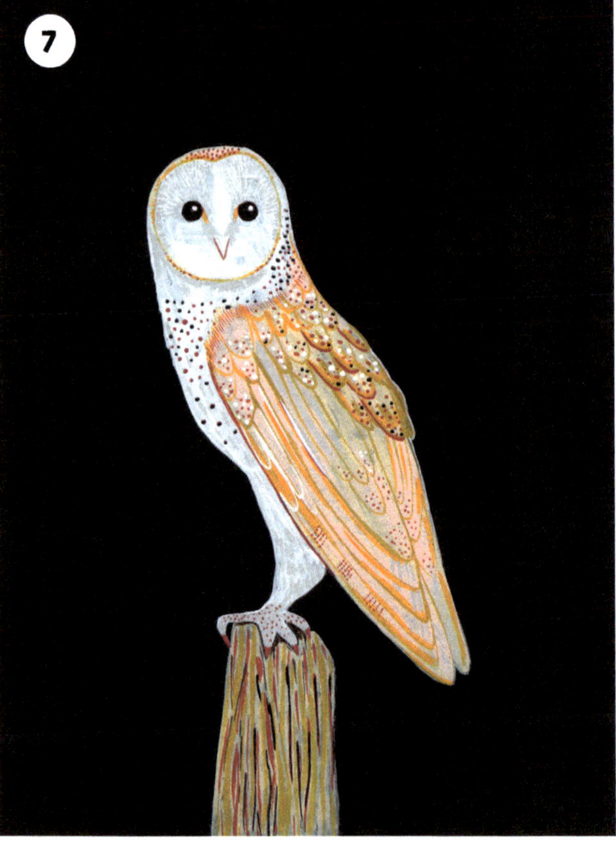

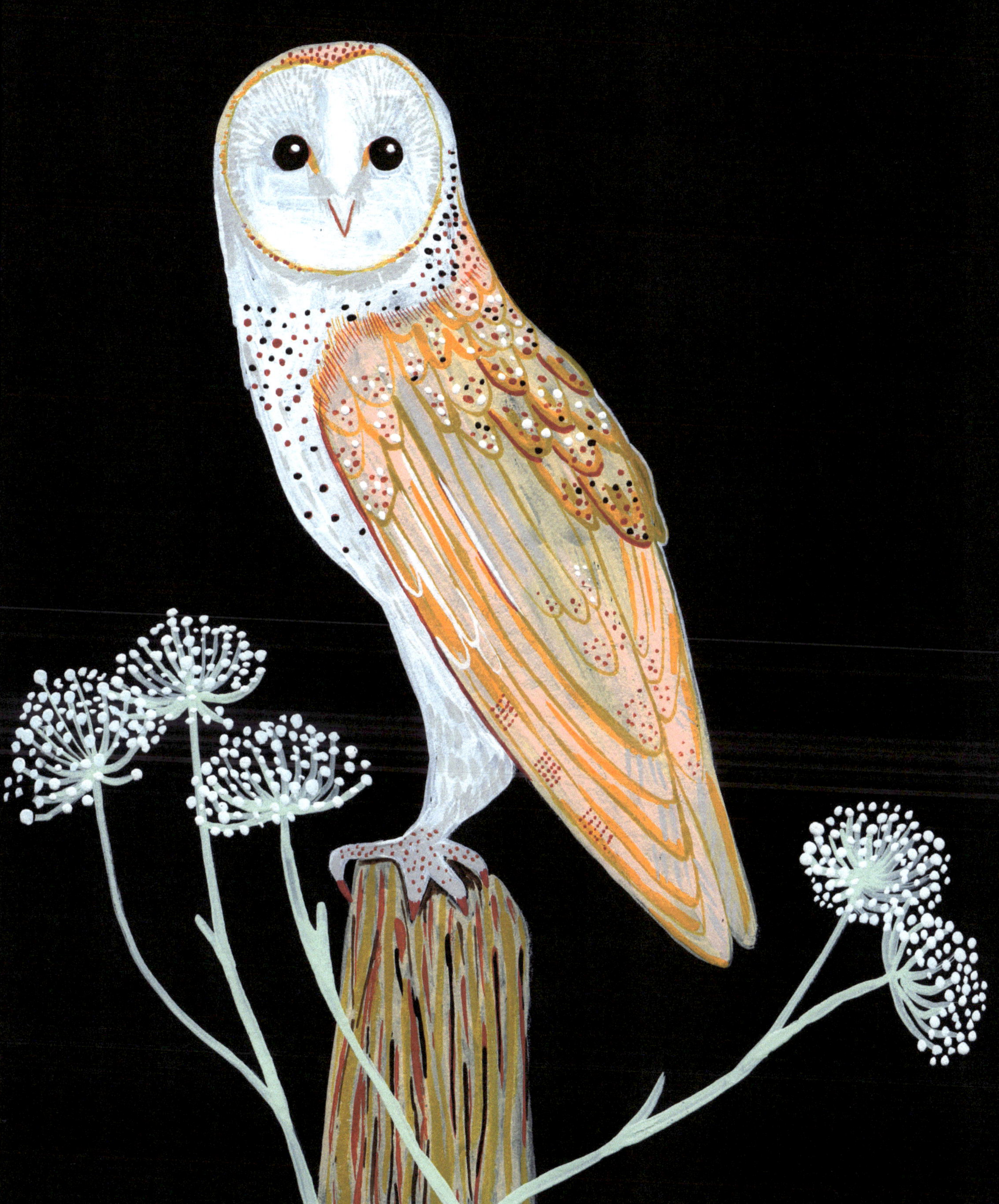

Once and Flor-al

Flowers can be approached in so many different ways, from a super-realistic botanical style at one end of the spectrum to a much more folk or naïve style, which is the direction we're going in for this project. This approach offers more opportunity to show off your personal style. We'll paint flowers freehand and in a fairly stylized way. Floral art is always in demand in the art world for greetings cards, fabrics and other products.

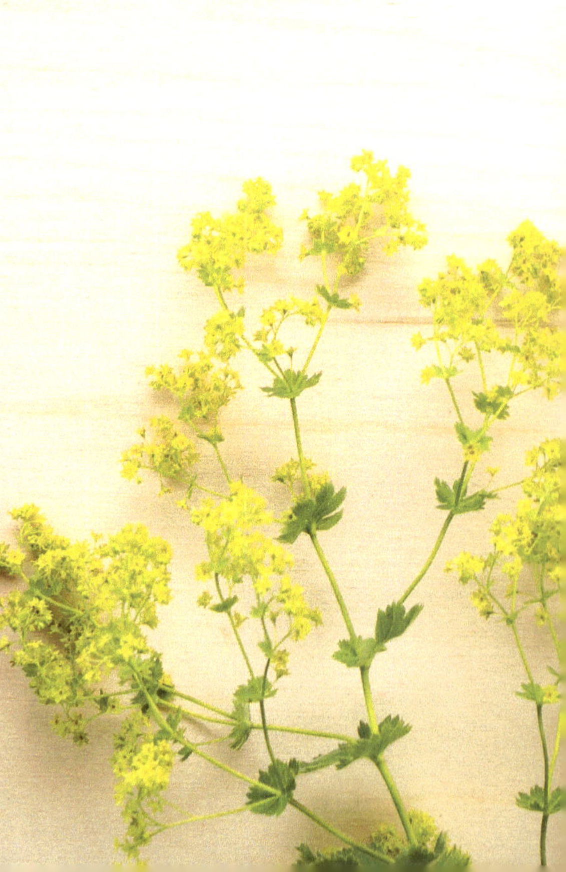

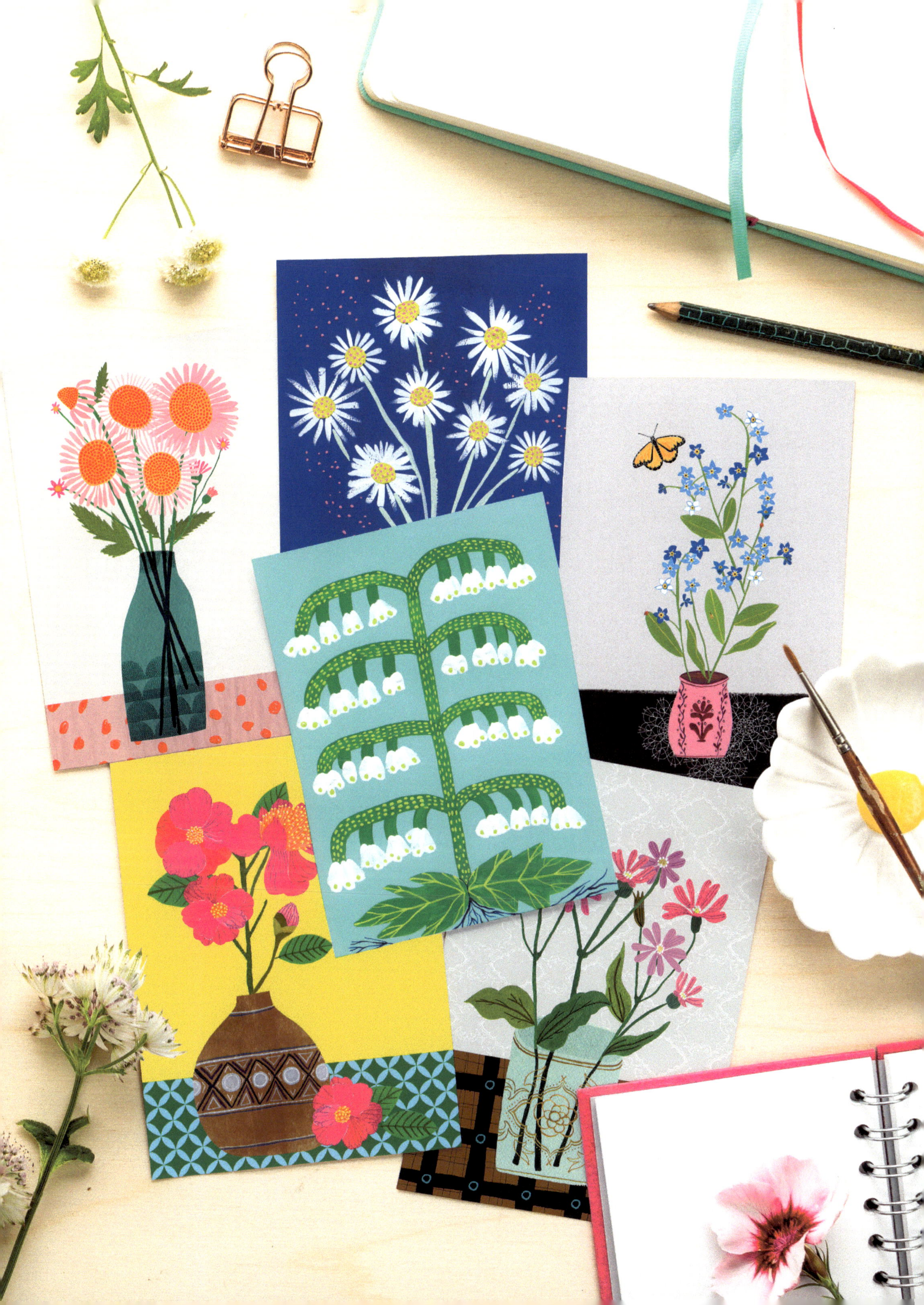

COLOUR

- Ice green
- White
- Navy blue
- Spectrum yellow
- Brilliant green

PAPER

Plain cartridge
or printer paper

Tracing paper

Watercolour
block paper

TECHNIQUES

Mark Making

Line Work

Overlaying

Detail

1. Begin by fully covering your paper in a bright colour. I chose an ice green and used it quite solid here rather than pooling in a watercolour wash, as I wanted a more graphic feel.

2. Once the background layer is dry, take some darker green paint and a square brush if you have one – don't worry if you don't, just use whatever brush you have. Paint on a stem in freehand, then add some branches and leaves.

3. Add white flower heads to dangle down from the branches. I simply loaded up my brush with white paint and placed the brush down on its side to achieve the petal shapes. They remind me of snowdrops.

4. Introduce more mark making and some line work by adding flashes of yellow detail to the petals, stem and leaves.

5. To finish off, using a much smaller, more pointed brush, freehand paint in some dark roots at the bottom of the plant. I used a navy blue for this finishing detail.

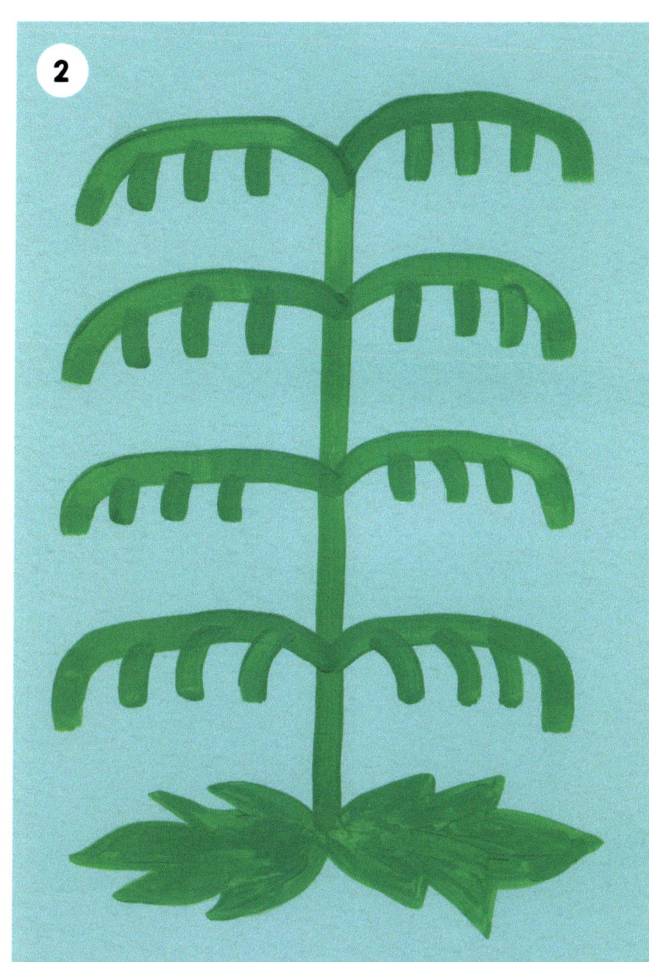

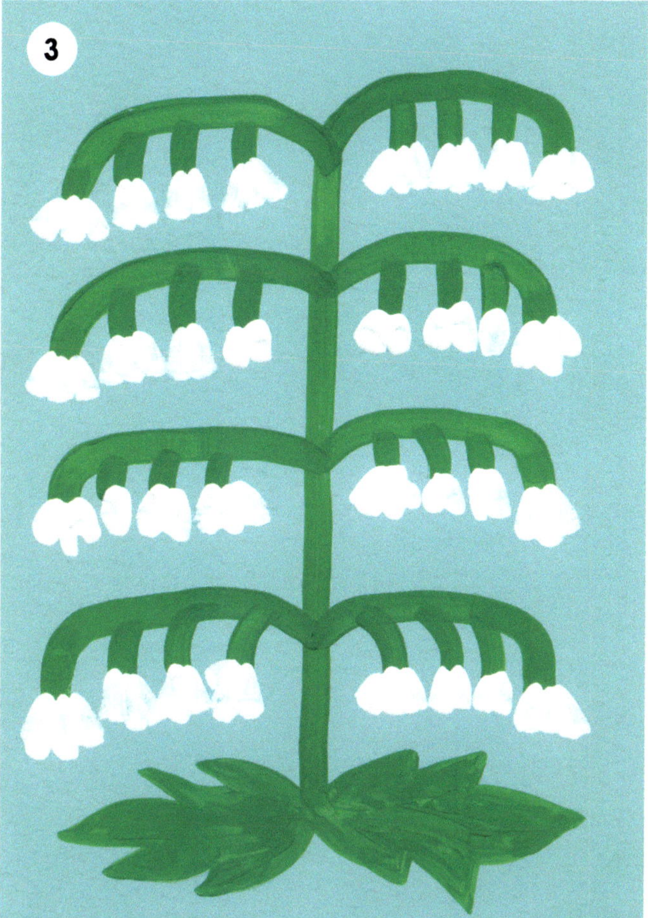

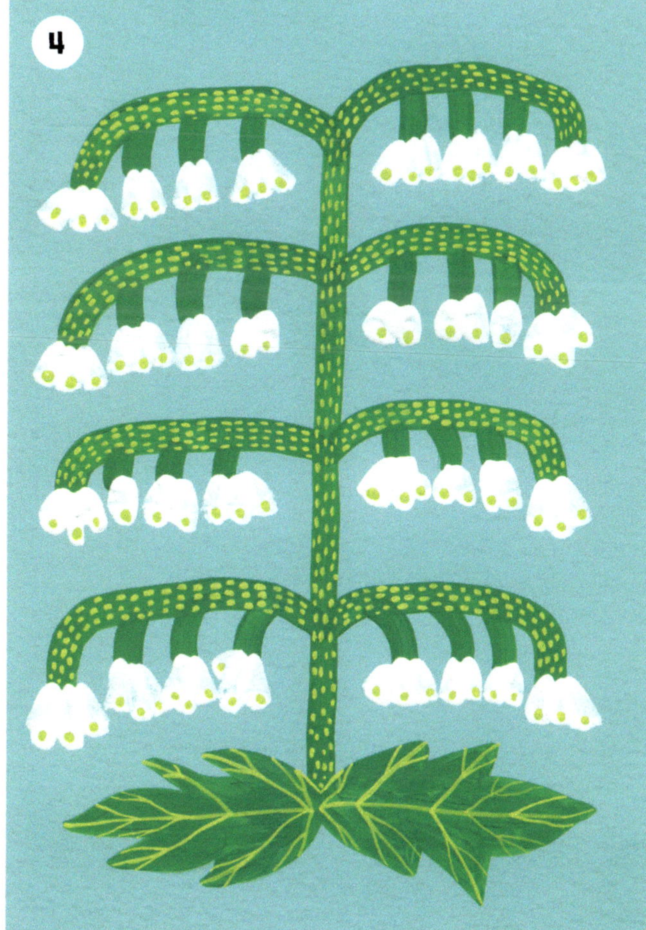

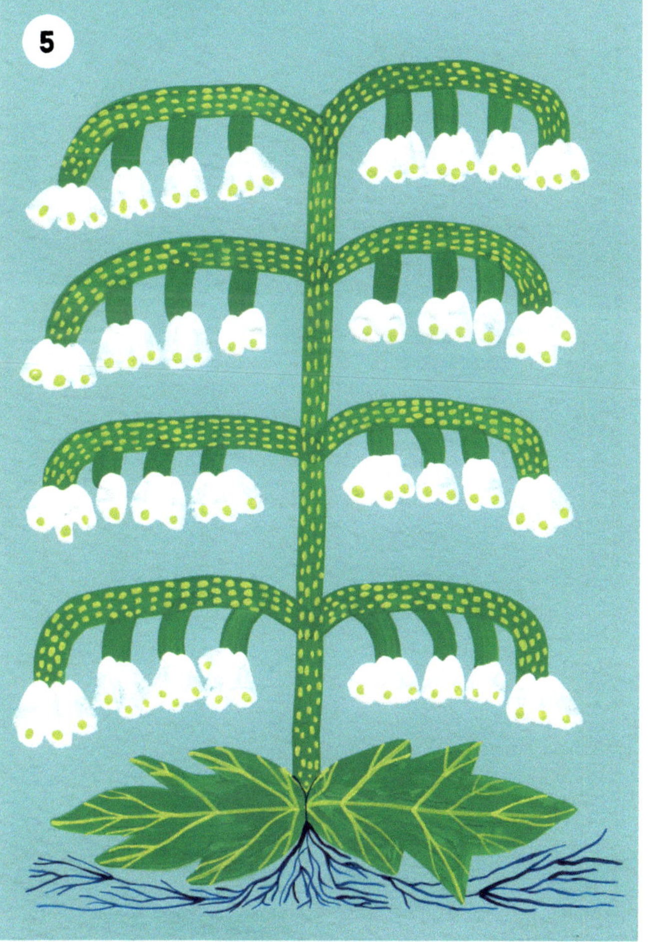

HERE ARE SOME OTHER FLORAL ILLUSTRATIONS THAT I
REALLY ENJOYED PAINTING. THEY ARE A LITTLE MORE ON
THE REALISTIC SIDE COMPARED TO THE MAIN PROJECT,
BUT I WANT YOU TO SEE THE DIFFERENT STYLES THAT ARE
ACHIEVABLE WITH GOUACHE. THESE FOUR PAINTINGS WERE
PART OF A LARGER PERSONAL PROJECT. WHILE THE FLOWERS
WERE PAINTED WITH GOUACHE, I FINISHED THEM ALL IN
PHOTOSHOP USING MY DIGITAL COLLAGE PROCESS. SOME
OF THESE FLORAL PAINTINGS HAVE BEEN FEATURED ON
GREETINGS CARDS AND NAPKINS.

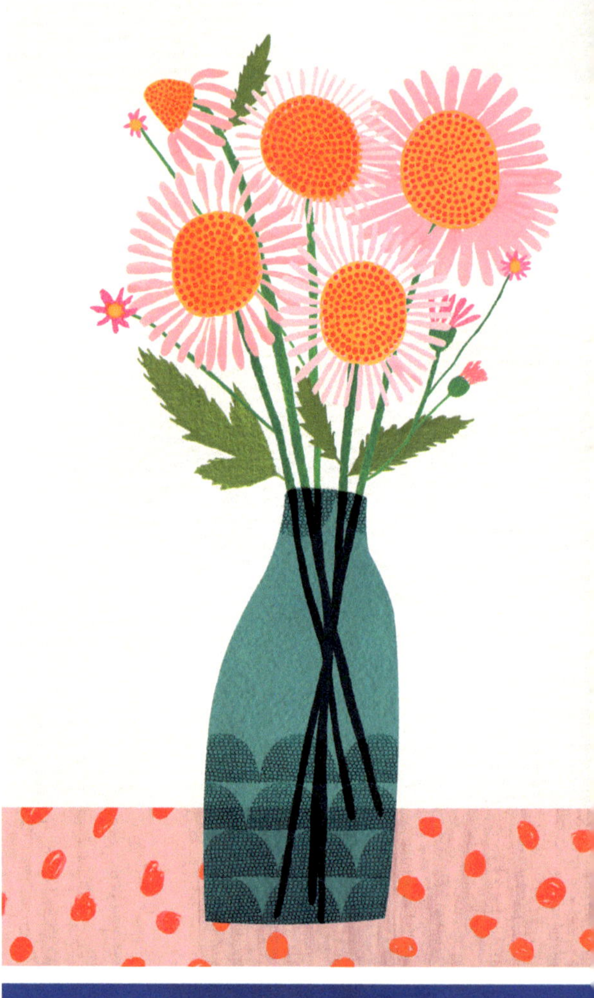

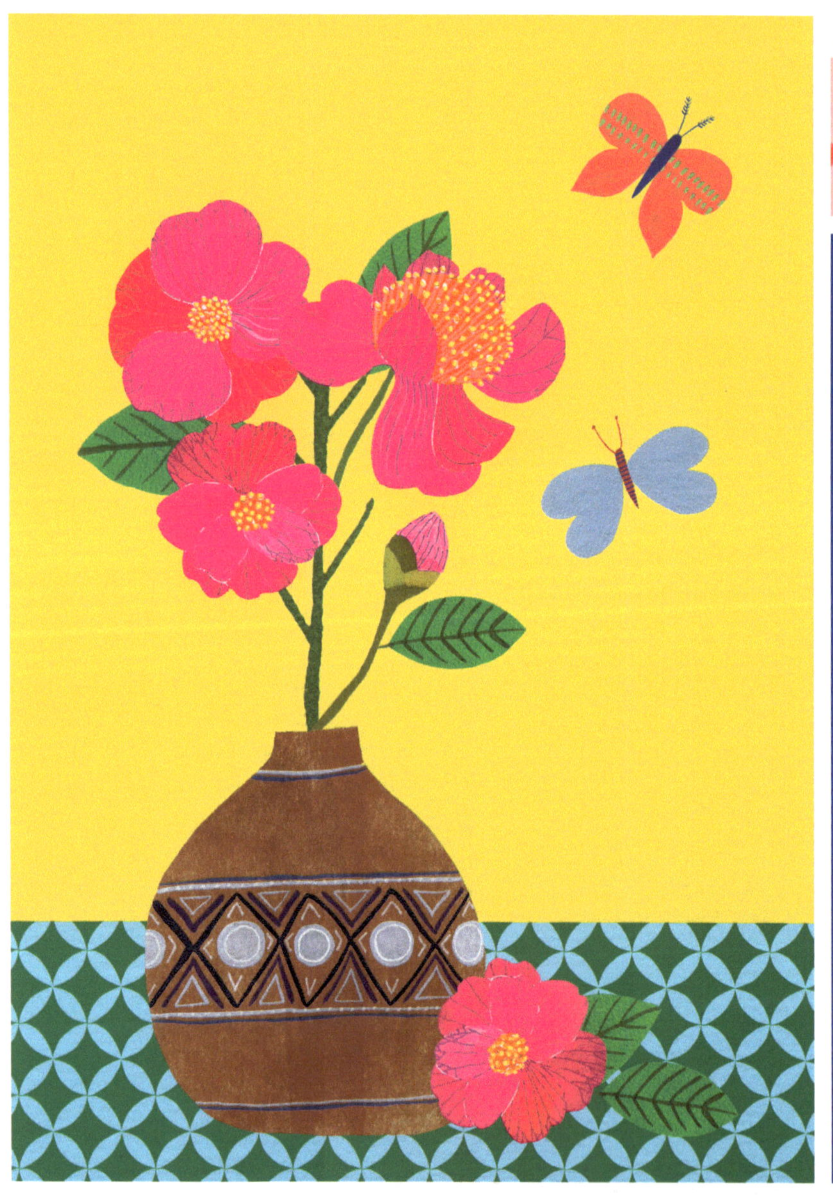

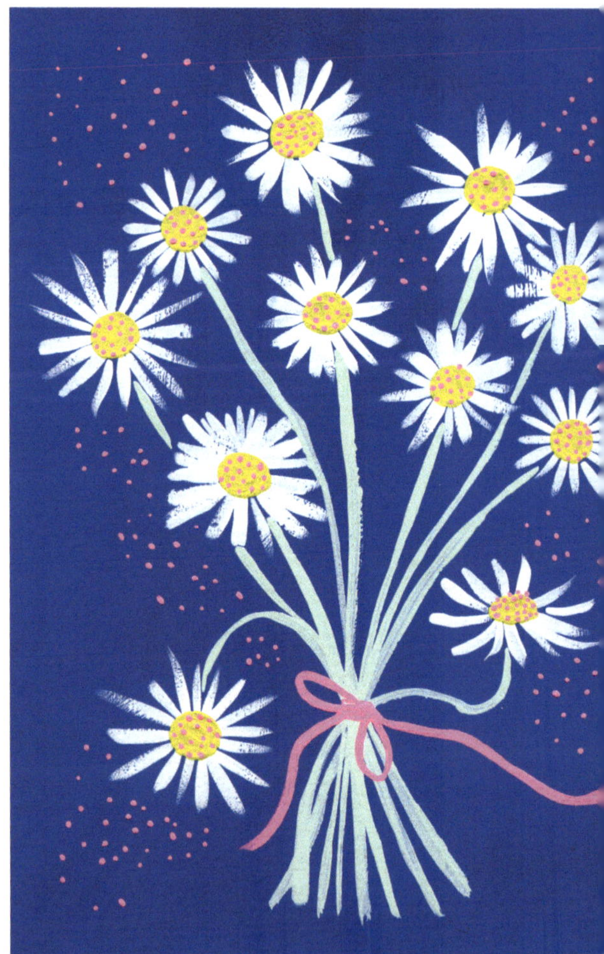

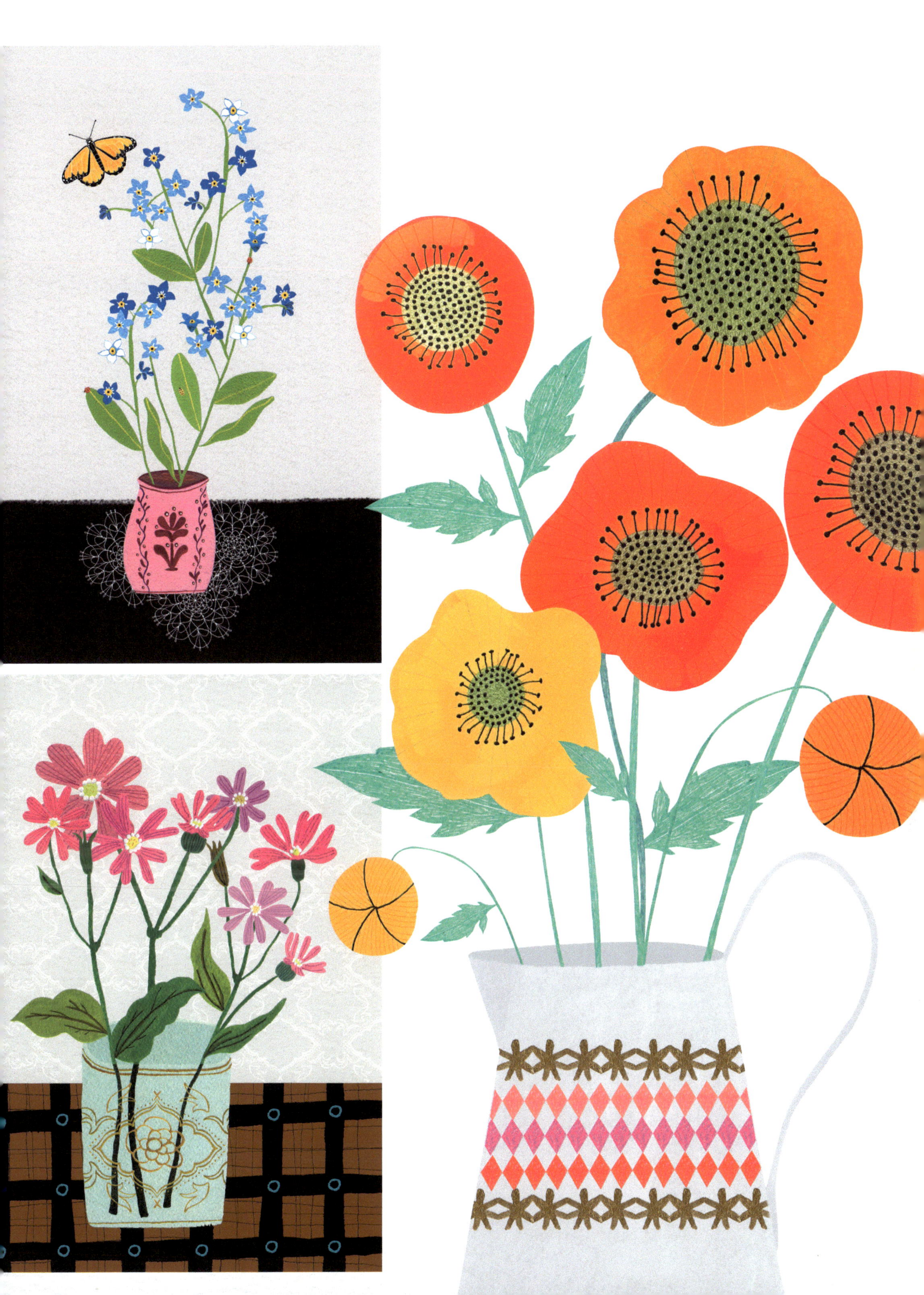

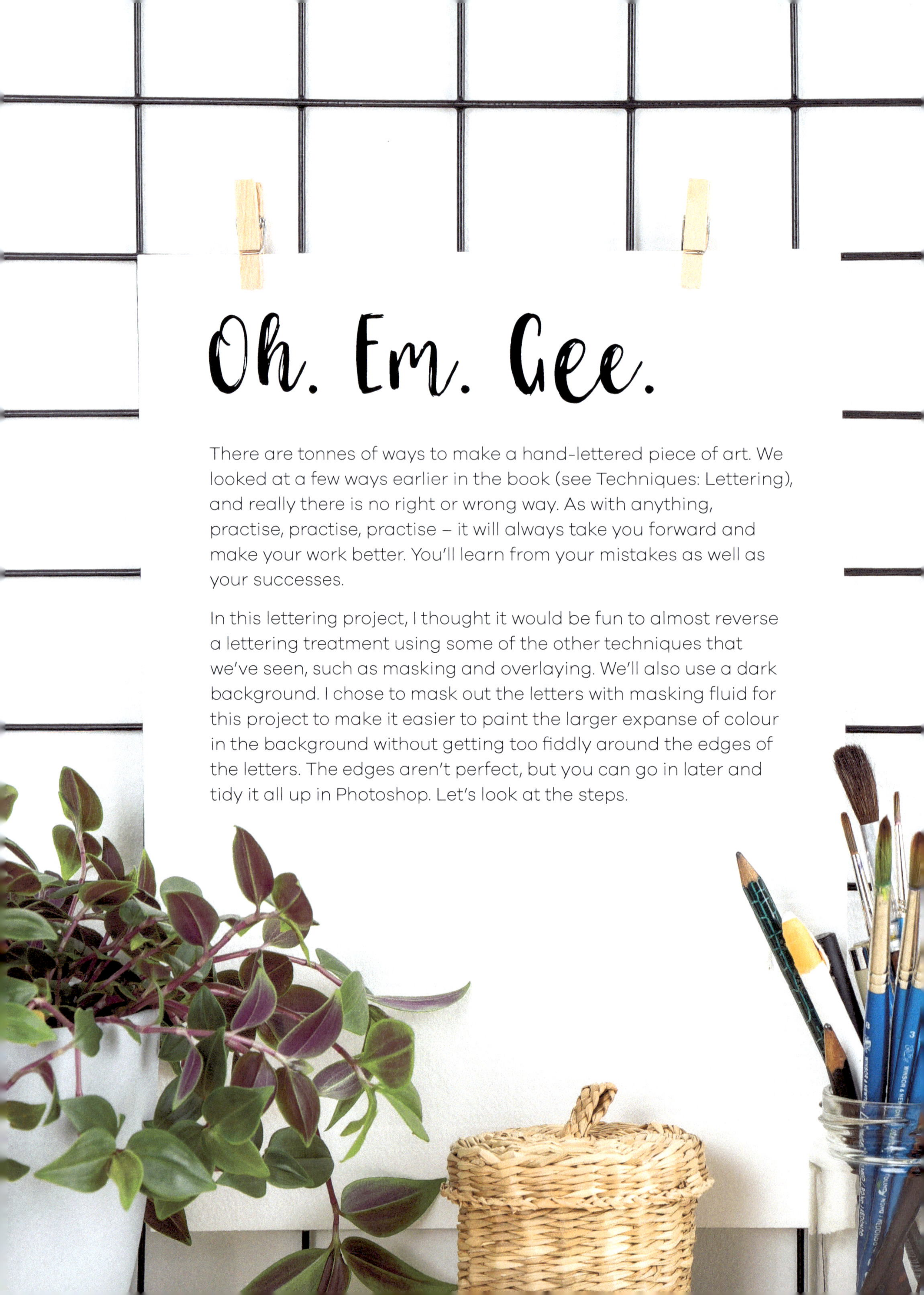

Oh. Em. Gee.

There are tonnes of ways to make a hand-lettered piece of art. We looked at a few ways earlier in the book (see Techniques: Lettering), and really there is no right or wrong way. As with anything, practise, practise, practise – it will always take you forward and make your work better. You'll learn from your mistakes as well as your successes.

In this lettering project, I thought it would be fun to almost reverse a lettering treatment using some of the other techniques that we've seen, such as masking and overlaying. We'll also use a dark background. I chose to mask out the letters with masking fluid for this project to make it easier to paint the larger expanse of colour in the background without getting too fiddly around the edges of the letters. The edges aren't perfect, but you can go in later and tidy it all up in Photoshop. Let's look at the steps.

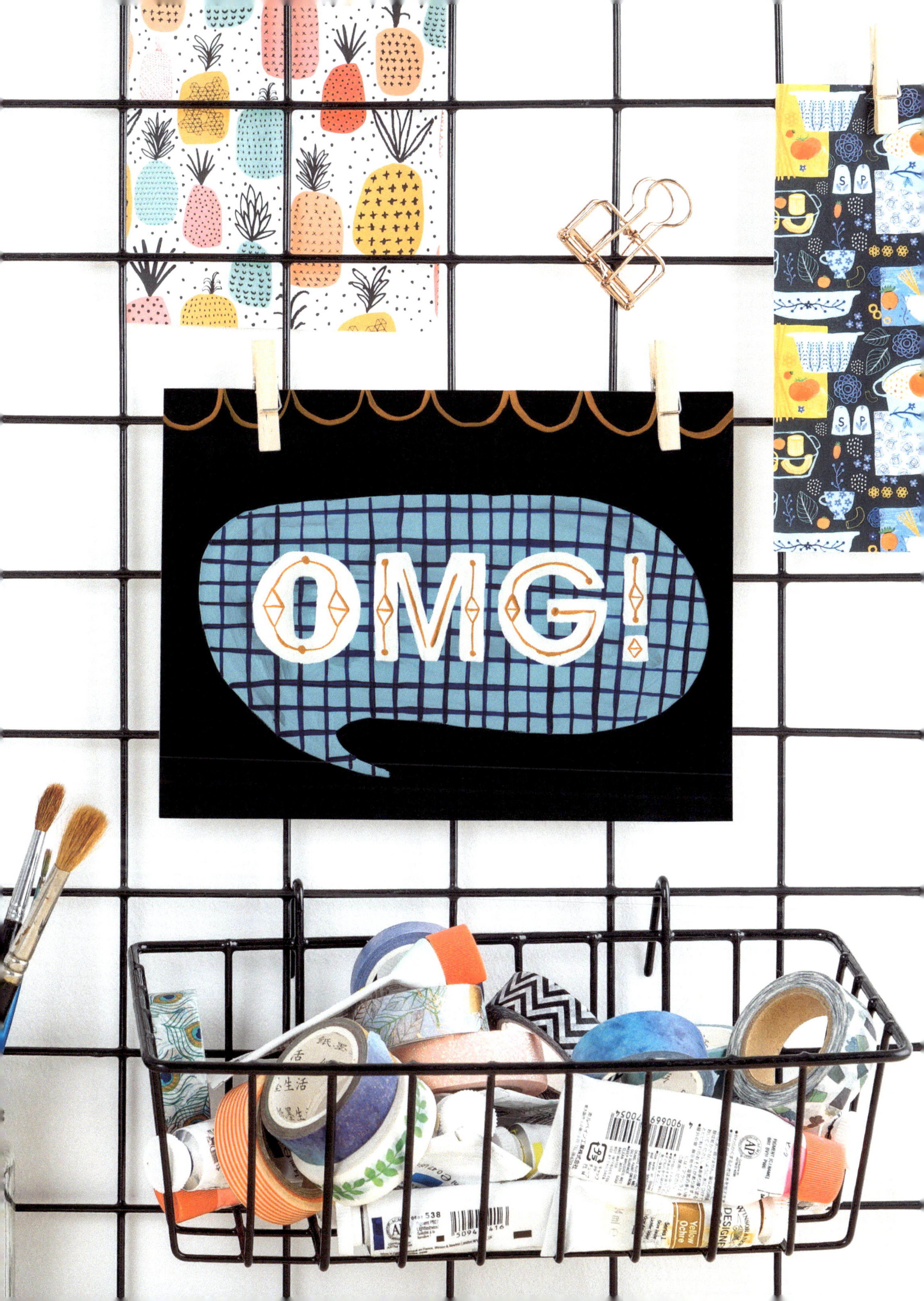
OMG!

COLOURS

- ● Ultramarine
- ● Burnt umber
- ● Aqua blue
- ● Metallic violet
- ○ White
- ● Cadmium yellow deep

PAPER

Plain cartridge
or printer paper

Tracing paper

Watercolour
block paper

TECHNIQUES

Sketching

Line Work

Shapes and Edges

Lettering

Detail

Dark Backgrounds

1. Begin by sketching out your letters. You can sketch freehand straight onto your watercolour paper or use the tracing technique to transfer the guidelines. If you do trace the letters, keep in mind that the letters will be back to front, so after you've first traced your sketch, you'll need to turn the tracing paper over and carefully retrace all the lines on the reverse. Flip it again so that the letters will be the right way around ready to transfer to the watercolour paper.

2. Once you're happy with the sketch, go ahead and fill in the letter shapes with masking fluid. Leave it to dry completely before moving on to the next step.

3. For this step, I mixed up a really dark, almost black colour by combining some ultramarine and burnt umber. Make sure that you mix enough to cover the full page while maintaining the opacity. Paint the dark colour over the whole page, including the areas covered with masking fluid. Leave this layer to dry completely.

4. Once the background is dry, choose your next colour – I used a light blue – and freehand paint a speech bubble shape over the previous layers. You can barely see the letters underneath now. Again, leave this layer to dry completely before moving on to the next step.

5. To add some interest, I painted this grid pattern over the top of the speech bubble, using my brush to draw the lines freehand. I like the wobbly, imperfect nature of these lines. Leave this layer to dry completely.

6. Now for the really fun part! Once everything is completely dry, take a clean eraser and begin rubbing away the masking fluid from the letters. You'll reveal a white background where we've blocked out the shapes. Depending on how you painted the masking fluid, the edges may be a little bumpy or ragged as they are in my example.

7. I wanted to tidy up the edges around the letters so I went in with some white paint and a small brush and smoothed them out by starting at the edges and filling in the shape. It doesn't have to be perfect; the imperfect lines and edges are what makes the image interesting.

8. In this final step, I added some linear details in orange on top of the white letters and across the top of the dark background. This is all done freehand with a small brush. You can continue adding details around the edge as a border or choose some different colours to add more dots, lines or shapes to your letters.

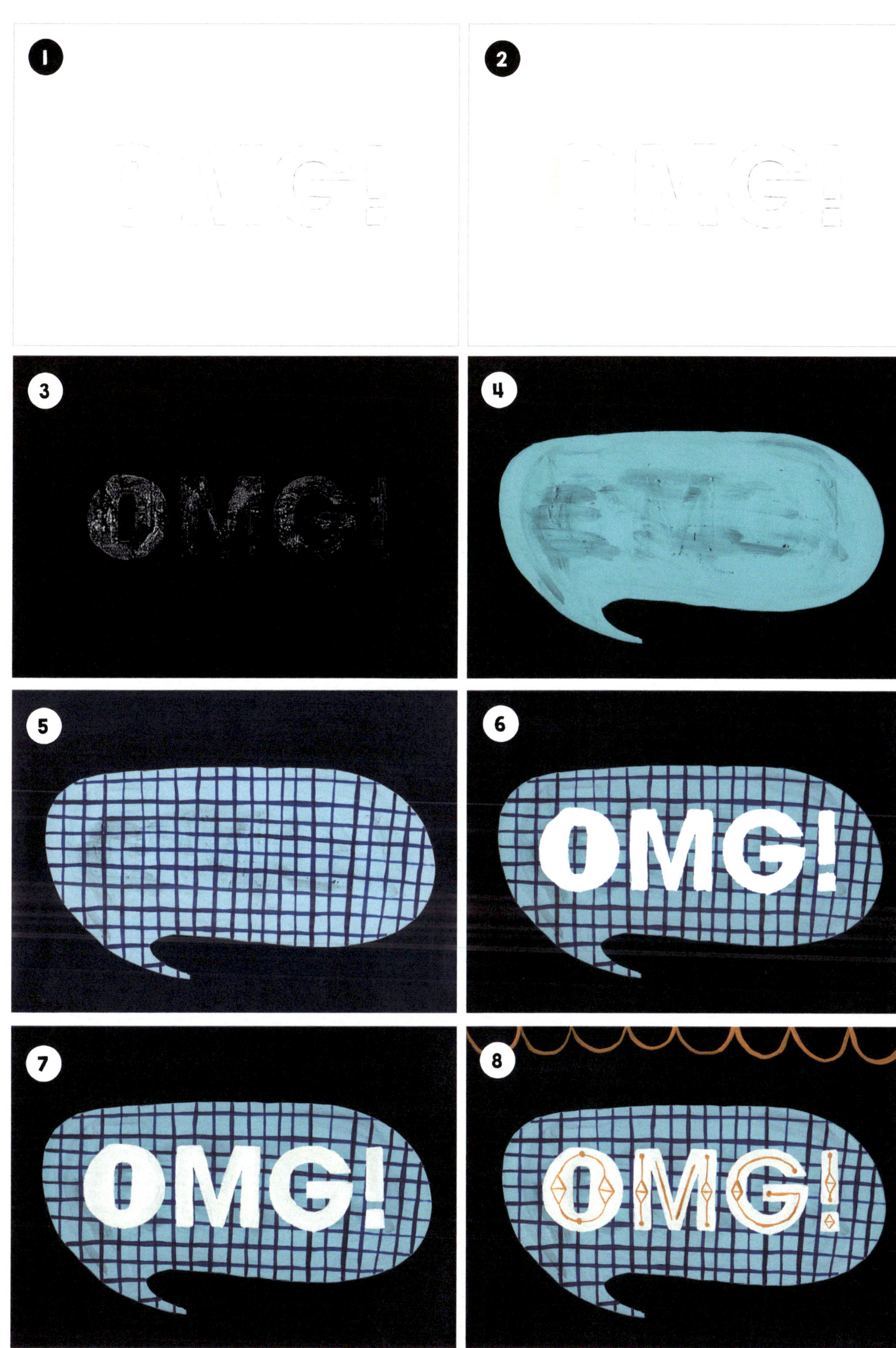
OMG!
OMG!
OMG!
OMG!

Curious Cat on the Mat

This project incorporates several gouache painting techniques, beginning with a sketch, then adding to the main shapes with a wash treatment. I've built up the image with detail, line work, overlaying and texture. I don't often paint scenes like this as one whole piece, but I thought that it would be a useful addition to see in terms of composition and execution.

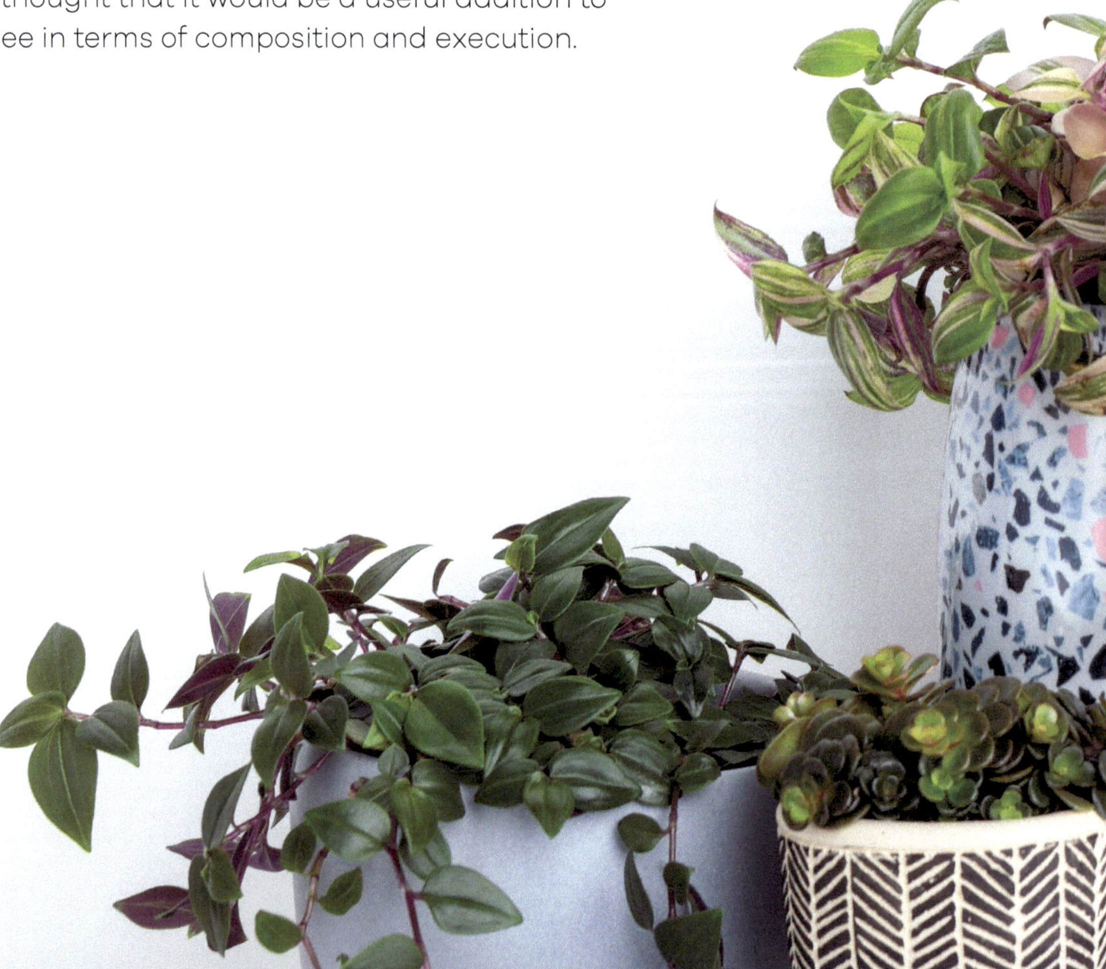

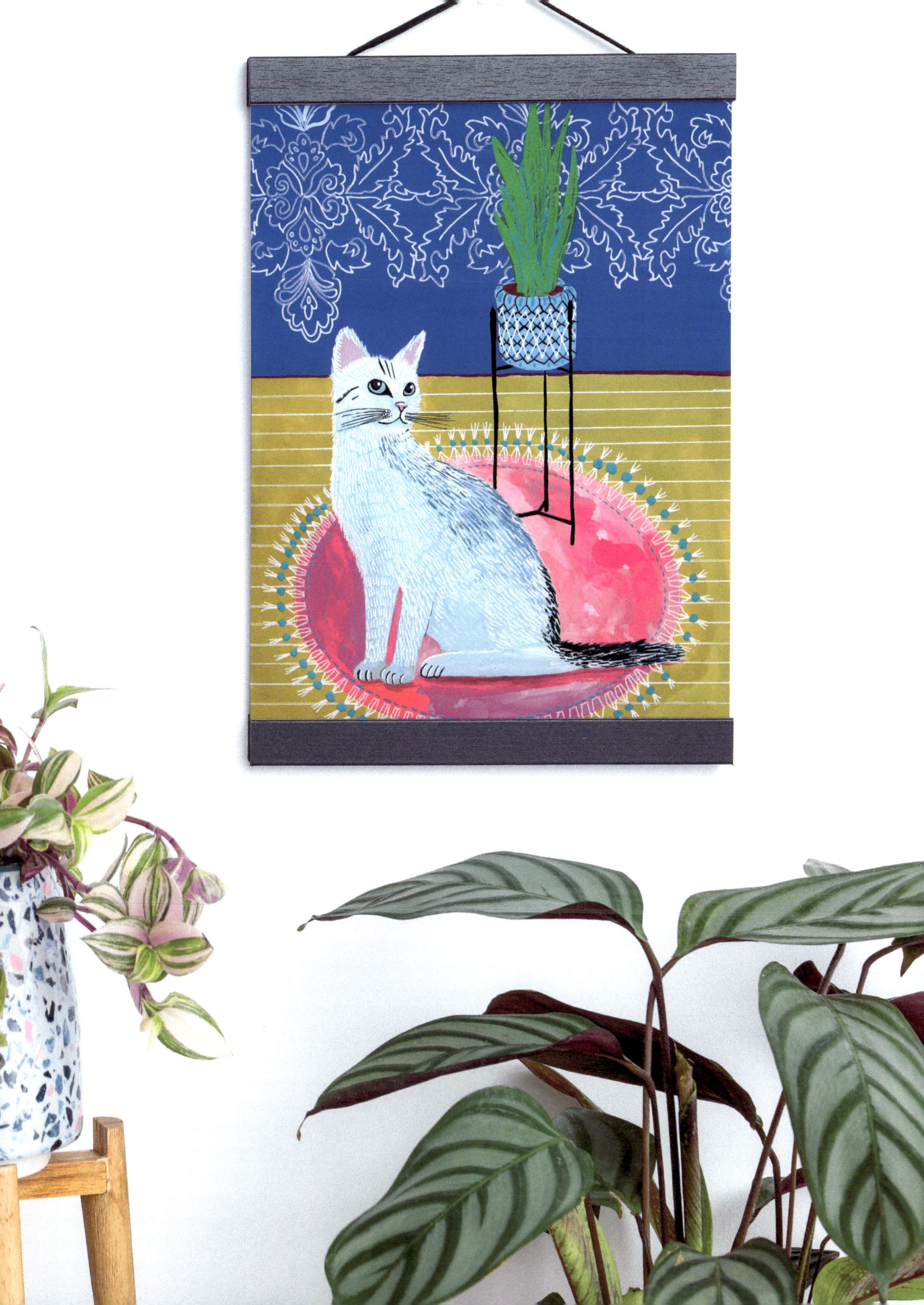

COLOURS

- Opera pink
- Ultramarine
- Burnt umber
- Spectrum yellow
- Yellow ochre
- White
- Cobalt turquoise light

PAPER

Plain cartridge
or printer paper

Tracing paper

Watercolour
block paper

TECHNIQUES

Sketching

Washes

Line Work

Overlaying

Detail

1. Begin by sketching the cat and a circular rug shape sitting underneath. You don't need to sketch anything else at this stage as there will be layers of paint covering up any pencil lines.

2. Block in the shape of the cat and then the rug with watered-down paints. I liked the texture on the rug so I decided to leave it like this.

3. Now block in the background wall and the floor. I also went back in over the cat to add a bit more texture and more of a grey colour. I haven't used any masking techniques where the colours meet; the edges are all freehand.

4. Next, I started to add fur and facial details to the cat. I've also painted a little darker shadow along the underside of its body so that it doesn't look as if it's floating in mid-air.

5. I wanted to add some interest to the blue wall in the background, so I drew a baroque-like motif. Let's transfer it to the painting using tracing paper to create a painting guide.

6. Once you've transferred the decorative element to the painting, use a white gel pen to draw the pattern on top of the paint. I drew on some lines for the floorboards in the same way.

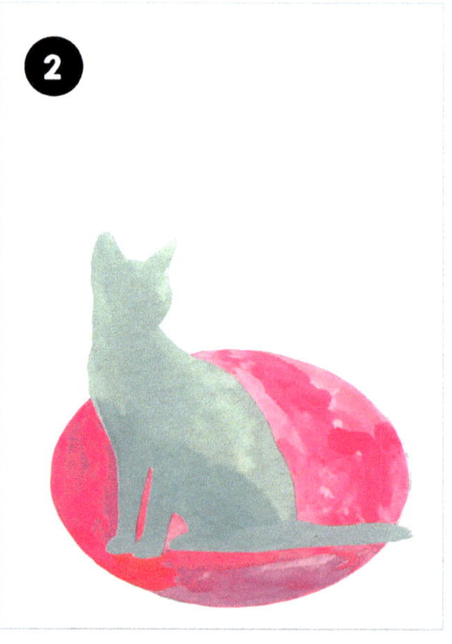

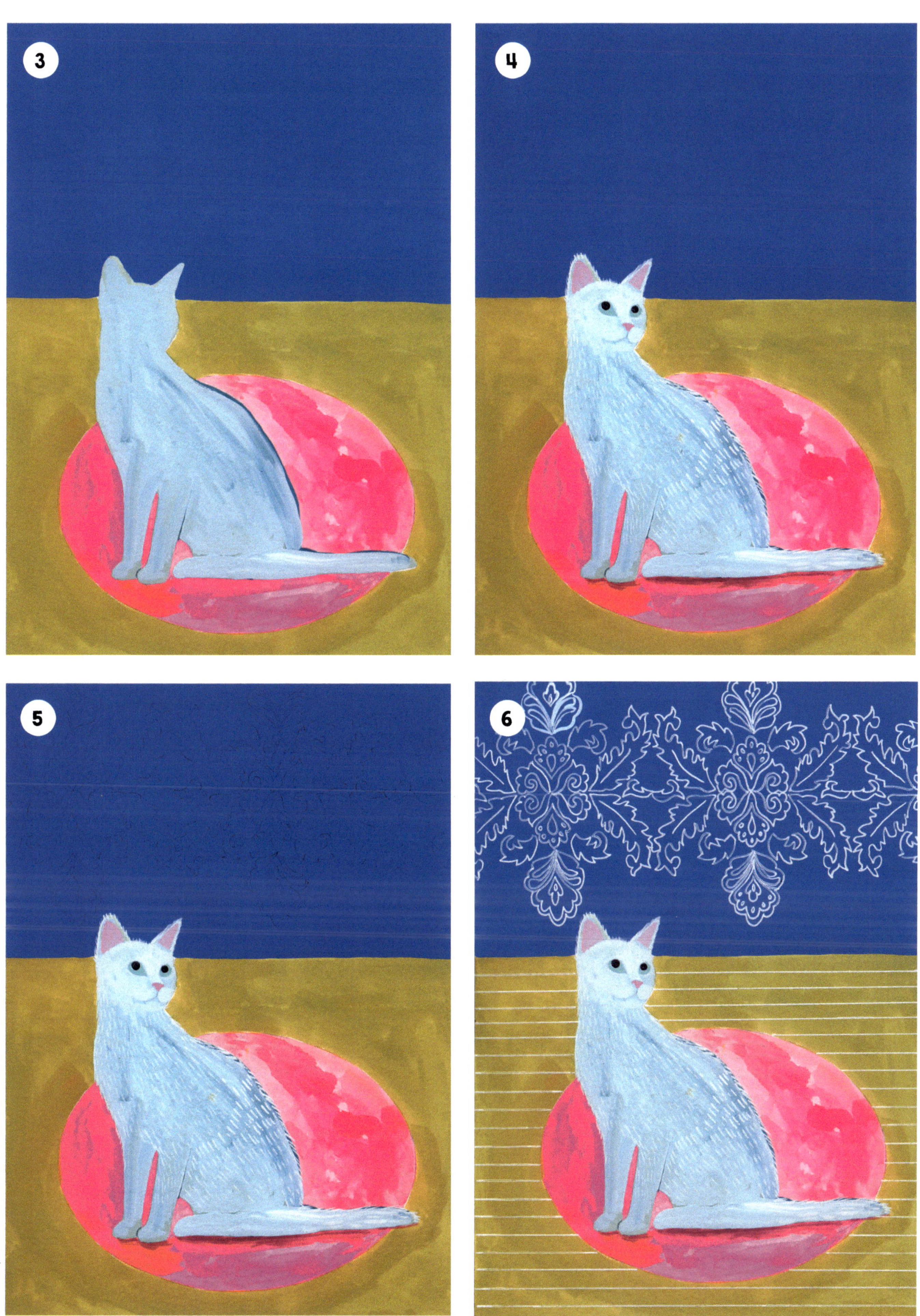

7. In this step, I added a bit of greenery to the composition. Notice how the cat's head is angled towards the plant – your eye is led up the painting and then across the wall pattern and back down to the cat in a sort of invisible triangle.

8. Up until this stage, the cat wasn't looking quite right because the eyes and facial features needed more detail. I used a darker navy mixed with burnt umber to get a dark, almost black colour to add to these details, improve the fur and begin the plant-pot pattern.

9. Draw just a few more details in white to the plant pot and rug and add the eye highlights. I used the white gel pen again for this.

10. In this last step, I added more white fur details to the cat's body and I finished off the rug by adding turquoise pom-poms, tassels and stitching.

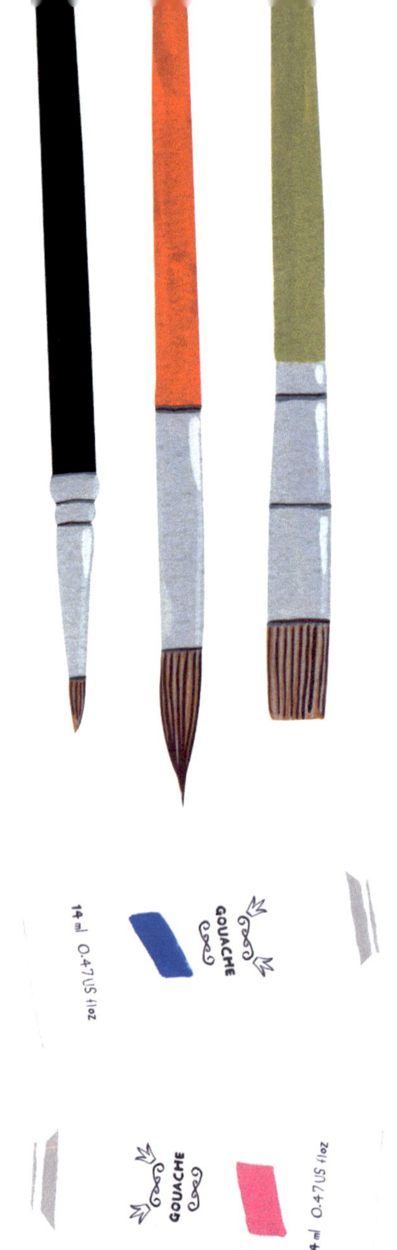

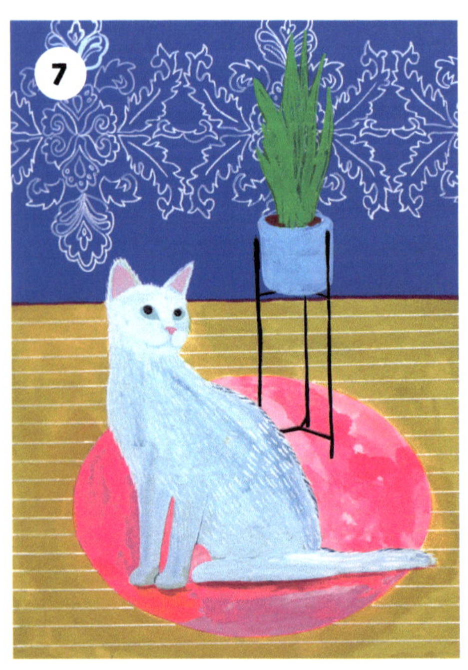

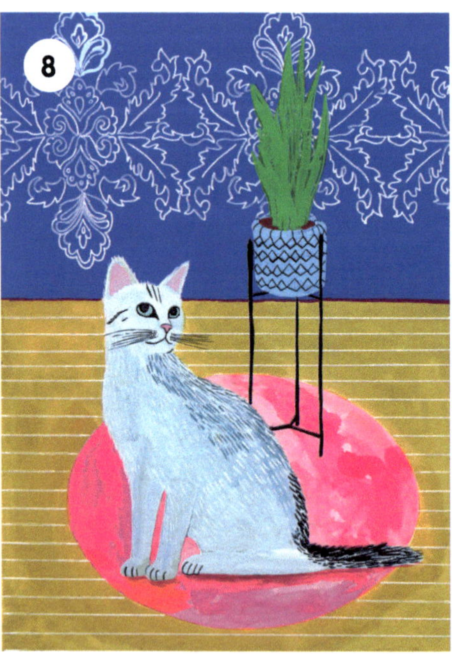

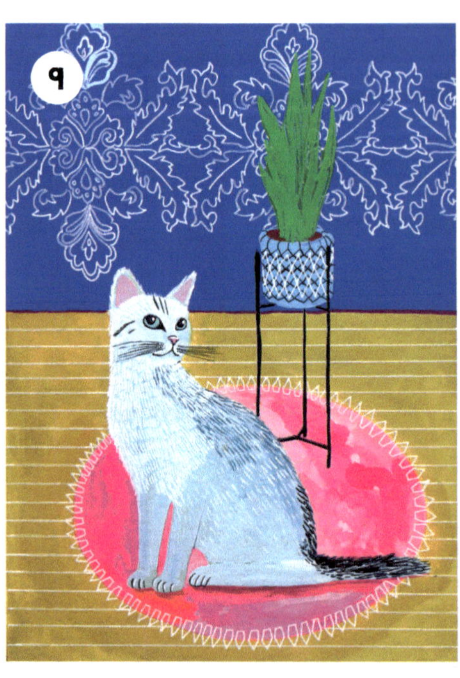

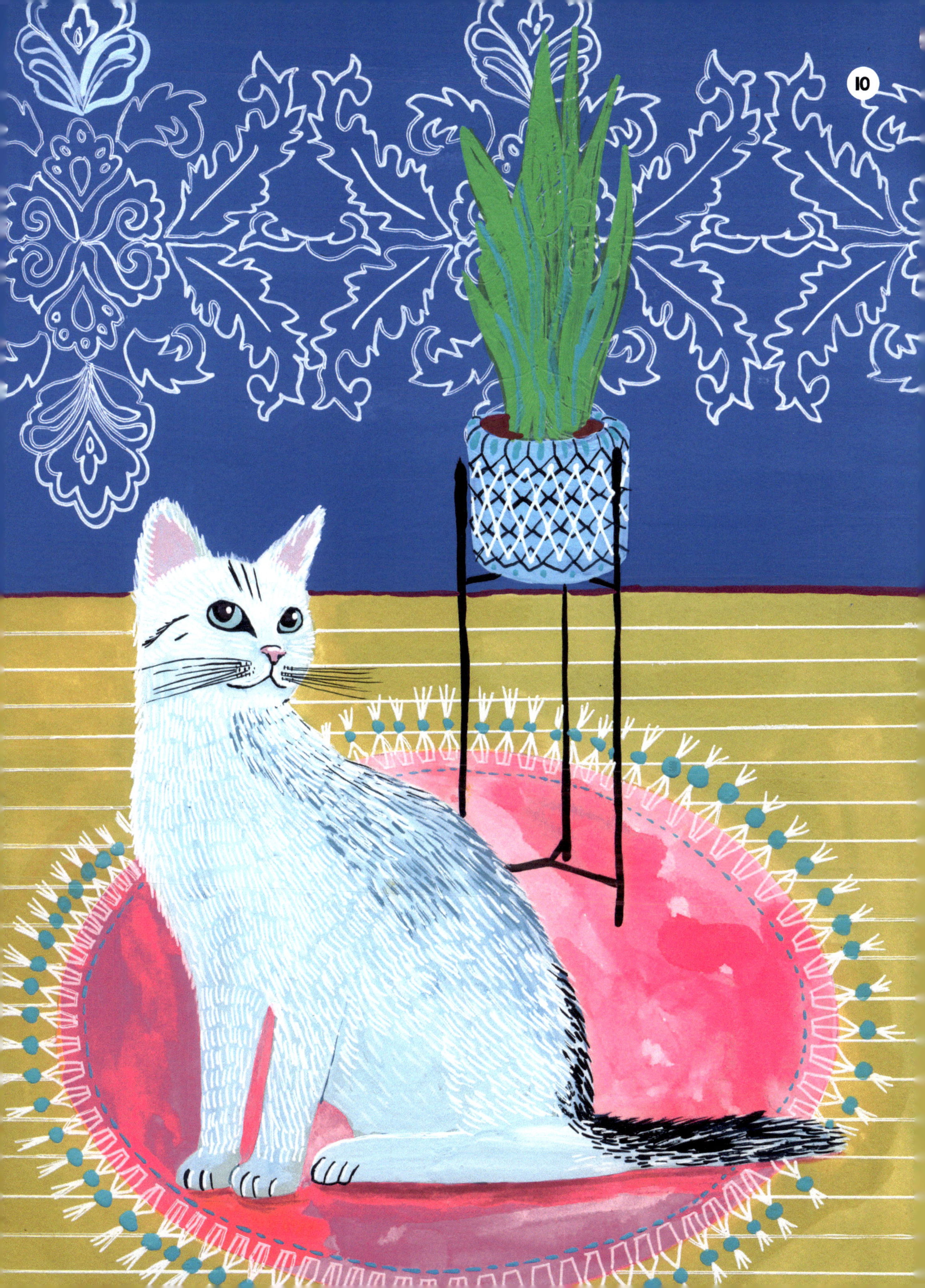

Fun and Floral Free-Flow

In this abstract piece I have used myriad techniques that we have looked at throughout the book. There are elements of overlaying, detail, shapes, mark making, line drawing and thinner wash areas.

This abstract piece came about very organically. I didn't have a plan for it and treated it more as an experiment of sorts, something I love to do in my sketch book. I encourage you to do the same without worrying about the end result too much. You'll learn so much from this practice, and it's a lot of fun! Just think about this kind of approach as building in layers. I've included a figurative drawing in my piece, because I like the contrast between the loose and free and tighter, more recognizable shapes and forms.

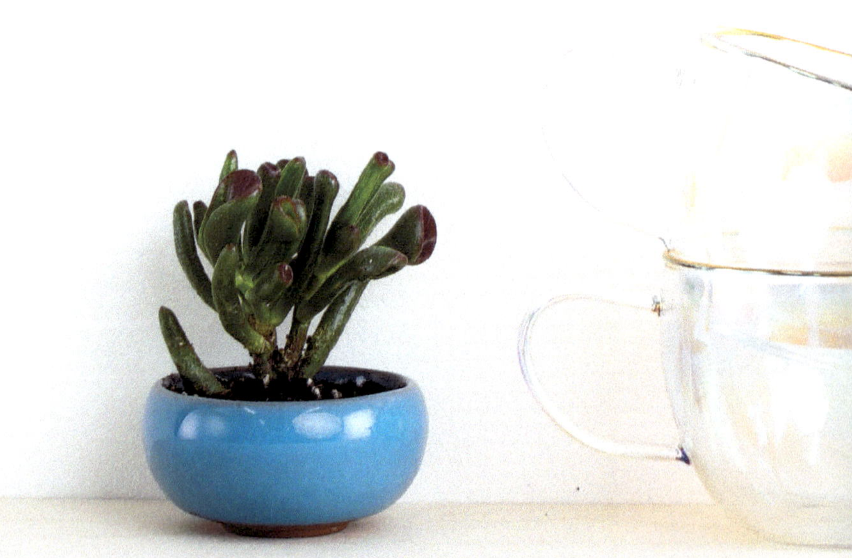

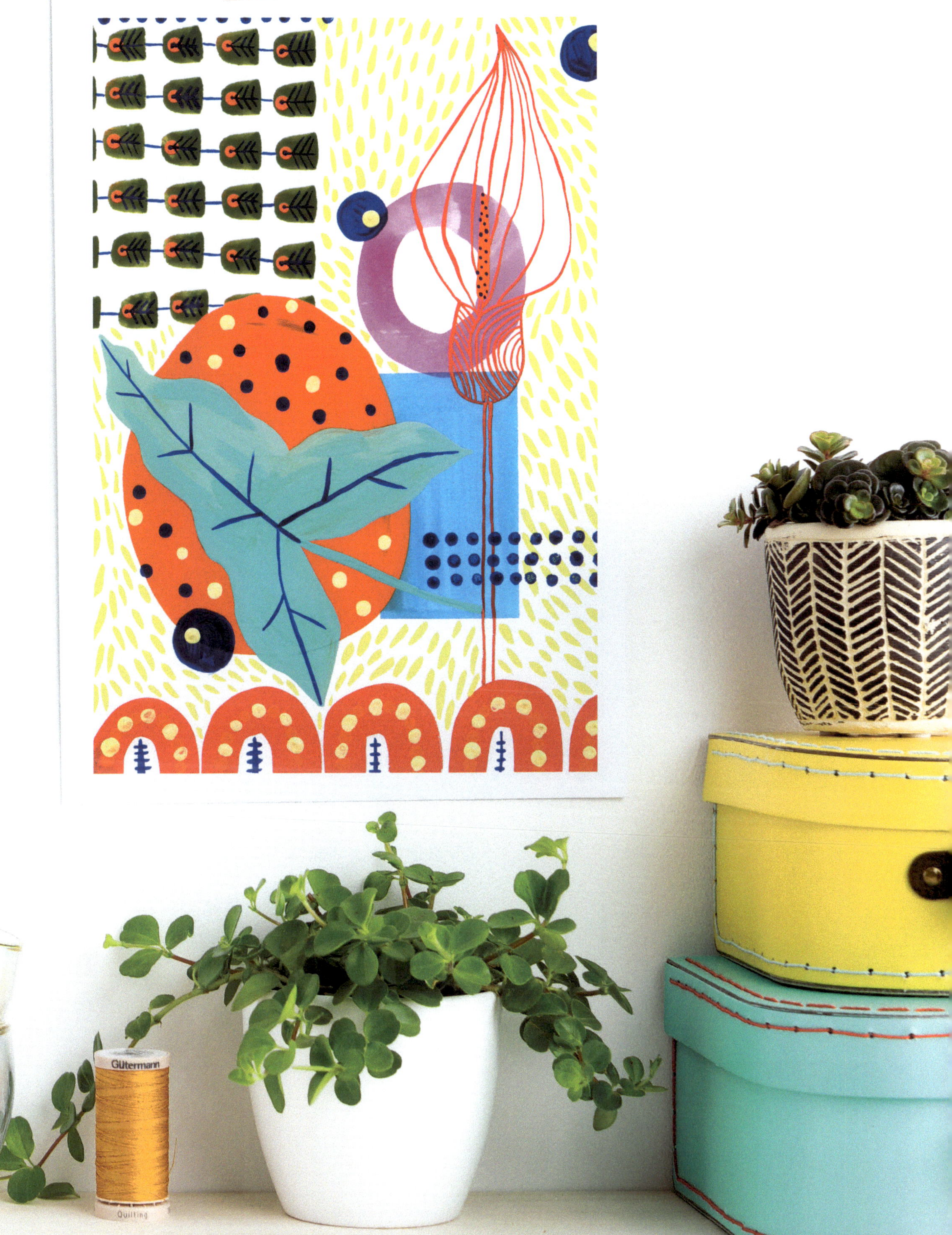

COLOUR

- ● Opera pink
- ● Spectrum yellow
- ● Orange
- ● Raw umber
- ● Sap green
- ● Phthalo blue
- ● Flame red
- ● Cobalt turquoise light
- ● Ultramarine
- ○ White

PAPER

Watercolour paper

Washi tape

TECHNIQUES

Washes

Mark Making

Line Work

Shapes and Edges

Overlaying

Detail

1. Beginning this project, I used washi tape around the edges of my paper to create a kind of frame or border – washi is enough of a barrier in this instance as I'm not using a wash background. I will peel the tape off at the end and it will give a nice sharp, neat edge. I started off by picking a super-bright pink and painted a simple circle. I mixed the paint up very thinly to make the effect more of a transparent wash. Wait for the paint to dry before moving to the next step.

2. Next, I added an orange circle – but this time, instead of stopping at just an outline, I filled the shape with the orange paint. The paint became dry on the brush, but I continued without loading up with more paint. Again, wait for the paint to dry before moving on. You can use a hairdryer to speed up the process.

3. I wanted to add a different shape this time, so I masked off a rectangular shape with washi tape and filled this rectangle with a thinly mixed blue colour. Once the paint had dried, I removed the tape to reveal the lovely crisp edge.

4. In this step, I chose a vibrant red and painted some chunky arch shapes along the bottom of the page. You can see that there are little areas where the paint has cracked on the washi tape border. This was due to the paint being a little thicker than usual and also because I dried it very quickly with a hairdryer.

5. In this step, I introduced another colour, this time a dark sap green. I used a square brush to lay down some marks to create another element of interest, slightly overlapping the orange shape. They remind me of petals or little feathers. Allow the paint to dry before moving on to the next step.

6. I used the orange again to add some dots to the red arches at the bottom and also on each of the green marks that I made in the previous step. I painted over the orange shape again as I felt it needed to be stronger and have clearer, crisp edges. In doing this, I painted over a small area of the green marks.

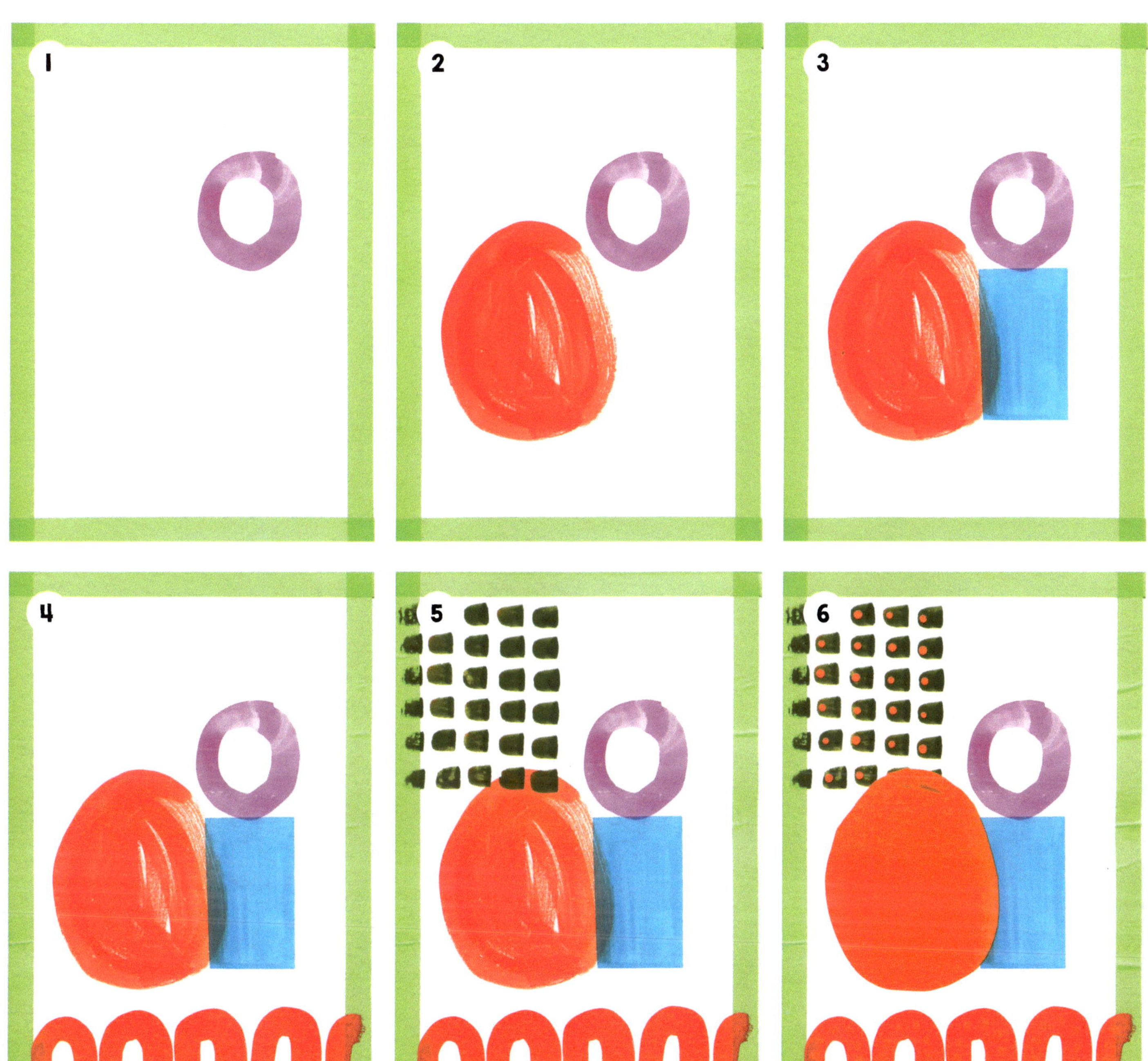

7. I really wanted to add some kind of floral element to this piece. I 'drew' a flower with a small brush and some of the red paint, overlaying it on top of the pink and blue shapes. I filled in part of the flower stamen with solid orange.

8. To break up that large expanse of orange on the left of the painting, I added a lightish blue leaf to contrast with the orange. The shape is fairly stylized and works with the abstract, graphic nature of this piece. I had to wait for this to dry and then go over it again, as the orange was showing through more than I wanted it to.

9. In step 8, while painting the blue leaf, I accidentally dropped a tiny bit of blue paint on the edge of the orange shape. To cover this and to add another element, I picked a much darker blue to add three circles. I used the same blue to draw in the line detail on the leaf, small dots on the stamen of the flower and lines and marks on the green marks and under the red arches.

10. In this last step, I wanted to add another element to bring everything together, so I used a bright yellow to create a flowing pattern in the unpainted white spaces. I added further details to the orange shape, the dark blue circles and the red arches. I also added some dark blue dots, in a grid-like fashion, over the stem of the flower. I used the end of the eraser from my pencil for this, and I love the fact that you can see the number '35' on some of this printed dots, which must have been on the eraser. Feel free to continue adding more details to make a full and exciting artwork, or try making three or four as a series, using similar colours, marks and drawing to tie everything together. Once you have finished, carefully peel the washi tape away from the edges of the paper (that part is so satisfying!) to reveal a lovely crisp edge.

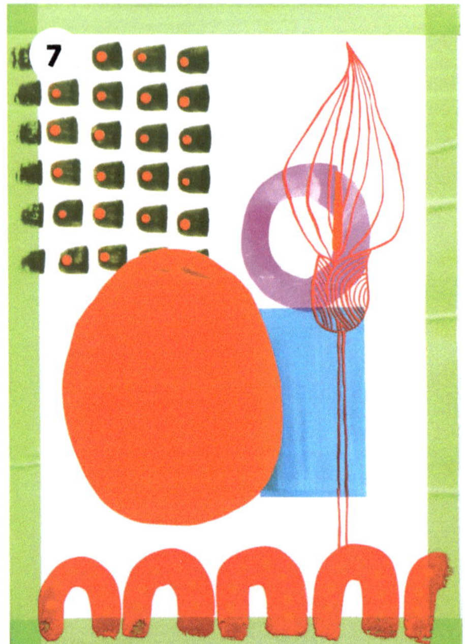

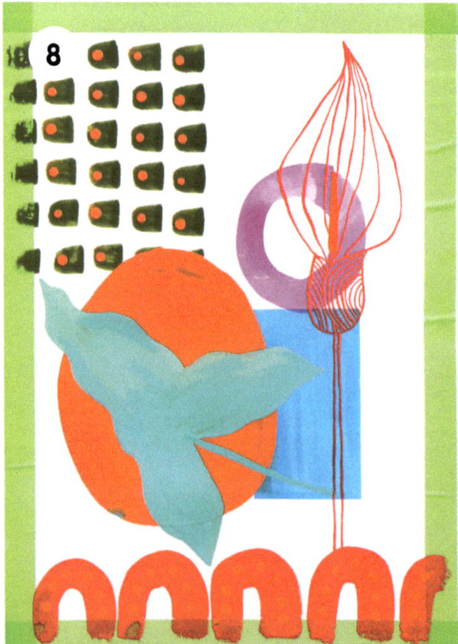

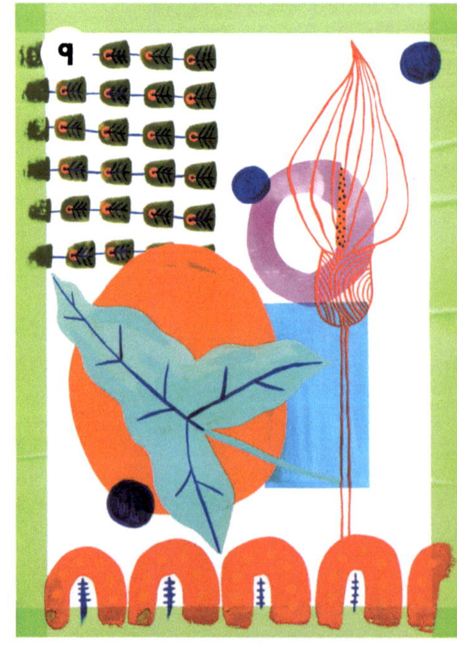

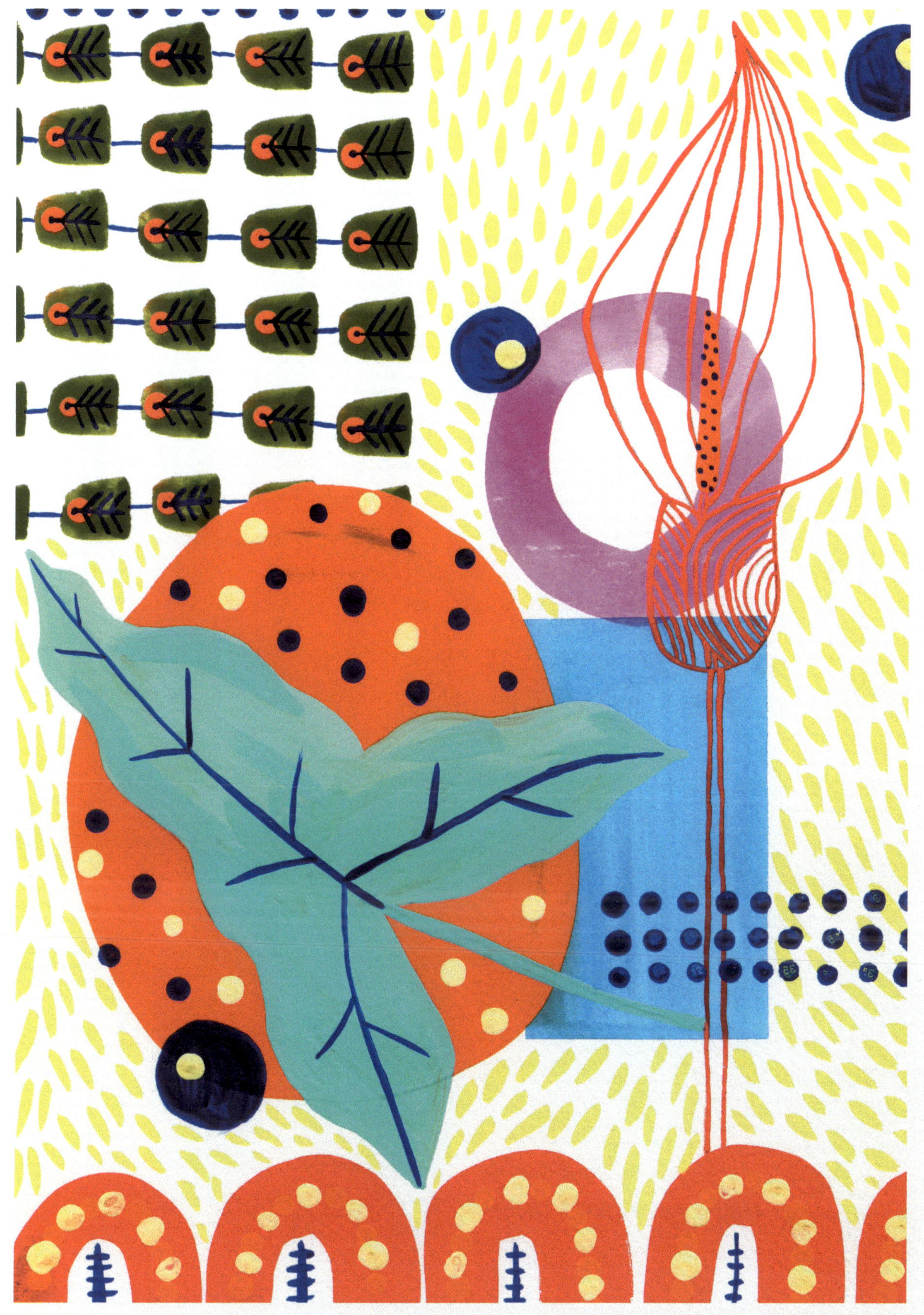

About the Author

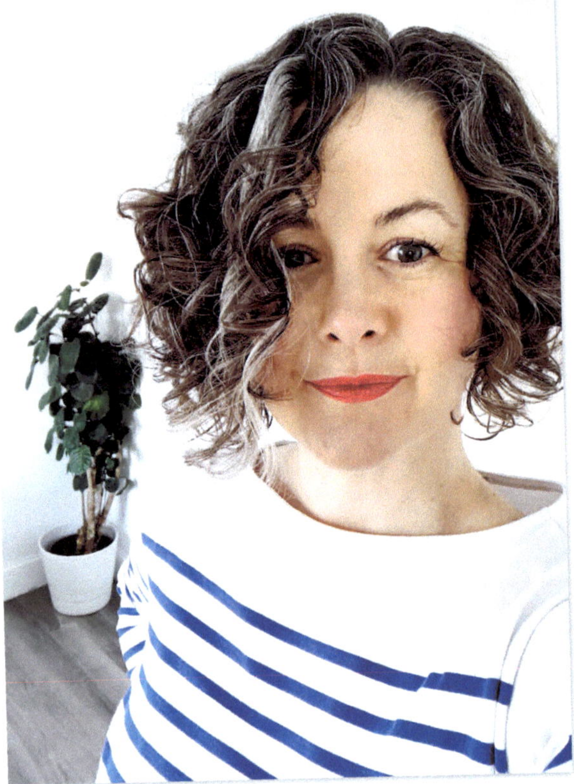

Zoë Ingram is an artist from Edinburgh in Scotland. She enjoys a career in the art and design world that has spanned over 20 years.

Before embarking on her career professionally, Zoë studied printed textiles for four years in the Scottish Borders town of Galashiels at the former Scottish College of Textiles, part of Heriot-Watt University. It was during her textile studies that she was introduced to the wonderful medium of gouache.

On leaving college, Zoë worked in design agencies on various projects from corporate reporting to web design. It wasn't until many years later, when she moved to Australia with her family in 2009, that she began to get in touch again with her true love of painting and making art.

In 2013, Zoë entered a global talent competition with around 1500 participants and went on to win the life-changing prize of representation with her now art agent, Lilla Rogers Studio. Zoë has been with the agency ever since and adores not only the LRS family but also the wide variety of opportunities and projects that she has been asked to work on.

After almost 10 years in Australia, Zoë returned to her Scottish home town in 2018 to set up her art practice, which is a lovely home studio space in a corner of her Edinburgh home.

Some of Zoë's clients are Walker Books, Creative Co-Op, Midwest CBK, Crate & Barrel, The Washington Post, Workman Publishing, Nosy Crow, Quarto, Live Happy magazine, Demdaco, Hallmark, HarperCollins, Oxford University Press, Peter Pauper Press, Penguin Random House and Ikea. As well as working with clients the world over, Zoë enjoys creating patterns for fabric and wallpaper, which she sells on Spoonflower, an online print-on-demand fabric printer.

Zoë would love to see how you're using the book and see your progress with gouache. Share your painting explorations using the hashtag #ohmygouache

ZOEINGRAM.COM
INSTAGRAM.COM/ZOEINGRAM.ILLUSTRATION
SPOONFLOWER.COM/PROFILES/ZOE_INGRAM
YOUTUBE.COM/CHANNEL/
UC6M1DFZ1OPNIDZLEQW3TGGG

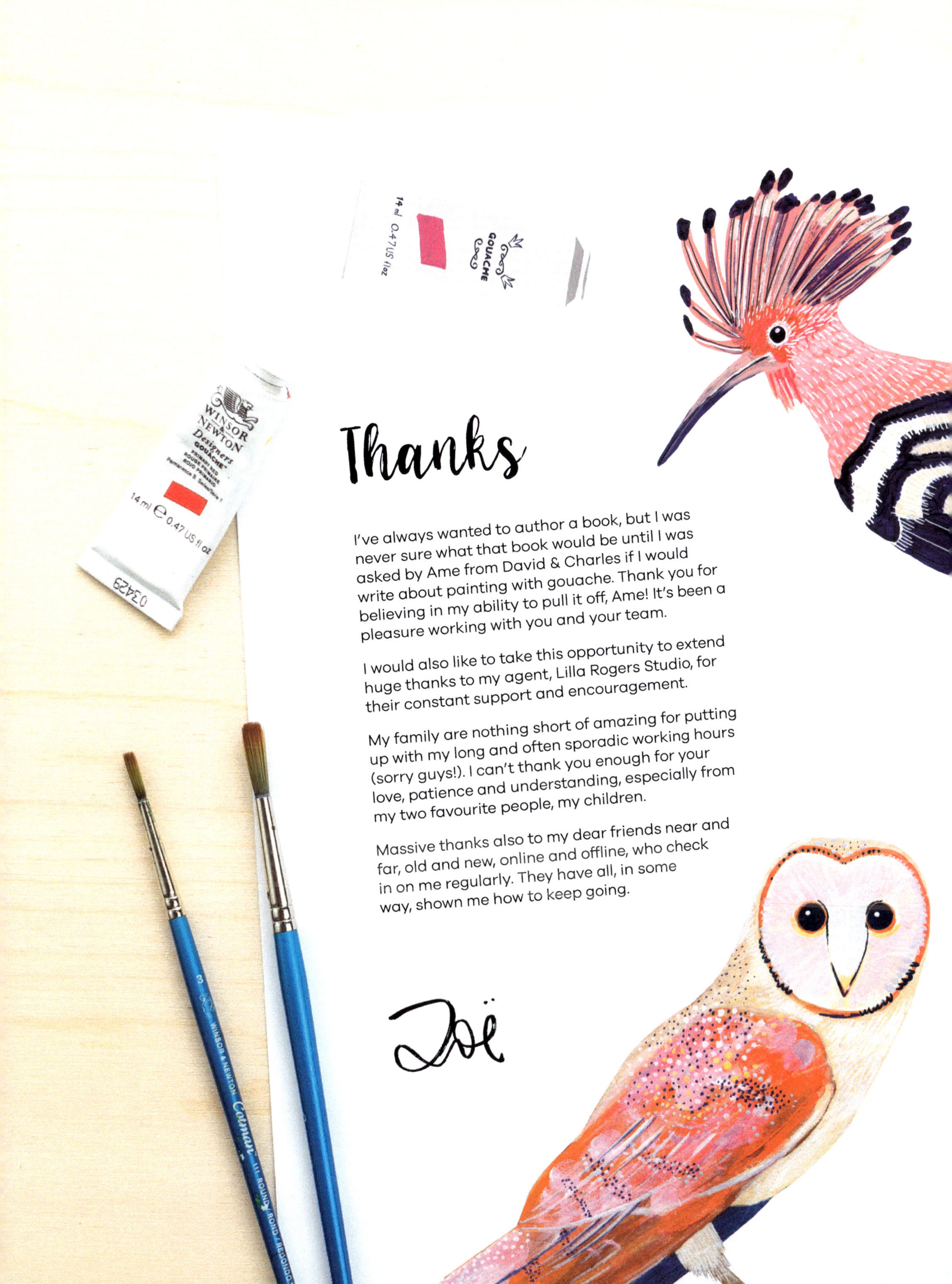

Thanks

I've always wanted to author a book, but I was never sure what that book would be until I was asked by Ame from David & Charles if I would write about painting with gouache. Thank you for believing in my ability to pull it off, Ame! It's been a pleasure working with you and your team.

I would also like to take this opportunity to extend huge thanks to my agent, Lilla Rogers Studio, for their constant support and encouragement.

My family are nothing short of amazing for putting up with my long and often sporadic working hours (sorry guys!). I can't thank you enough for your love, patience and understanding, especially from my two favourite people, my children.

Massive thanks also to my dear friends near and far, old and new, online and offline, who check in on me regularly. They have all, in some way, shown me how to keep going.

Resources

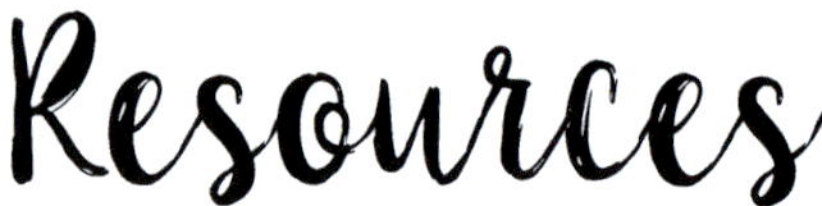

Online inspiration

Pinterest
pinterest.com

Instagram
instagram.com

Materials

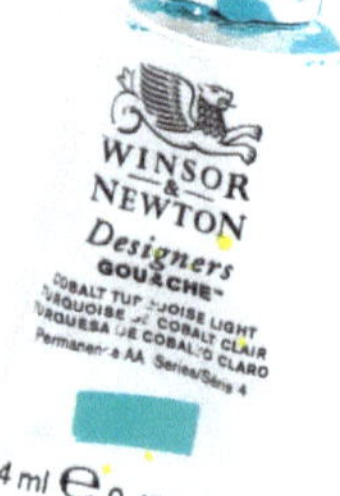

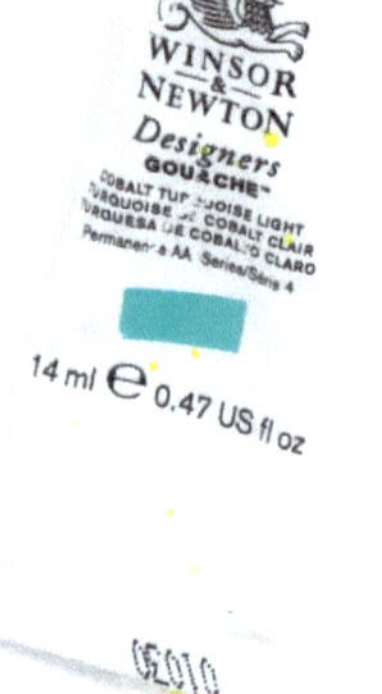

Arches watercolour paper
arches-papers.com

Bockingford watercolour paper
stcuthbertsmill.com

Holbein acryla gouache
holbeinartistmaterials.com

Liquitex acryla gouache
liquitex.com

Pentel twist-erase pencil
pentel.co.uk

Strathmore watercolor
400 series art journal
strathmoreartist.com

Winsor & Newton
gouache and brushes
winsornewton.com

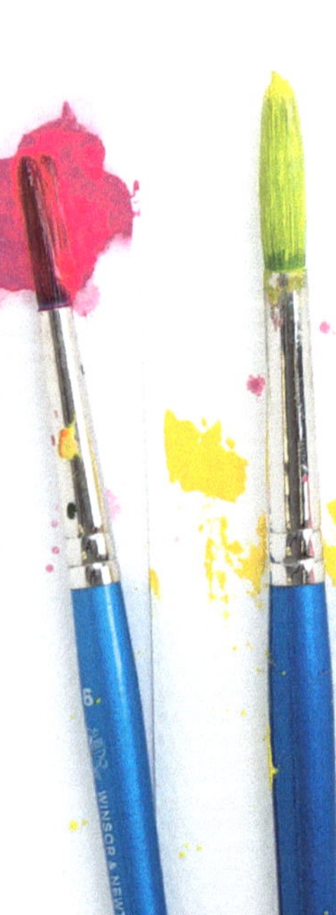

Gloss medium

For collage work,
I use Golden gloss medium
goldenpaints.com

Scanners & printers

In my work, I use an Epson
Perfection V370 Photo Scanner and
an Epson SureColor P600 printer
epson.co.uk

Online art stores

UK

artsupplies.co.uk

cassart.co.uk

edinburghartshop.co.uk

greyfriars-art-shop.co.uk

jacksonsart.com

USA

dickblick.com

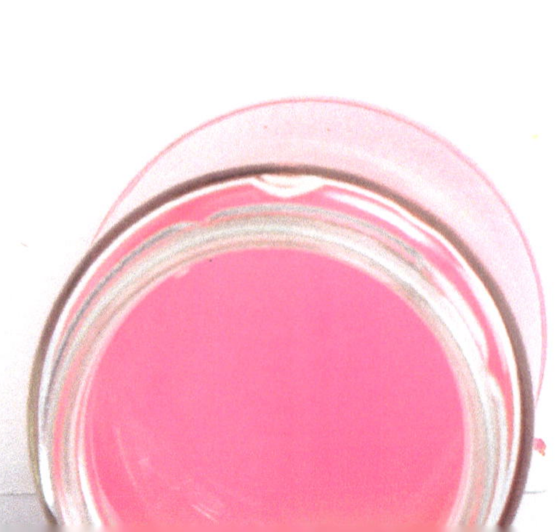

Index

A DAVID AND CHARLES BOOK
© David and Charles, Ltd 2021

David and Charles is an imprint of David and Charles, Ltd
Suite A, Tourism House, Pynes Hill, Exeter, EX2 5WS

Text and Designs © Zoe Ingram 2021
Layout and Photography © David and Charles, Ltd 2021

First published in the UK and USA in 2021

A catalogue record for this book is available from the British Library.

ISBN-13: 9781446308318 paperback
ISBN-13: 9781446381144 EPUB

This book has been printed on paper from approved suppliers and made from pulp from sustainable sources.

MIX
Paper | Supporting responsible forestry
FSC® C013604

Printed by CPI Group (UK) Ltd for:

David and Charles, Ltd
Suite A, Tourism House,
Pynes Hill, Exeter, EX2 5WS

Publishing Director: Ame Verso
Managing Editor: Jessica Cropper
Project Editor: Claire Coakley
Head of Design: Anna Wade
Pre-press Designer: Ali Stark
Illustrations: Zoe Ingram
Book Design, Art Direction and Styling: Anna Wade
Photography: Jason Jenkins
Production Manager: Beverley Richardson

David and Charles publishes high-quality books on a wide range of subjects. For more information visit **www.davidandcharles.com.**

Share your art with us on social media using #dandcbooks and follow us on Facebook and Instagram by searching for @dandcbooks.

Layout of the digital edition of this book may vary depending on reader hardware and display settings.

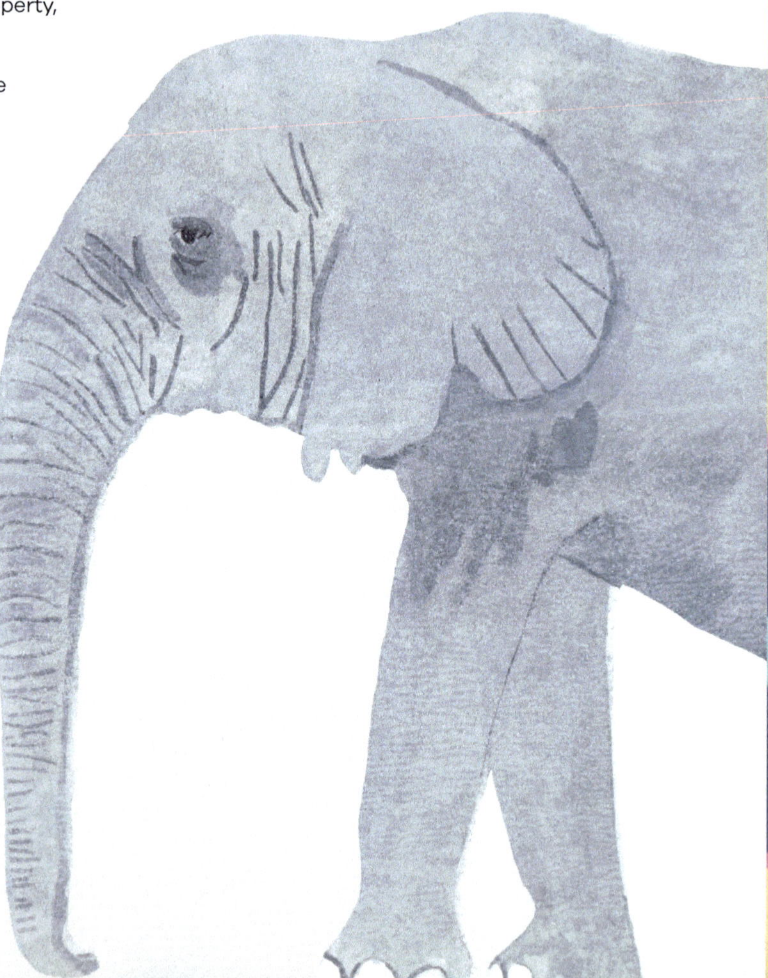

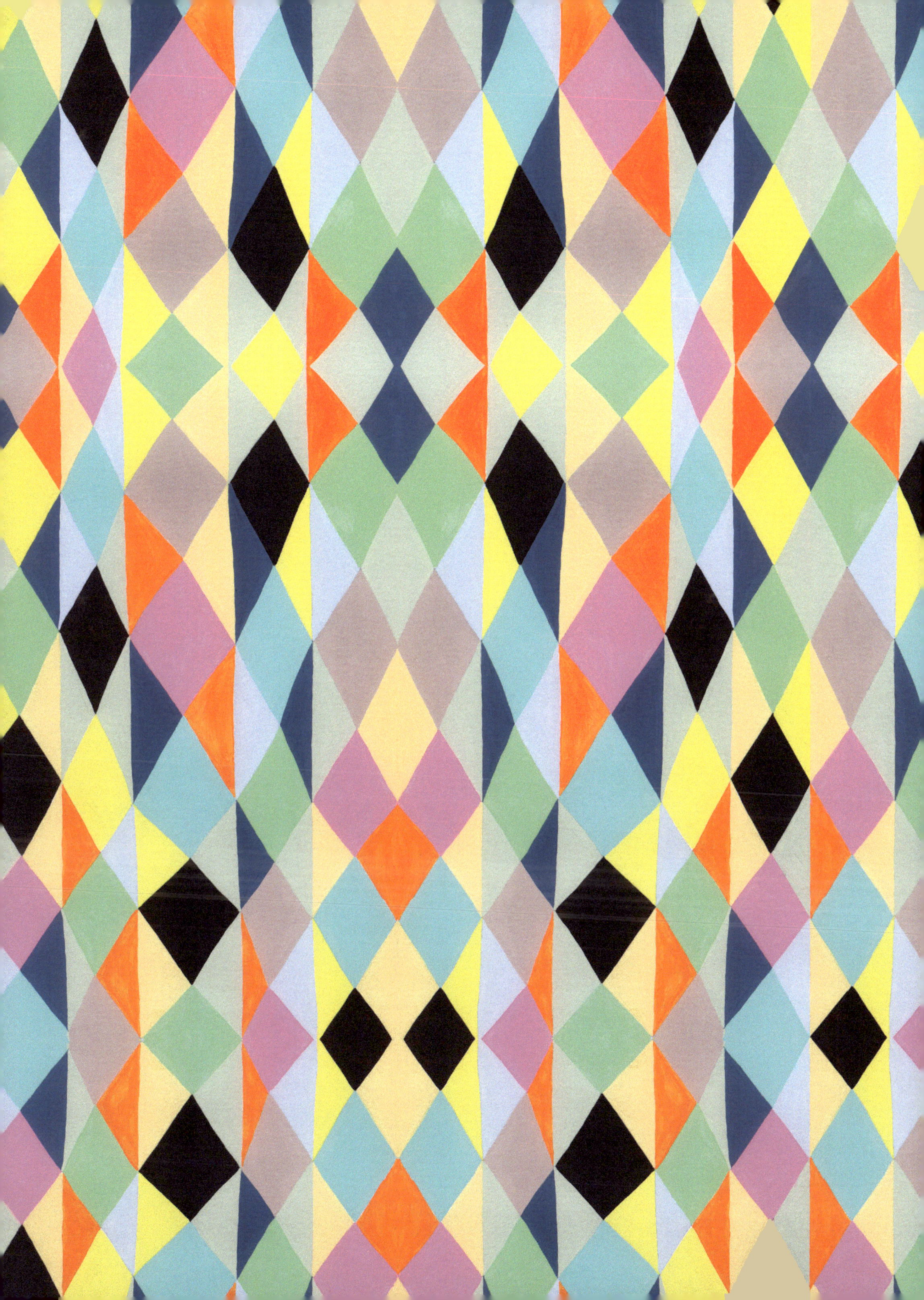

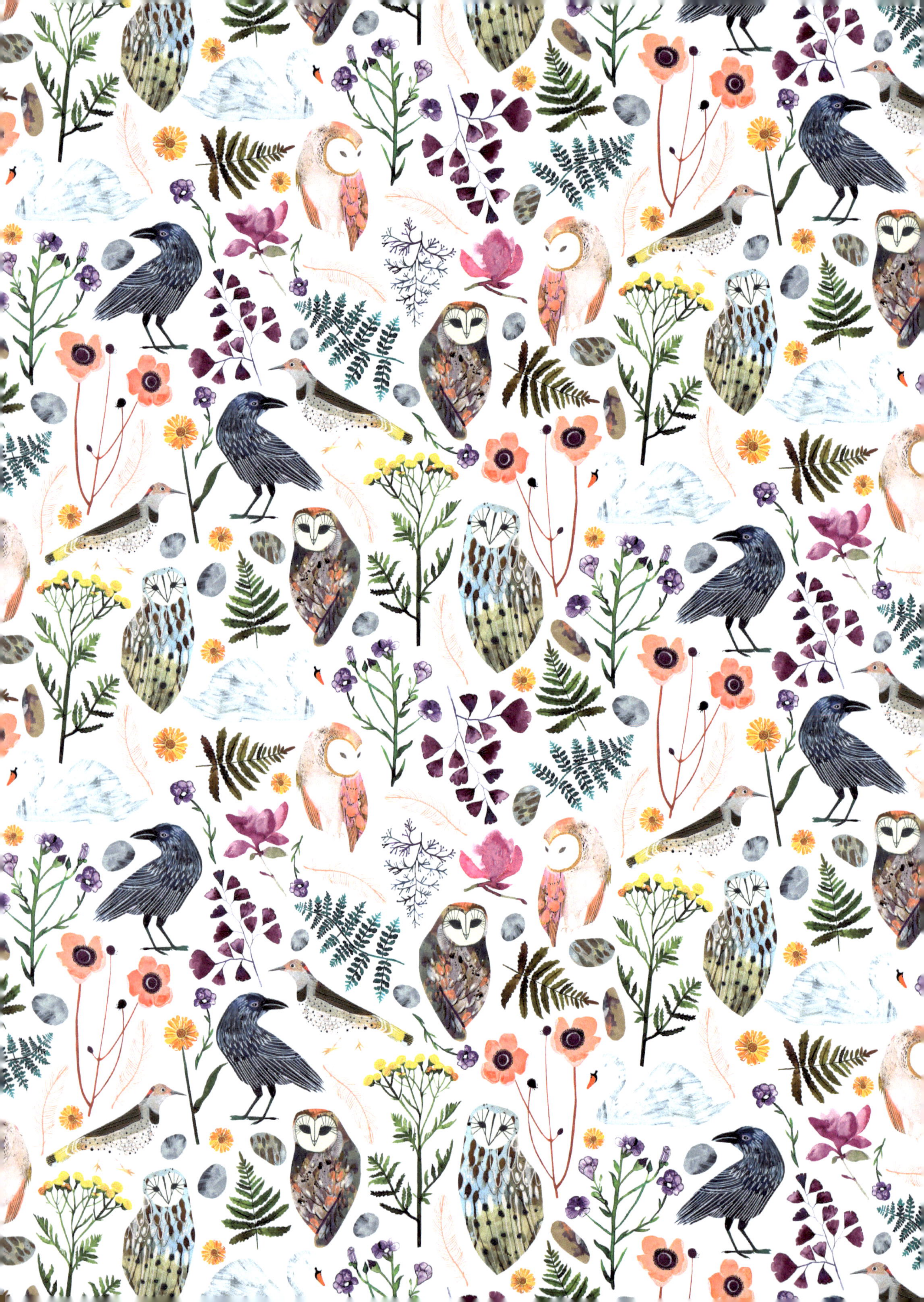